WRITERS
AND
PHILOSOPHERS

WRITERS

AND

PHILOSOPHERS

A Sourcebook of Philosophical Influences on Literature

EDMUND J. THOMAS
and
EUGENE G. MILLER

GREENWOOD PRESS

New York • Westport, Connecticut • London

Library of Congress Cataloging-in-Publication Data

Thomas, Edmund J.
    Writers and philosophers : a sourcebook of philosophical
influences on literature / Edmund J. Thomas and Eugene G. Miller.
        p.   cm.
    Includes bibliographical references.
    ISBN 0–313–25684–5 (lib. bdg. : alk. paper)
    1. Philosophy in literature. 2. Literature—Philosophy.
I. Miller, Eugene G.   II. Title.
PN49.T447   1990
809′.9338—dc20   90–34139

British Library Cataloguing in Publication Data is available.

Library of Congress Catalog Card Number: 90–34139
ISBN: 0–313–25684–5

First published in 1990

Greenwood Press, 88 Post Road West, Westport, CT 06881
An imprint of Greenwood Publishing Group, Inc.

Printed in the United States of America

The paper used in this book complies with the
Permanent Paper Standard issued by the National
Information Standards Organization (Z39.48–1984).

10   9   8   7   6   5   4   3   2   1

Contents

Preface

___

Throughout our careers as teachers of literature and philosophy, we have become increasingly aware of the debt owed by western literary figures to the philosophical speculations of thinkers from the time of the ancient Greeks to the present and to the mysticism of the Orient. At any level of instruction, the teacher of literature and literary criticism draws inevitably, often unknowingly, on philosophical theory in the examination of poetry, fiction, and drama. Platonism in the works of the Romantic poets and, more recently, Martin Heidegger, Karl Jaspers, and Jean-Paul Sartre are cases in point. Discussions with teachers of undergraduate courses in literature and with graduate students in English and our own observations over the past twenty-five years have led us to recognize a serious need among teachers and students for guidance to the philosophical influences that contributed, at times profoundly, to the work of major literary figures and to literary criticism. The teacher and student alike must bring to the study of literature an awareness of philosophical sources.

Thus, we were led to the compilation of this sourcebook. Our goal is to provide a resource which will help develop to a greater depth concepts with which teachers and students of literature may have some familiarity. It is hoped that the entries will serve as useful points of departure for further study and research and will contribute to an increased understanding and enjoyment of literature.

It is important to affirm the character of this text as a source of philosophical influences in fiction, poetry, and drama and to assert that, although we are aware that the entries cannot preclude an interpretive element, our intent is to provide brief, factual, basic information about literary figures and their philosophical sources. The literary figures selected are those whose works most commonly appear in high school and college literature anthologies or are most frequently studied in undergraduate and graduate literature courses. The entries do not attempt to provide full biographical data or literary criticism; these are the concerns of other reference books. Rather, the text describes major philosophical influences reflected in the writings of each author as well as references to philosophical works that are known to have played a part in the author's intellectual and aesthetic development. Several poets and novelists for whom specific philosophical linkages are not readily apparent, either from examination of their works or from study of available criticism, have been included because of philosophical elements implicit in their works. For example, Stoicism can be discerned in Ernest Hemingway and existential elements in Emily Dickinson and Sylvia Plath, which justify their inclusion. On the other hand, certain well-known, frequently anthologized authors whom one might have expected to find in this volume, such as F. Scott Fitzgerald and Joyce Carol Oates, are not included as the research has not revealed clear linkages to individual philosophers or particular philosophical systems.

The entries on 123 writers, arranged in alphabetical order, are supplemented by a section of brief bio-bibliographical profiles of 77 relevant philosophers and a glossary of philosophical terms, concepts, and movements. Appended to each author study is a selected bibliography of sources suggested as reading to further an understanding of the writings and their underlying philosophy. A bibliography at the end of the volume offers more general sources on literary theory and philosophy, stressing their interrelationships.

A cross-referencing system is provided for the convenience of readers. Within the entries on writers, single asterisks following names of philosophers mentioned refer the reader to the section that profiles philosophers and their works. Double asterisks refer the reader to the glossary of terms, concepts, and movements. The notation q.v. refers to entries on other writers within the body of the text.

We cannot hope to mention by name all who have helped so generously in the compilation of this sourcebook. The library reference staff at Niagara County Community College, especially Gail Staines and Kathleen M. Greenfield, must be acknowledged for their tireless efforts, always successful, to provide us with texts and information not readily available. The humanities faculty, especially E. R. Baxter, Norman Tederous, Brandon Warden, and the late Dr. William Warthling, must be thanked for their encouragement and for their reviews and criticisms of the developing manuscript, which could not have been completed without the dedicated effort and commitment of Ann Johnston, secretary to the Humanities Division at Niagara County Community College. Finally, our wives, Dr. Candalene McCombs Thomas and Roseanne Miller, must be recognized as overseers and editors. It is our hope that our collective experiences and awarenesses will be of use in serving the needs of our readers.

Key to Journal Titles and Abbreviations

AJES	*The Aligarh Journal of English Studies*
AmLS	*American Literary Scholarship: An Annual*
AntigR	*The Antigonish Review*
ArQ	*Arizona Quarterly*
ATQ	*American Transcendental Quarterly: A Journal of New England Writers*
BuR	*Bucknell Review*
Callaloo:	*An Afro-American and African Journal of Arts and Letters*
CEMF	*Collected Essays by the Members of the Faculty* (Kyoritsu Women's Junior College)
CIBS	*Communications from the International Brecht Society*
CJPhil	*Canadian Journal of Philosophy*
ClioI	*CLIO: A Journal of Literature, History, and the Philosophy of History*
Clues:	*A Journal of Detection*
CML	*Classical and Modern Literature: A Quarterly*
CollL	*College Literature*
Conradiana:	*A Journal of Joseph Conrad Studies*
CRevAS	*Canadian Review of American Studies*
CSL	*Cambridge Studies in Linguistics*
CVE	*Cahiers Victoriens et Edouardiens*
DAI	*Dissertation Abstracts International*
DicS	*Dickinson Studies*
DVLG	*Deutsche Vierteljahrschrift Fur Literaturwissenschaft und Geistesgeschichte*
EON	*The Eugene O'Neill Newsletter*
ESA	*English Studies in Africa: A Journal of the Humanities*
ESQ:	*A Journal of the American Renaissance*
Expl	*Explicator*
FR	*The French Review: Journal of the American Association of Teachers of French*

Francofonia:	*Studie e Ricerche Sulle Letterature di Linqua Francese*
FurmS	*Furman Studies*
GPQ	*Great Plains Quarterly*
GR	*Germanic Review*
HTR	*Harvard Theological Review*
HumanS	*Human Studies: A Journal for Philosophy and the Social Sciences*
JAmS	*Journal of American Studies*
JEP	*Journal of Evolutionary Psychology*
JJQ	*James Joyce Quarterly*
JKSA	*Journal of the Kafka Society of America*
JML	*Journal of Modern Literature*
KSJ	*Keats-Shelley Journal*
KulturaP	*Kultura: Szkice, Opowiadania, Sprawozdania* (Paris, France)
LCrit	*The Literary Criterion* (Mysore, India)
LFr	*Lanque Francaise*
LY	*Lessing Yearbook (Jahrbuch)*
MD	*Modern Drama*
MELUS:	*The Journal of the Society for the Study of Multi-Ethnic Literature of the Untied States*
MFS	*Modern Fiction Studies*
MLQ	*Modern Language Quarterly*
MLR	*The Modern Language Review*
MP	*Modern Philology: A Journal Devoted to Research in Medieval and Modern Literature*
MQ	*Midwest Quarterly: A Journal of Contemporary Thought*
MR	*Massachusetts Review: A Quarterly of Literature, The Arts and Public Affairs*
MSE	*Massachusetts Studies in English*
MSH	*Michigan Studies in the Humanities*
MSpr	*Moderna Sprak* (Stockholm, Sweden)
NCF	*Nineteenth-Century Literature*
Neophil	*Neophilologus* (Groningen, Netherlands)
NewC	*The New Criterion*
NHQ	*The New Hungarian Quarterly*
ON	*The Old Northwest: A Journal of Regional Life and Letters*
Paideuma:	*A Journal Devoted to Ezra Pound Scholarship*
PEGS	*Publications of the English Goethe Society*
PLL	*Papers on Language and Literature: A Journal for Scholars and Critics of Language and Literature*
PMLA	*Publications Modern Language Association of America*
POMPA	*Publications of the Mississippi Philological Association*
PoT	*Poetics Today*
PSt	*Prose Studies*
R&L	*Religion and Literature*
RCLL	*Revista de Critica Literaria Latin Americana*
RR	*Romantic Review*
SAJL	*Studies in American Jewish Literature*
Scan	*Scandinavka: An International Journal of Scandinavian Studies*

ScanR	*Scandinavian Review*
SBN	*Saul Bellow Journal*
SoAR	*South Atlantic Review*
SSEng	*Sydney Studies in English*
SSI	*Short Story International*
T&K	*Text and Kontext*
TCL	*Twentieth Century Literature: A Scholarly and Critical Journal*
TWN	*The Thomas Wolfe Review*
Viator:	*Medieval and Renaissance Studies*
VIJ	*Victorians Institute Journal*
VP	*Victorian Poetry*
WascanaR	*Wascana Review*
WC	*The Wordsworth Circle*
WHR	*Western Humanities Review*
WLT	*World Literature Today: A Literary Quarterly of the University of Oklahoma*
YR	*The Yale Review*

LITERARY FIGURES
AND
PHILOSOPHICAL
INFLUENCES

_____

A

AIKEN, CONRAD. B. August 5, 1889, Savannah, Georgia. D. August 17, 1973, Savannah, Georgia. American poet, short-story writer, and critic.

Conrad Aiken attended private schools and then Harvard where he was a friend of T. S. Eliot (q.v.). Aiken lived in the United States and England until 1947, when he settled in Massachusetts. Between 1915 and 1920 he attempted to create poetry that resembled music. After 1920 he wrote a series of narrative poems and several volumes of lyrics and meditations. The best of his poetry can be found in *Collected Poems* (1953), which includes "Preludes to Definition," considered by some critics to be his masterpiece. Aiken was very successful as a short-story writer; "Silent Snow, Secret Snow" is his most popular one. *Short Stories* was published in 1950.

Aiken is included in Harold Bloom's book *The Anxiety of Influence,* which lists twelve American poets whom Bloom considered to be "the strongest America poets" born in the last three decades of the nineteenth century (Bloom, 8). Bloom also maintains that these twelve poets were conscious of indebtedness to Friedrich Nietzsche* and Sigmund Freud.* Aiken never denied these influences. From 1911 to 1914 he met regularly with T. S. Eliot, and Aiken's biographers tell us that their discussions ranged from Aristotle* to George Santayana* but often were concentrated on Nietzsche and Freud. Joseph Killorin says of these conversations: "Aiken held in these conversations, against Eliot's skepticism, that Freud's study of neuroses through dreams was revolutionary for understanding the relation of an artist to his art" (Killorin, 37).

Aiken's debt to Freud is well documented; for example, in a *Paris*

Review interview he said emphatically, "Freud was in everything I did" (reported by Spivey, 99). It is, however, not as easy to verify the influence of Carl Jung* on the poet, but a 1980 article by Ted Spivey traces Jungian psychology in a convincing way in poems like "The Divine Pilgrim" where Aiken employs the archetype** of the anima.** Spivey states at the end of his study: "Although Aiken said he was influenced by Jung, he seldom quoted him. Yet their journeys were similar because they were based on a similar vision" (Spivey, 111).

There are two additional philosophical influences on Aiken. First was Emersonian transcendentalism**; finally, during his Harvard years he came under the influence of the renowned teacher and philosopher, Santayana.

REFERENCES

Bloom, Harold. *The Anxiety of Influence: A Theory of Poetry.* New York: Oxford University Press, 1973.

Butscher, Edward. *Conrad Aiken: Poet of White Horse Vale.* Athens: University of Georgia Press, 1989.

Killorin, Joseph. "Conrad Aiken's Use of Autobiography." *Studies in the Literary Imagination* 13, no. 2 (Fall 1980): 27–48.

Marten, Harry. *The Art of Knowing: The Poetry and Prose of Conrad Aiken.* Columbus: University of Missouri Press, 1988.

Spivey, Ted R. "Conrad Aiken's Fusion of Freud and Jung." *Studies in the Literary Imagination* 13, no. 2 (Fall 1980): 99–112.

ALBEE, EDWARD. B. March 12, 1928, Washington, D.C. American playwright.

Edward Albee was educated at Choate School and Trinity College in Hartford, Connecticut. His initial attempts to write poetry were not successful, and in the late 1950s he turned to drama. His first published works were three one-act plays: *The Zoo Story* (1959), *The Death of Bessie Smith* (1960), and *The Sandbox* (1960). His first full-length play, *Who's Afraid of Virginia Woolf?* (1962), received numerous awards. This was followed by *Tiny Alice* (1964), *A Delicate Balance* (1966), and *Seascape* (1975). Both of the last two plays won Pulitzer Prizes. After 1962 Albee worked as a producer and coproducer of dramas.

It is difficult to place Edward Albee in a definite literary school because such successful plays as *Who's Afraid of Virginia Woolf?*, *The Zoo Story*, *Seascape,* and many others are too divergent in theme and concept. At times he is a bedfellow of the theatre of the absurd, at times he is in the camp of existentialism,** and according to Julian Wasserman at times he is even allied with Platonism** and Neoplatonism.** In any case, the serious critic of Albee will see that he is a writer whose ideas range from absurdity** to nihilism** and far beyond to Platonism. The German writer Ruth Eva Schulz-Seitz illustrates this clearly in her book on Albee, *Dichter Philosoph der Bühne* (Poet-Philosopher of the Stage).

It is fitting that we first discuss absurdity in Albee's works because he has gained fame and fortune in the American theatre which he himself considers absurd. There are many examples of absurdism in his plays, but one of the most pointed examples is the case of Julian in *Tiny Alice* who faces "nothingness," and who, in complete isolation at the moment of death, turns to Christianity. Now the most interesting aspect of the absurdity theme in this work is the fact that Alice feels that the absurdity of human existence should be faced bravely and with courage. This reaction appears to be the answer of existentialism. To absurdity in the universe Albert Camus (q.v.) tells us in the myth of Sisyphus that one does not despair or resort to suicide but continually struggles and lives in good faith. Mary Castiglie Anderson sums up absurdism in *The Zoo Story:* "Although variously explained as a sociopolitical tract, a pessimistic analysis of human alienation, a modern Christian allegory of salvation, and an example of absurdist and nihilistic theatre, Albee's *The Zoo Story* has managed to absorb these perspectives without exhausting its many levels of meaning" (Anderson, 93).

REFERENCES

Amacher, Richard E. *Edward Albee.* Boston: Twayne Publishers, 1982.
Anderson, Mary Castiglie. "Ritual and Initiation in *The Zoo Story,*" in *Edward Albee: An Interview and Essays,* edited by Julian N. Wasserman. Houston, Tex.: The University of St. Thomas, 1983.
Bloom, Harold, ed. *Edward Albee.* New York: Chelsea, 1987.
Guo, Jide. "Albee and the Theatre of the Absurd." *Foreign Literature Studies* (China) 33, no. 3 (September 1986): 22–28.
Roudane, Matthew C. *Understanding Edward Albee.* Columbia: University of South Carolina Press, 1987.
————. "Thematic Unity in the Theatre of Edward Albee." *POMPA* (1986): 93–100.
Wasserman, Julian N. *Edward Albee: An Interview and Essays.* Houston, Tex.: The University of St. Thomas, 1983.

ANDREYEV, LEONID. B. August 21, 1871, Orel, Russia. D. September 12, 1919, Kuokkala, Finland. Russian short-story writer, novelist, and playwright.

Leonid Andreyev was educated at Moscow University where he began to write. In 1897, he took a job as a reporter, first on the *Moscow Herald* and later on *The Courier*. In 1898 he published *Bargamot and Garaskd,* a short story showing considerable promise that attracted the attention of Maxim Gorky, who became Andreyev's mentor. In 1901 Andreyev published his first book of short stories and at once became a literary celebrity. After 1905 he achieved substantial status as a playwright with such popular successes as *To the Stars* (1905), *The Life of Man* (1906), *King Hunger* (1907), *The Black Maskers* (1908), *Anathema* (1909), *The Waltz of the Dogs* (1914), and *He Who Gets Slapped* (1916). After the Bolshevik Revolution of 1917, Andreyev emigrated to Finland, where he attacked the Communists who controlled his homeland.

Friedrich Nietzsche's* attack on middle-class values and his perception of traditional "lies" which have enslaved modern men appealed to Andreyev and gave him inspiration for his own writings. "But for Nietzsche the human crisis had its source in the contradiction between the Christian philosophy and the world as it presents itself to man, for Andreyev it arose from man's detachment from the metaphysical entity" (Woodward, 40). Nietzsche scorned metaphysics, and his disbelief in the oneness of men ran contrary to Andreyev's convictions. Andreyev created an ideal framework for the salvation of man, one which of course differed from Christian salvation but also repudiated the Will to Power and the Superman concept which was Nietzsche's pattern for the final evolution of man.

In 1900 Andreyev wrote *The Story of Sergey Petrovich,* an important work and a social document that attested to the influence of Nietzsche's ideas on the mind of the average Russian intellectual in the mid–1890s. At this time, new life came into the social thought of Russian intellectuals, and Andreyev's depiction of the rebel and the cult of individualism documented this change in the Russian intellectual life. Sergey Petrovich becomes for Andreyev the Nietzschean superman (at least in the mind of the hero) who isolates himself from the world, subjects himself to intense self-analysis, and dreams of unlimited power. When he realizes that he is unable to attain the freedom and strength of Nietzsche's hero, he decides to take Zarathustra's advice: "[U]nto many life is a failure, a poisonous worm eating through unto their heart. These ought to see to it that they succeed better in dying" (Nietzsche, 95–96). And so Petrovich commits suicide, but the scene is depicted by the author as taking place in such squalor that the suicide is portrayed as a misguided and foolish act.

Another philosopher, again a German, whom Andreyev read and followed from his earliest years was Arthur Schopenhauer.* Even in the mid–1890s, when the ideas of Karl Marx* aroused the interest and enthusiasm of Russian intellectuals, Schopenhauer remained for Andreyev his principal intellectual inspiration. The *Principium Individuationis* of Schopenhauer especially fascinated Andreyev; he agreed with the German philosopher that man was imprisoned within the walls of his individuality and that only the intellect could free him. Nevertheless, Andreyev was an independent thinker, and he often disagreed with his philosophical masters. "One example would concern the knowledge of ultimate reality. Knowledge of ultimate reality does not presuppose for him, as it does for Schopenhauer, its rejection; he sees the achievement of such knowledge not simply as the conquest of death, but as the sole foundation for an abiding love of life" (Woodward, 31).

Unfortunately, although Andreyev was considered by his contemporaries as one of Russia's most original and gifted writers, he has received scant attention in the west. His works display not only an artistic technique, but also a preoccupation with the abstract and the philosophical—a characteristic that is understandable once one realizes the extent to which he was immersed in the writings of Nietzsche and Schopenhauer.

REFERENCES

Martini, Angela. "Andrejev: Die sieben Gehenkten." In *Die Russische Novelle*, edited by Bodu Zelinsky. Düsseldorf, West Germany: Bagel, 1982.
Nietzsche, Friedrich. *Thus Spake Zarathustra*. Leipzig, East Germany, 1898.
Woodward, James B. *Leonid Andreyev: A Study*. Oxford, England: Clarendon Press, 1969.

ARNOLD, MATTHEW. B. December 24, 1822, Laleham, England. D. April 15, 1888, Liverpool, England. English poet and critic.

Matthew Arnold was educated at Oxford and after his university years took the post of private secretary to Lord Lansdowne in 1847. In 1851 he became an inspector of schools, a position he held for thirty-five years. "Arnold's career as a writer can be divided into three periods. In the 1850's most of his poems appeared; in the 1860's his literary and social criticism; in the 1870's his second set of essays in literary criticism" (Abrams, 1330). His major works include *Essays in Criticism* (1865), *Culture and Anarchy* (1869), and *Literature and Dogma* (1873). The third work concerns studies of the Bible, and it is considered to be a sequence to his social criticism. Arnold's poetry is often pessimistic in nature, and his prose attacks puritanism** and the Victorian age.

There is evidence that, during his Oxford years, Matthew Arnold understood Epicureanism** in its distorted sense, namely, the tradition of wine and mirth. After 1847, when his long stay at Oxford came to a close, he wrote several poems that could be thought to be Epicurean and in some instances Stoic (see Stoicism**) as well. The eighth stanza of "To a Gypsy Child by the Sea Shore" (1849) reveals an awareness of the Stoic tradition.

"Among other 1849 poems written, 'To a Friend' is a reminder that Stoicism guided Arnold's thought for at least forty years. In the poems written between 1849 and 1852, one finds Stoicism as a central theme: 'To George Cruikshank' (1849) states that man can control the least of his days; and *Courage* (1852) declares, with the Stoics, that we must submit our wills to the laws of nature, bear in silence our evil fortune and learn to wait, renounce, withdraw" (Anderson, 138–39).

Arnold alludes repeatedly to Socrates,* Plato,* and Aristotle*; indeed, he reveals in much of his work a deep familiarity with their teachings. In *Literature and Science* (1883), he defends the ideals of Platonic education and expresses his belief that Plato's Paideutic aims are still valuable in the Victorian school system (see Platonism**). In *Culture and Anarchy,* he writes,

> Having been brought up at Oxford in the bad old times, when we were stuffed with Greek and Aristotle . . . my head is still full of a number of phrases we learnt at Oxford from Aristotle, about virtue being in a mean, and about excess and defect and so on. (VI, 62)

Much of Arnold's writing deals with the heritage of Rome; and among his articles on Virgil and Horace, there is an essay "On the Modern Element in Literature" which discusses the Epicurean Latin poet, Lucretius.* Here Arnold stresses Lucretius's message that one must learn the nature of things.

On reading Matthew Arnold, one realizes that he was thoroughly imbued with Greek and Roman culture. Although Arnold is chiefly aligned with literary figures, his work was strongly influenced by Greek and Roman philosophers.

REFERENCES

Abrams, M. H., ed. *Norton Anthology of English Literature*. 5th ed. 2 vols. New York: W. W. Norton, 1986.

Anderson, Warren D. *Matthew Arnold and the Classical Tradition*. Ann Arbor: University of Michigan Press, 1965.

Arnold, Matthew. *Culture and Anarchy*. Cambridge, England: Cambridge University Press, 1932.

Culler, Dwight A. *Imaginative Reason: The Poetry of Matthew Arnold*. New Haven, Conn.: Yale University Press, 1966.

Johnson, Stacy W. *The Voices of Matthew Arnold*. New Haven, Conn.: Yale University Press, 1961.

ARRABAL, FERNANDO. B. August 11, 1932, Melilla, Spanish Morocco. Spanish dramatist.

After a self-imposed exile in Paris, Fernando Arrabal began to produce plays in the 1950s, including the surrealistic and violent *The Two Executioners* and *The Car Cemetery* (both 1958), which outraged critics and shocked audiences. In the 1960s he instituted what became known as "Panic Theatre"; the best example is *The Architect and the Emperor of Assyria* (1967). A later phase of Arrabal's theatre was political beginning with the appearance of *They Put Handcuffs on the Flowers* (1973).

Arrabal has openly acknowledged few philosophical influences; however, his works express the existential notion of absurdity** in the universe (see also existentialism**) and a sense of angst** that is reminiscent of Søren Kierkegaard.* His externalizing of psychological traumas and dreams shows the influence of Sigmund Freud,* and his obsession with man possessed by the anima** can be traced to Carl Jung.* Arrabal's use of tautologies, the obsessive repetition of situation, and the metamorphosis of characters encourage the audience to arrive at a Jungian archetypal analysis of his plays.

Much has been written about Arrabal's interest in the grotesque, which associates him with the theatre of the absurd. From Arrabal's reading of Kierkegaard and other existentialist writers, the author has created in his strange and original plays situations that go beyond reason. "Life (then)," as Peter Podol puts it, "becomes a game without fixed rules, a puzzle without a concrete solution, a kaleidoscope of changing configurations and patterns" (Podol, 29).

More must be said about Arrabal's weltanschauung,** which presents the illogical and absurd world of man. Some examples of this absurdity occur in *Picnic on the Battle Field* (1959) where the horrors of war are underscored by the innocence of the characters. In *The Tricycle* (1958), in *Fando and Lis* (1955), and, in fact, in most of his early plays, the existentialist influence is evident in, for example, the impossibility of communication, the inability of his characters to deal with a devious and unstable world, and, in short, the chaos and disharmony rampant in the universe.

REFERENCES

Diaz, Janet. "Theatre and Theories of Fernando Arrabal." *Kentucky Romance Quarterly* 16 (1969): 143–54.

DuGresne, Nicole. "Bacchanalia and Fete Panique: Myth, Play and Sacrifice in Euripides and Arrabal." *BuR* 26, no. 2 (1982): 84–96.
Podol, Peter L. *Fernando Arrabal*. Boston: Twayne, 1978.
Taylor, Steven M. "Wonders in Wonderland: Fantasy in the Works of Carroll and Arrabal." In *Aspects of Fantasy*, edited by William Coyle. Westport, Conn.: Greenwood Press, 1986.

AUDEN, W[YSTAN] H[UGH]. B. February 21, 1907, York, England. Naturalized American citizen, 1946. D. September 29, 1973, Vienna, Austria. British/American poet.

W. H. Auden studied English at Oxford from 1925 to 1928, and in the 1930s he worked as a schoolmaster and wrote travel books. In 1936 he married Thomas Mann's (q.v.) daughter Erika, and her subsequent British citizenship helped her escape Nazi persecution. After 1939 Auden lived in New York and later alternated between America and Austria. His major works include *Poems* (1930) and *Look, Stranger* (1936). *For the Time Being* (1944) and *The Sea and the Mirror* (1944) were considered poetical reflections rather than poems. Two other volumes, *Nones* (1951) and *Epistle to a Godson* (1972), were favorably received by the critics, some of whom felt that Auden was the most outstanding poet of his generation.

W. H. Auden, a master at light verse as well as serious poetry, particularly respected the work of such thinkers as Sigmund Freud,* Carl Jung,* Reinhold Niebuhr,* Søren Kierkegaard,* and other existentialists (see existentialism**).

Especially impressed with Freud, Auden states in "The Essence of Freud's Teaching" (1935) that "The introduction of self-consciousness is a complete break in development, and all that we recognize as evil or sin is its consequence" (Auden, 339). "In Memory of Sigmund Freud" (1939) is one of Auden's better known occasional poems, and in 1953 he wrote "The Greatness of Freud," a review for the *Listener*. In fact, during the 1950s he emerged as an expert reviewer of books on and by Sigmund Freud (Callan, 275).

Existentialists like Karl Jaspers,* Martin Heidegger,* and Kierkegaard made such an impact on Auden that existentialist vocabularies worked their way into his poetry. An example of the extent to which existential concepts influenced Auden's poetry occur in *The Sea and the Mirror*, which borrows its theme from William Shakespeare's *The Tempest*. In the opening lines of Auden's poem, Prospero quotes from Kierkegaard's discussion of anxiety, and later in the work Auden expounds the necessary existential struggle in "this rough world." *Another Time* (1937) reflects the influence of both Kierkegaard and Heidegger.

Among the various existentialists, Kierkegaard was apparently the most influential; he is much in evidence in a major work of Auden's, *The Age of Anxiety* (1947). Here, as Kierkegaard had done earlier, Auden identifies anxiety as one of man's basic problems. Kierkegaard's presence is obvious throughout much of Auden's work, as it is in "New Year Letter" (1941) which includes material that corresponds to Kierkegaard's triad.

REFERENCES

Auden, Wystan Hugh. *The English Auden: Poems, Essays and Dramatic Writing, 1927–1939*. London: Faber, 1977.

Bloom, Harold, ed. *W. H. Auden*. New York: Chelsea, 1986.

Boly, John R. "Auden and Hopkins: On Harrowing the House of the Dead." In *Hopkins among the Poets: Studies in Modern Responses,* edited by Richard F. Giles. Hamilton, Ontario, Canada: International Hopkins Association, 1985.

Callan, Edward. *Auden: A Carnival of the Intellect*. New York: Oxford University Press, 1983.

Jarrell, Randall. "Freud to Paul: The Stages of Auden's Ideology." *Partisan Review* 12 (Fall 1945): 437–57.

Roth, R. M. "The Sophistication of W. H. Auden: A Sketch in Longinian Method." *Modern Philology* 48 (February 1951): 193–204.

Spender, Stephen. *World Within World*. London: Hamish Hamilton, 1951. (Autobiographical)

B

BARBU, ION. B. March 19, 1895, Cimpulung, Romania. D. August 11, 1961, Bucharest, Romania. Romanian poet and mathematician.

Ion Barbu made his entrance into Romanian literature in 1918 with poems that described Balkan life. By 1925 he had applied a mathematical vision of the world to his poetry, and the consequence was a body of poetry that was obscure and cryptic. His collected verse appeared in 1930 and established him as a major Romanian writer. "Barbu's preoccupation with the analogies between poetry and mathematics produced a verse characterized by mathematical metaphor, by the symmetrical regularity of stanzas, and yet where striking sonority and musicality prevail" (Bullock and Woodings, 39).

Barbu, a mysterious and difficult poet, is considered to be one of the greatest Romanian poets of the twentieth century. His biographer, Alexander Cioranescu, speaks of the difficulty of Barbu's poetry: "The peculiar dialectical difficulties are complicated by an enormous field of references, analogies, and association of ideas and with the plastic representation of existences which have neither mass nor shape, transforming his poetry into a cryptic message" (Cioranescu, preface). One of the keys to this poetry seems to be the philosophy of Friedrich Nietzsche.* That Barbu was a disciple of the German philosopher can be seen in the Nietzschean ideas that are interwoven into Barbu's poetry. The poet was introduced to Nietzsche when, as a young mathematics student, he became friends with Tudor Viana, an aspiring doctoral candidate in philosophy. In 1914 or 1915, Barbu read Nietzsche's *The Birth of Tragedy* (1872) and probably had the opportunity to discuss the work with Viana who had a more formal training in philosophy. From this point on, Nietzsche's philosophy became the fundamental component of Barbu's poetry.

Barbu's acceptance of Nietzsche's questionable vision of classical Greece is reflected in the poems of his first phase. This vision of Greece included the concept of "pantheistic intoxication," which can be seen in his poem *Pantheism* (see pantheism**). It is obvious to the student of Barbu that Barbu rejected the Apollonian** in favor of the Dionysian** aspect of Hellenic culture, which was emphasized and advocated by Nietzsche, as can be seen in his poem entitled *Dionysiac*.

REFERENCES

Bullock, Alan, and R. B. Woodings, eds. *Twentieth-Century Culture*. New York: Harper & Row, 1983.
Cioranescu, Alexander. *Ion Barbu*. Boston: Twayne, 1981.
Petrescu, Ioana Em. "Copacul inecat." *Steaug* 35, no. 441 (February 1984): 20. Discusses Barbu's philosophy.

BAROJA, PIO. B. December 28, 1872, San Sebastian, Spain. D. October 30, 1956, Madrid, Spain. Spanish novelist.

Pio Baroja was a medical doctor who did not begin writing until the age of thirty. The trilogy of *The Quest* (tr. 1922), *Weeds* (tr. 1923), and *Red Dawn* (tr. 1924) included his first successful novels. His attention to the Madrid underworld resulted in a novel called *City of the Discreet* (1917). In 1928 he published an important philosophical novel entitled *The Tree of Knowledge*. After 1912 Baroja devoted himself primarily to the genre of the historical novel with a series of twenty-two volumes called *The Memoirs of a Man of Action* (1913–1934). Baroja has influenced the post–civil war generation of Spanish writers as well as the American writers Ernest Hemingway (q.v.) and John Dos Passos (q.v.).

In order to grasp the essentials of Baroja's thought and art, one must be aware of the fact that he was increasingly engrossed in philosophy. Much of his life was spent in the study of such thinkers as Immanuel Kant,* Søren Kierkegaard,* Arthur Schopenhauer,* and Friedrich Nietzsche,* and their thinking naturally worked itself into his writing.

Baroja's study of Schopenhauer and Nietzsche culminated in *The Tree of Knowledge* (1928) in which the characters of Hurtado and Iturrioz reflect the teaching of both philosophers. Yet, in this work, Baroja's preoccupation with Kant led him to Hortado's explanation of Kantian philosophy to a doubting Iturrioz. In her analysis, Beatrice P. Pratt suggests, "If Baroja can be classified at all, he is a Kantian insofar as he conceived of the world as a representation, a creation of the subject, the transcendental ego" (Pratt, 117).

Pratt's statement is probably accurate, especially since Baroja stated that Kant was the greatest of all philosophers but that he, Baroja, was also a token Epicurean (see Epicureanism**). Baroja had a lifelong desire to avoid strong emotions; he practiced a philosophy of disengagement; and he renounced pleasure and expected thereby to be spared pain.

It is dangerous, however, to attempt to restrict Baroja to one philosopher because his works suggest he was an eclectic.** He was, for example, a great admirer and follower of Kierkegaard, Schopenhauer, and Nietzsche. For one who criticized collective religious creeds, it is remarkable that Baroja accepted the difficult Christianity of Kierkegaard. For one as liberal as Baroja, it is likewise difficult to comprehend his acceptance of the pejorative comments of Nietzsche and Schopenhauer on the masses of society or, as Nietzsche called them, "the despicable herd."

REFERENCES

Galerstein, Carolyn. "The Crisis of Reason in Baroja's *The Tree of Knowledge*."
    LFr 2, no. 1 (January 1982): 34–41.
Golson, Emily Becker. "Pio Baroja and John Dos Passos: The Evolution of
    Two Political Novelists." *DAI* 43, no. 4 (October 1982): 1138A.
Macklin, J. J. "The Modernist Mind: Identity and Integration in Pio Baroja's
    Camine de Perfeccion." *Neophil* 67, no. 4 (October 1983): 540–55.
Pratt, Beatrice P. *Pio Baroja*. New York: Twayne, 1971.

BARTH, JOHN. B. May 27, 1930, Cambridge, Maryland. American novelist.

John Barth studied at Johns Hopkins University and graduated with an M.A. in 1952. In the following year, he began to teach at Pennsylvania State University and moved to the State University of New York at Buffalo in 1965 as writer in residence. Barth's first two novels, *The Floating Opera* (1956) and *The End of the Road* (1958) are realistic novels about men who are burdened with a sense of futility. His last three works— *The Sot-Weed Factor* (1960), *Giles Goat-Boy* (1966), and *Lost in the Funhouse* (1968)—abandon realism and assume a bizarre and grotesque posture in a modern setting.

One of the most interesting writers since the 1950s, Barth has probably not been influenced by individual philosophers (at least this would be difficult to prove) but rather by the philosophical movements of nihilism** and existentialism.** "Barth is interested in dramatizing ideas in character, and his most interesting and important achievement to date is the embodiment of philosophical ideas in a form both tragic and comic" (Noland, 26).

Number and Nightmare by Jea E. Kennard (Archon, 1975) and *A Dangerous Crossing* by Richard Lehan (Southern Illinois University, Edwardsville, 1973) trace the influence of French existentialism on Barth's books. Evidence of existential thought occurs in the early novel, *The Floating Opera* (1956), where the characters either have no values or create values in isolation. The novel begins and ends with the problem of suicide, which Albert Camus (q.v.) claims is central to existential thought. "There is but one truly serious philosophical problem," Camus says, "and that is suicide. Judging whether life is or is not worth living amounts to answering the fundamental question of philosophy" (Camus, 3). Richard Noland argues that Barth's novels are existential because they are a mixture of tragedy and comedy and deal with the absurd. Ihab Hassan supports Noland's opinion when he states that the existential novel is neither completely tragic nor completely comic. "The existentialist novelist, therefore, must present this world in a form which contains an awareness of relativity, a form which includes both terror and laughter" (Noland, 20).

As a philosophical movement, nihilism is a "doctrine that nothing exists, or is knowable, or is valuable. Thus Gorgias[*] held that (1) nothing exists: (2) even if something did exist it could not be known" (Runes, 210). Beverly Gross claims that Barth's *The Sot-Weed Factor* and *Giles Goat-Boy* are nihilistic novels because they deny "the possibility of meaning, identity, and answers in a world in which these things are always shifting, masked and unattainable" (Gross, 31).

Barth's critics believe that his novels follow the philosophical traditions of nihilism and existentialism. Gross sums it up with the following statement: "The comedy in Barth's novels is the mockery of emotions and moral values . . . all issues in Barth's novels come down to some sort of game. . . . The suicide issue of *The Floating Opera* (1956) is an existential put-on . . . love is simply a comic absurdity, another game" (Gross, 31).

REFERENCES

Camus, Albert. *The Myth of Sisyphus*. Translated by Justin O'Brian. Cambridge, Mass.: Schoenhof, 1942.

Gerhard, Joseph. *John Barth*. Minneapolis: University of Minnesota Press, 1970.

Gross, Beverly. "The Anti-Novels of John Barth." In *Critical Essays on John Barth*, edited by Joseph J. Waldmeir. Boston: G. K. Hall, 1980.

Hassan, Ihab. "The Existential Novel." *The Massachusetts Review* 3 (Autumn 1961–Summer 1962): 795–97.
Hauck, Richard Boyd. *A Cheerful Nihilism: Confidence and "The Absurd" in American Humorous Fiction.* Bloomington: Indiana University Press, 1971, pp. 201–36.
Hoffmann, Gerhard. "The Absurd and Its Forms of Reduction in Postmodern American Fiction." In *Approaching Postmodernism,* edited by Douwe Kokkema and Hans Bertens. Amsterdam, Netherlands: Benjamins, 1986.
Noland, Richard. "John Barth and the Novel of Comic Nihilism." In *Critical Essays on John Barth,* edited by Joseph J. Waldmeir. Boston: G. K. Hall, 1980.
Runes, Dagobert David, ed. *Dictionary of Philosophy.* New York: Philosophical Library, 1983.

BEAUVOIR, SIMONE de. B. January 9, 1908, Paris, France. D. April 14, 1986, Paris, France. French novelist and essayist.

Simone de Beauvoir studied philosophy at the Sorbonne where she met the leader of the modern existentialist movement (see existentialism**), Jean-Paul Sartre* (q.v.). In the autobiographical volumes, *The Prime of Life* (1962) and *The Force of Circumstance* (1965), Beauvoir wrote of her intellectual and romantic association with Sartre. Her major novel *The Mandarins* (1954) won the Prix Goncourt. Simone de Beauvoir's nonfiction includes *The Ethics of Ambiguity* (1948), *The Second Sex* (1949), *The Coming of Age* (1972), and *All Said and Done* (1974). Beauvoir is considered one of the most prominent French literary figures of the twentieth century.

Simone de Beauvoir was a prolific writer of unusually broad dimensions. Her published works include seven novels, one play, and numerous philosophical tracts and books. Her relationship to Sartre dates back to 1929 when she was a student at the Sorbonne. Chauvinistically believing that intellect was an exclusively masculine characteristic, Sartre once said, "The marvellous thing with Simone de Beauvoir is that she has the intelligence of a man . . . and the sensibility of a woman" (reported by Winegarten, 39). Sartre, however, admitted that she knew as much about philosophy as he did. Winegarten sums up the Sartre-Beauvoir relationship: "As intellectual partners, their union appears remarkable; it is not common to find two important writers of different gender so intimately linked over so long a period in intellectual exchange" (Winegarten, 37).

Writing, for Simone de Beauvoir, was an obsession, a means of achieving an understanding of herself, of achieving the existentialist virtue of "authenticity."** Her major works such as *The Mandarins* and *L'Invitée* draw with profound intensity on her personal experiences. Her autobiographical volumes provide an invaluable source for understanding her fiction as well as the philosophical, social, and intellectual milieu in which she lived and wrote. Beauvoir's Sartrian existentialist views provide for her an essentially materialistic posture (see materialism**), reflected in her fiction, which precludes in her life even minimal concern with the spiritual. She devoted her considerable energies "to the process of living, to the life of the mind, to the major trends and crises of the day" (Winegarten, 4).

From her earliest years Simone de Beauvoir's major commitment was to writing—"Writing was for her an adventure. She found it a kind of exhaltation" (Winegarten, 1). Her awareness of herself as a woman writer was late in coming but finally found expression in *The Second Sex*.

REFERENCES

Ascher, Carol. *Simone de Beauvoir: A Life of Freedom*. Boston: Beacon Press, 1981.
Hatcher, Donald L. *Understanding "The Second Sex."* New York: Peter Lang, 1949.
Jardine, Alice. "Death Sentences: Writing Couple and Ideology" *PoT* 6, no. 102 (1985): 119–13.
Okely, Judith. *Simone de Beauvoir*. New York: Pantheon, 1986.
Winegarten, Renee. *Simone de Beauvoir*. Oxford, England: Berg, 1988.

BECKETT, SAMUEL. B. April 13, 1906, Dublin, Ireland. D. December 22, 1989, Paris, France. Irish dramatist and novelist.

Samuel Beckett lived in France after 1932 and wrote more in French than in English. His first novel, *Murphy* (1938), was followed by *Watt* (1953) and the trilogy *Molloy* (1951). However, Beckett is known primarily for his drama, and his most well-known and successful plays are *Waiting for Godot* (1956) and *Endgame* (1958). He received the Nobel Prize for Literature in 1969.

Since Beckett has been obsessively preoccupied with Christianity and Christian themes and since he frequently considers the problem of evil, the question of free will, and the possibility of redemption, it is not surprising that he has been influenced by Christian thinkers.

> The influence of St. Augustine,[*] [René] Descartes,[*] and Dante [q.v] upon Beckett has already been established by many critics and schol-ars . . . but further study demonstrates that at least part of the similarity between [T. S.] Eliot [q.v.] and Beckett occurs because they draw on common sources: Heraclitus,[*] St. Augustine, Dante, [Blaise] Pascal,[*] Herbert, the mystical tradition in Christianity generally. (Baldwin, 10)

There are elements in Beckett's works that satirize man's frailties—the problems of old age and infirmity—elements that are often surrealistic and absurd. Baldwin also points out the influence of Pascal on Beckett. "Pascal, of course, took the Augustinian side in his dispute with the Jesuits, another link with Beckett, whose interest in St. Augustine is well known" (Baldwin, 27).

In *Malone Dies* (1946), one finds multiple allusions to Plotinus,* St. Augustine, Meister Eckehart,* and St. John of the Cross. Baldwin discusses the influence of St. John of the Cross in *Malone:*

> He [Malone] wonders if he died in the forest, but concludes he did not. He discusses the nature of the light; it is neither dark nor bright, but a grayish light, as it was for Molloy. This midnight seems to correspond not only to the modern purgatorial world, but to the first dark night of St. John of the Cross, the night of the senses. (Baldwin, 61)

There are critics who accept Beckett's ideas yet have difficulty accepting Augustine's and Geulincx's* influence on his thinking. However, they have no trouble accepting the influence of Descartes. All three philosophers concluded that reason can only go so far in explaining the mysteries of the universe. Baldwin sums it up with the following statement: "Thus Beckett is in the odd position, for a supposed atheist, of having been influenced by three of the most intelligent men in the history of the world who managed to reconcile reason and intuition, intellect and insight, the visible and the invisible" (Baldwin, 27).

Beckett accepts Geulincx's view that mind and matter are mutually exclusive. Beckett's characters, in a world where matter is alien to them, often look upon their bodies with disgust. Hassan says, "[M]eantime, however, mind is set free from decaying matter; it turns endlessly upon itself, droning and dribbling words, and playing with number and system" (Hassan, 129).

When one reads Beckett and finds his works complex and often intellectually puzzling, one is not surprised to discover that he has drawn from many of the great thinkers of the past. As Hassan says, "His pessimism frequently sends him to [John] Calvin,[*] Augustine, Paul, to the gospels and the Eucharist, in search of images of man's ambiguous fate" (Hassan, 130).

Much has been written concerning Beckett's use of philosophical thought. For example, Ruby Cohn and John Fletcher have written articles that deal explicitly with philosophical influences on Beckett. "John Fletcher traces the ideas of the pre-Socratics in Beckett's early fiction:

Pythagoras[*] and Empedocles,[*] Heraclitus, ''the lachrymose philosopher,' and Democritus,[*] 'the laughing philosopher,' who appear in *More Pricks than Kicks* (1934) and *Murphy* (1957)'' (Hassan, 131).

REFERENCES

Baldwin, Helen L. *Samuel Beckett's Real Silence*. University Park: The Pennsylvania State University Press, 1981.
Cohn, Ruby. *Back to Beckett*. Princeton, N.J.: Princeton University Press, 1973.
Fletcher, John. ''Samuel Beckett and the Philosophers.'' *Comparative Literature* 17 (Winter 1965): 50–54.
Hassan, Ihab. *The Literature of Silence: Henry Miller and Samuel Beckett*. New York: Knopf, 1967.
Watts, Eileen H. ''The Language of Doubt: Post Cartesian Rationalism and the Language of Beckett's Novels.'' *DAI* 47, no. 5 (November 1986): 1724A–1725A.
Webb, Eugene. *Samuel Beckett: A Study of His Novels*. Seattle: University of Washington Press, 1973.

BELLOW, SAUL. B. July 10, 1915, Lachine, Quebec, Canada. American novelist.

Saul Bellow grew up in Montreal, Canada, and moved with his parents to Chicago, Illinois, after which he earned a B.A. in anthropology at Northwestern University. His first novel, *Dangling Man* (1944), was followed by his powerful and successful work *The Adventures of Augie March* (1953). He further established his reputation as a novelist with *Henderson the Rain King* (1959), a work set in a mythical Africa. His greatest novel is probably *Herzog* (1964), in which Bellow reveals his deep concern with the ethical dilemmas of modern life. Finally, *Humboldt's Gift* won him the Nobel Prize for Literature in 1976.

Bellow started his career as an anthropologist** who, when he turned to writing fiction, astounded the reading public with his intellectual stance and a style of writing that contrasted with the clinical, impersonal writing that had been described as ''modernity.'' In fact, Bellow took a stand against the many ''isms,'' including existentialism** and nihilism,** both of which have been the vogue in modern writing.

The heart of Bellow's disagreement with existentialism concerns its theory of self. Jean-Paul Sartre* (q.v.) maintains that, since there are no essences, there is no human nature. This belief is completely contrary to Bellow's belief that each of us has a God-given soul and is a living and breathing individual and person. In addition, Bellow repudiates Sartre's teaching that the idea of God is contradictory; in many of his novels, his characters end in a mystical stage where they experience peace with God.

One who reads Bellow must see at once that he is at opposite poles from the French (atheist) existentialists, and one should not then be surprised that Bellow satirizes existentialism in the Lucas Asphalter episode. In *Herzog* the protagonist questions Martin Heidegger's* degradation of the ordinary life and "the Fall into the Quotidian." Daniel Fuchs adds to this: "In criticising the philosopher for his lack of civility, of a sense of community, of ignorance of the other, Professor Herzog is joining a distinguished company" (Fuchs, 159).

One must marvel at the brave individualism of Bellow in opposing popular philosophical movements. He took the unpopular position and opposed absurdity** in literature as well as the godless stance of the existentialists and nihilists. Bellow is an intellectual who has read and digested the philosophy of the greatest thinkers from St. Augustine* to Friedrich Nietzsche* and Sigmund Freud* as well as to modern existentialists such as Sartre and Albert Camus (q.v.). Bellow made his "Kierkegaardian" choice as a writer, and the results are "a cross between Jewish sanctification and Christian grace" (Fuchs, 157). One important thing is evident: Saul Bellow has read many of the modern philosophers but has rejected them. As a consequence, his works result in traditional religious novels in which the heroes never commit suicide in an absurd world, never give in to "existential anguish," but move to a final mystical state in a world where there is still hope and a god.

REFERENCES

Brachenhoff, Mary. "Humboldt's Gift: The Ego's Mirror—A Vehicle for Self-Realization." *SBN* 5, no. 2 (Spring-Summer 1986): 15–21.

Clayton, John J. *Saul Bellow's Seize the Day: A Study in Mid-Life Transition.* *SBN* 5, no. 1 (Winter 1986): 34–47.

Fuchs, Daniel. *Saul Bellow: Vision and Revision.* Durham, N.C.: Duke University Press, 1984.

Galloway, David D. *The Absurd Hero in American Fiction: Updike, Styron, Bellow, Salinger.* Austin: University of Texas Press, 1966.

Porter, M. Gilbert. *Whence the Power? The Artistry and Humanity of Saul Bellow.* Columbia: University of Missouri Press, 1974.

Yetman, Michael C. "Toward a Language Irresistible: Saul Bellow and the Romance of Poetry." *PLL* 22, no. 4 (Fall 1986): 429–47.

BELY, ANDREY. B. October 26, 1880, Moscow, Russia. D. January 8, 1934, Moscow, USSR. Russian poet, novelist, and critic.

Raised in an educated milieu, Andrey Bely made his literary debut early in his life with a collection of poetry called *Simfoniia* (1902). In 1913 Bely became a follower of the Austrian social philosopher Rudolf

Steiner (1861–1925) and joined his anthroposophical colony in Basel, Switzerland. He welcomed the 1917 Bolshevik Revolution but later, because of the executions of several literary colleagues, Bely became dispirited and left Russia. He returned to his homeland in 1923. His first novel, *The Silver Dove* (1909), concerns a mystical Russian sect; it was followed by *Petersburg* (1913). Bely's autobiography expresses his realist view of life.

Bely, poet, novelist, and one of the most talented Russian writers at the turn of the century, lived at a time when, as Konstantin Mochulsky, his biographer, says, "the Marxists were addicted to philosophy and the philosophers to theology" (Mochulsky, 35). In 1904, he was appointed to the philosophy faculty in Moscow where he attended the lectures of Trubetsky on Greek philosophy and seminars on Plato.* But Bely's love was Kantianism,** which he studied assiduously. Consequently, he became absorbed in the Marburg School and in the neo-Kantian ideas of Hermann Cohen,* who also influenced the thinking of the young Boris Pasternak (q.v.). Bely's *The Symphony* (1900) and his theoretical article "Forms of Art" reflect the influence of both Friedrich Nietzsche* and Arthur Schopenhauer.*

In January 1908, Bely travelled to Petersburg and there delivered a lecture entitled "Friedrich Nietzsche and the Portents of the Present." This incident is important because it documents the fact that he was not just a novelist and poet but a recognized authority in philosophy, especially the philosophy of Nietzsche and Immanuel Kant,* the two most significant influences on his thought. In fact, his biographer arrives at the conclusion that "neo-Kantian idealism is carried to the ultimate extreme in Bely's system" (Mochulsky, 115).

REFERENCES

Anschuetz, Carol. "Bely's Petersburg and the End of the Russian Novel." In *The Russian Novel from Pushkin to Pasternak,* edited by John Garrard. New Haven, Conn.: Yale University Press, 1983.
Cassedy, Steven, ed. and trans. *Selected Essays of Andrei Bely.* Berkeley: University of California Press, 1985.
Elsworth, J. D. *Andrey Bely: A Critical Study of the Novels.* Cambridge, England: Cambridge University Press, 1983.
Mochulsky, Konstantin. *Andrei Bely; His Life and Works.* Ann Arbor, Mich.: Ardis, 1977.

BLAKE, WILLIAM. B. November 28, 1757, London, England. D. August 12, 1827, London, England. English poet, engraver, and visionary.

William Blake was the son of a shopkeeper. He received formal elementary education but, because of his family's circumstances, was forced to learn a trade. At the age of ten, he studied drawing and at fourteen was apprenticed to an engraver. He was, for a brief period, a member of the antiques class at the Royal Academy, after which he set up shop as an engraver. In 1809 he held a successful exhibition of sixteen paintings, and in 1821 he was commissioned to provide the drawings and engravings for the Book of Job. Blake's literary works include *Poetical Sketches* (1783), *Songs of Innocence* (1789), *Songs of Experience* (1794), *The Marriage of Heaven and Hell* (1790–1793), *Milton* (1808), and *Jerusalem* (1820).

When one enters into the world of William Blake, one enters into the world of a rebellious genius who, misunderstood in his own time, expressed his rejection of the intellectual and religious tradition in his unique and disturbing art and poetry. Blake was a compulsive scholar. As a youth he had carefully read and annotated John Locke's* *Essay on the Human Understanding,* but "in Blake's poetry Locke, along with [Francis] Bacon[*] and Newton, is constantly a symbol of every kind of evil, superstition and tyranny and whatever influence he had on Blake was clearly a negative one" (Frye, 14).

William Blake, undoubtedly one of the most erudite and intellectually sophisticated men of his era, was schooled in classical learning, was familiar with the teachings of Plato* and Aristotle,* and was as well acquainted with the philosophers of his own time whom he most often opposed. His rejection of the popular notion of eighteenth-century primitivism** is expressed nicely by Northrop Frye who states that "Blake had no use for the noble savage or for the cult of the natural man; he disliked [Jean-Jacques] Rousseau [q.v.] enough to give an attack on him a prominent place in *Jerusalem*" (Frye, 36).

Blake disagreed with Locke about the origin of ideas. According to Locke, ideas come from space into the mind; for Blake, space is a state of mind. Blake also held Locke responsible for deism** since his teaching was the source of the separation of the divine and the human. Frye points out, "It is an error of fact to call Locke a Deist, but it is not an error of interpretation to see many affinities between Deism and Locke's theory of knowledge" (Frye, 187). It should also be mentioned that Blake saw deism and not atheism** as the real foe of Christianity. Frye remarks on the antipathy that Blake held for the deists as well as his dislikes for Voltaire* and Rousseau, the pillars of reason and nature: "It was only in the age of reason that Rousseau could have thought up his conception of nature, and only a deist age which accepted the goodness of the natural man could have produced the rationalism of Voltaire. Blake's dislike of

Voltaire was at least as great as Voltaire's admiration for Newton and deist England'' (Frye, 377, 378).

Blake's familiarity with Platonism** is apparent in his numerous references to Plato. He disagreed with Plato's theory of knowledge: "to Plato, knowledge was recollection and art imitation; to Blake, both knowledge and art are recreation" (Frye, 85). However, in general, Blake leaned heavily toward Plato's philosophy because he saw that the philosopher offered an infinity of responses instead of demanding a single one. But Blake was not a Platonist; in fact, it is a conspicuous feature of Blake's thought that he disliked classical culture which focused on the state rather than the individual, and he expressed a preference for the Hebrew tradition.

If Blake was not a Platonist, he was indeed a Swedenborgian (see Swedenborgianism**). Blake accepted Emanuel Swedenborg's* rejection of the doctrine of a threefold God and embraced the Swedenborgian emphasis on the role of the imagination in his philosophy and theology. Blake's acceptance of Swedenborg as his master and ally is based to some extent on a common interest in Hebrew theology, which both considered superior to the pagan and classical traditions. Acceptance of any thinker as a master is surprising in so unique and isolated a spirit as Blake.

REFERENCES

Bloom, Harold. *Blake's Apocalypse*. Garden City, N.Y.: Doubleday, 1963.
Frye, Northrup. *Fearful Symmetry: A Study of William Blake*. Boston: Beacon Press, 1947.
Harper, George Mills. *The Neoplatonism of William Blake*. Chapel Hill: University of North Carolina Press, 1961.
Korteling, Jacomina. *Mysticism in Blake and Wordsworth*. New York: Haskell House, 1966.
Singer, June K. *The Unholy Bible: A Psychological Interpretation of William Blake*. New York: G. P. Putnam's Sons for the C. G. Jung Foundation, 1970.
Stieg, Elizabeth Joy. "William Blake and the Prophetic Process." *DAI* 47, no. 3 (September 1986): 916A.

BORGES, JORGE LUIS. B. August 24, 1899, Buenos Aires, Argentina. D. June 14, 1986, Geneva, Switzerland. Argentine short-story writer, essayist, and poet.

Very early, Jorge Luis Borges immersed himself in European culture, as a result of his family's emigration to Europe in 1914. In 1920 he joined the ultraist movement in Spain and returned the following year to

Buenos Aires where he is credited with the founding of the ultraist movement in South America. His first works consisted of a volume of philosophical poetry called *Buenos Aires Fervor* (1923). *Ficciones* appeared in 1941, followed by *The Aleph and Other Stories* (1933–1969), *Poemas* (1922–1943), and *Selected Poems* (1923–1967). The nonpolitical nature of Borges's work resulted in his being suspected by the Latin American left and identified with the right, which may well have kept him from winning the Nobel Prize.

Although there is no evidence that Borges ever studied the works of Jean-Paul Sartre* (q.v.) and Albert Camus (q.v.), a reading of Borges's works reveals significant similarities with the French existentialists, especially those writers concerned with the absurd human condition (see existentialism** and absurdity**). "The absurdity conveyed by Borges's works derives principally from three basic themes: the distrust of language as a means of depicting reality, the failure of human reason to unveil the mysteries of the universe and the rejection of absolute moral or philosophical values" (McMurray, 3).

Borges's protagonists are constantly on a quest for knowledge and salvation, a quest that usually ends in failure. Borges has no faith in the philosophers to point out the way. Like the existentialists who stress man's search to define himself, Borges sees each philosophical school as "provisional." For Borges, then, philosophy does not establish a mirror of reality, but rather an artificial system of thought that is superimposed on the real world.

Borges has injected into his writings the various forms of idealism** espoused by George Berkeley,* David Hume,* and Arthur Schopenhauer,* philosophers who are probably the most visible and the most useful for depicting the tenuousness of things.

The idealists, with whom Borges has aligned himself, maintain that material objects exist only in our minds and have no independent existence. Thus, in the poem "Daybreak," Borges "describes the dawn in Buenos Aires as a perilous moment for the city because it is not being perceived by its sleeping inhabitants and therefore could cease to exist" (McMurray, 53). Many of Borges's stories illustrate and explain idealistic philosophy. "The Circular Ruins" is probably his best fictional treatment of idealism. "The story's principal theme, that reality is a dream, is inextricably linked to Idealism, especially to the Idealism of Schopenhauer, who stresses the unreality of art and views life as the manifestation of will" (McMurray, 68).

Other than idealism, pantheism** is the philosophy that occurs most frequently in the works of Borges. Borges once wrote an essay entitled

"Pascal's Sphere," which verifies the fact that Borges was indeed familiar with ancient and modern philosophy because, in the essay, Borges traces the concept of the divinity from ancient Greece to the seventeenth century. Blaise Pascal* emerges in this essay as "a kind of existential pantheist" (McMurray, 78).

Borges is then not only an enlightened twentieth-century writer, but one who is well grounded in both ancient and modern philosophy, one who enhanced his art with the incorporation of philosophical thought.

REFERENCES

Acheana, Jon T. *The Prose of Jorge Luis Borges: Existentialism and the Dynamics of Surprise*. New York: Lang, 1984.
McMurray, George R. *Jorge Luis Borges*. New York: Ungar, 1980.
Paoli, Roberto. "Borges & Schopenhauer." *RCLL* 11, no. 24 (1986): 173–208.
Singh, Karnail. "Jorge Luis Borges (1899–1986): An Introduction." *LCrit* 21, no. 3 (1986): 14–17.

BRECHT, BERTOLT. B. February 10, 1898, Augsburg, Bavaria, West Germany. D. August 14, 1956, East Berlin, East Germany. German poet and dramatist.

As a drop-out medical student, Bertolt Brecht wrote songs and poems, and at first hesitated between the theatre and the silent film. With his play *Trommeln in der Nacht (Drums in the Night)* (1922), he won the Kleist prize and a national reputation. He moved to Berlin in 1924 where he scored a great popular success with the *Drei-Groschenoper (The Threepenny Opera)* (1928). This was followed by *Mahogonny* (1930), a work on which he collaborated with Kurt Weill. In 1929, he wrote his didactic "Lehrstücke" and aligned himself with the Communist party in its fight against the Nazis. He was exiled to Scandinavia in the 1930s, and here he wrote his longest play, *Galileo* (1938). The war forced him to move to the United States where he settled in California in 1941 and tried in vain to establish himself as a film writer. His chief work from this period was *Der Kaukasische Kreidekreis (The Caucasian Chalk Circle)* (1944). He returned to Europe in 1947 and wrote the *Short Organum*. From 1949 until his death in 1956, he lived in East Berlin where he staged his Thirty Years War play *Mutter Courage (Mother Courage)* (written, 1939, performed, 1941) and helped found the Berliner Ensemble, whose productions made him world famous.

There is probably no modern playwright, who is, at once, as innovative and didactic as Bertolt Brecht. Drama became for Brecht a didactic medium through which he hoped to influence, and to change, German politics. His aim was not to entertain, but to teach. He attacked capitalism; he satirized gangsterism and exploitation as the inevitable results of the capitalistic society. To promote Marxist (see Marxism**) concepts, Brecht initiated the idea of Epic Theatre (and its so-called *Verfremdung-seffekt*), which rejects Aristotelian theatre because its aim is not to arouse the spectators' emotions but to educate them in Marxist philosophy. The *Verfremdungseffekt* is a form of alienation which prevents the audience from entering into the Aristotelian state of illusion. In his play *Galileo,* for example, Brecht does not intend the audience to be mesmerized into believing that Galileo himself, as portrayed by the actor, walks the boards; he insists that the actor maintain his own identity as an actor in the critical awareness of the audience. "No writer has taken a keener delight in the contradictory nature of reality than Brecht, who for this very reason perhaps, found the dialectical philosophy of [Georg Wilhelm] Hegel[*] and [Karl] Marx[*] so congenial, and who rated the publication of Mao-Tse-Tung's book *On Contradiction* the outstanding literary event of 1954'' (Dickson, 3). Brecht was politically a Marxist who had spent a lifetime in the study of Marx, but his philosophical mentor was Hegel, from whom he learned that the criterion of authenticity** in art is achieved in the identity of form and content. Brecht's biographer Keith Dickson states that

> the relationship between form and content in a given work of art is so intimate that any change in the one immediately affects the other. If Brecht had ignored this basic Hegelian principle, forcing his revolutionary message into traditional moulds, it would not have the ring of truth about it that so many have discerned. (Dickson, 227)

REFERENCES

Bornemann, Ernest. "Credo quia Absurdum: An Epitaph for Bertolt Brecht."
    Kenyon Review 21 (1959): 169–80.
Dickson, Keith. *Toward Utopia: A Study of Brecht.* Oxford, England: Clarendon
    Press, 1978.
Esslin, Martin. *Brecht: The Man and His Work.* New York: Doubleday, 1960.
Gray, Ronald. *Bertolt Brecht.* New York: Grove Press, 1961.
Hecht, Werner. "The Development of Brecht's Theory of Epic Theater: 1918–
    1933." *The Tulane Drama Review* 6 (1961): 40–97.
Jesse, Horst. "The Young Bertolt Brecht and Religion." *CIBS* 15, no. 2 (April
    1986): 17–27.

C

CAMUS, ALBERT. B. November 7, 1913, Mondovi, French Algeria. D. January 4, 1960, Petit-Villeblevin, Yonne, France. French writer.

In 1942 and 1943, the publication in Paris of *L'Étranger* (trans. S. Gilbert, *The Outsider,* London, 1946) and *Le Mythe de Sisyphe* (trans. J. O'Brien, *The Myth of Sisyphus,* London, 1975) brought immediate fame to Albert Camus. The liberation of 1944 revealed him as having been active in the resistance movement during World War II. Camus described his next work *La Peste* (Paris, 1947; trans. S. Gilbert, *The Plague,* London, 1948) as his most anti-Christian work. However, the double rejection of communism and Christianity was expressed in more philosophical terms in *L'Homme Revolt* (Paris, 1951; trans. A. Bower, *The Rebel,* London, 1953). This publication led in 1952 to a violent quarrel with Jean-Paul Sartre* (q.v.). In 1957 Camus was awarded the Nobel Prize for Literature.

In 1935, Camus rewrote a book of his friend Jean Guitton on Plotinus* and St. Augustine.* At this time he expressed his admiration for Plotinus because the philosopher believed that intuition rather than reason was the bridge between man and the universe. Camus's biographer Patrick McCarthy says of the finished product, "He [Camus] admires the dualism of the early Christians and of his pessimistic Augustine but he cannot give up the dreams of oneness which he finds in Plotinus" (McCarthy, 73).

The fact that Camus's *L'Homme Revolt* is a study of Georg Wilhelm Hegel,* Karl Marx,* Friedrich Nietzsche,* the surrealists (see surrealism**), and other prophets of revolt is ample proof that Camus had immersed himself in philosophical writings. *L'Homme Revolt* is, in fact, a philosophical essay that expounds the moral and political values that lay beyond nihilism.**

Camus discovered Arthur Schopenhauer* and Nietzsche very early, while he was a student at the lycée. Philosophy was part of the obligatory school program, and the text he was reading was the *Manuel de Philosophie* by Armand Cuvillier. In September 1939, Camus began a serious study of the works of Nietzsche. Camus's biographer Herbert Lottman makes the point that

> He pursued his reading of Nietzsche, finding rules of behavior which he would like to follow . . . the house itself was surrounded by almond trees; here he would begin the brief essay *Les Amandiers* which offered, to himself first of all, a way toward inner peace in a time of troubles, making ample use of the lessons he was learning from Nietzsche. (Lottman, 216)

Continuing his study of Nietzsche, in 1943 Camus agreed to edit a volume of selected writings of Nietzsche and to write a preface for part of a series called *Classique de la Liberté*. Interviewed during a 1955 visit to Greece, Camus claimed that whereas most of his fellow French writers had been nourished on German literature, *he* had been raised on Greek. He then stated that Plato* was more important to him than Hegel but admitted the influence of Nietzsche (reported in McCarthy). At the scene of the auto accident that caused Camus's death in Villeblevin on January 3, 1960, the police found the author's black leather briefcase in the muddy soil. Among personal photographs, his passport, and other important documents was a copy of Nietzsche's *Le Gai Savoir*.

The Camus-Sartre relationship must be discussed here because it is often misunderstood. There was never a long period of friendship between the two men, and they had, in fact, little in common. However, the popular press linked the two writers and branded them as existentialist (see existentialism**), which angered Camus. Camus disagreed with Sartre over the primacy awarded to existence, and he did not consider himself an existentialist. On November 15, 1945, Camus told an interviewer of *Les Nouvelles Littéraires:* "No, I'm not an existentialist." He then went on to explain that the only book of ideas he himself had published, *Le Mythe de Sisyphe,* was, in fact, directed against so-called existentialist philosophers. Lottman mentions this interview and elaborates on the author's denial of being an existentialist: "In an interview published a month later Camus spelled out his difference with Existentialism, both the religious type of [Søren] Kierkegaard [*] and [Karl] Jaspers [*] and the atheist Existentialism of [Edmund] Husserl [*], [Martin]

Heidegger [*], and Sartre'' (Lottman, 372). Two interviews that appear in the Pleiade edition of Camus's work are important in clarifying Camus's philosophical position and demonstrate his extensive knowledge of the existentialist philosophers.

REFERENCES

Cohn, Robert Greer. ''The True Camus.'' *FR* 60, no. 1 (October 1986): 30–38.
Hanna, Thomas. *The Thought and Art of Albert Camus*. Chicago: Henry Regnery, 1958.
Lottman, Herbert. *Albert Camus*. New York: Doubleday, 1979.
McCarthy, Patrick. *Camus*. New York: Random House, 1982.
Shrivastava, K. C., and G. D. Mehta. ''The Greatness of the Novel as an Art Form: The Views of D. H. Lawrence and Albert Camus.'' *Prajna* 29, no. 1 (1983): 115–24.
Sterling, Elwyn F. ''Albert Camus' *La Peste:* Cottard's Act of Madness.'' *CollL* 13, no. 2 (Spring 1986): 177–85.

CARLYLE, THOMAS. B. December 4, 1795, Ecclefechan, Dumfries-shire, Scotland. D. February 5, 1881, London, England. Scottish essayist and historian.

Thomas Carlyle taught for several years, until 1819. In the 1820s, he published *Sartor Resartus*, and in 1834 he moved to London, where he wrote his greatest work, *The French Revolution* (1837). In 1865, he served as the rector of Edinburgh University, but on his wife's death in 1866, he became a partial recluse.

Although Carlyle is best known as a biographer—he wrote an exemplary biography of Friedrich von Schiller (q.v.)—and as a social theorist whose work focused on heroism, work, and duty, he was also a writer who was deeply concerned with philosophical ideas, especially those of Friedrich Nietzsche* and Karl Marx.*

As a rebel and a somewhat disturbing misfit in a Victorian society, Carlyle, with his sometimes fierce cynicism toward the social traditions that he considered either wrong or outmoded, had much in common with Nietzsche. As Albert J. LaValley stated, ''Carlyle and Nietzsche have both suffered for their fascism, whether lauded and made all-important or condemned and used as an occasion for dismissing their seriousness of purpose'' (LaValley, 11). Carlyle's work *Cromwell* (1845), in which he searched for heroes, clearly displayed Nietzschean elements in the glorification of the strong character who will overturn society and become a hero for all ages.

Carlyle's *Latter-Day Pamphlets* of 1850, in which he himself played the hero, excoriating the advocates of democracy and philanthropy with a lofty contempt and building a doctrine of a strong new aristocracy much in the manner of the later Nietzsche, had, he felt, alienated him from everyone; but unlike Nietzsche, he seems to have viewed this alienation as inflicted from without. (LaValley, 269)

Although the works of Carlyle often parallel Marxian theory, Carlyle's vision and its application are somewhat different. Marx was more philosophical than Carlyle, yet both attack what they consider to be unreal systems that fail to deal with reality. "Carlyle begins with the idle workers, estranged and alienated from their work, their fellowmen, nature, and themselves, before the St. Ives Workhouse; Marx, with the condition of 'estranged labor,' an economic state which is every bit as psychological as it is social'' (LaValley, 222). With the growing rift between laborer and management, both Carlyle and Marx see society breaking apart and both argue in the interest of unity for a fair distribution of economic wealth. Both affect the reader in the same way; theirs is the common voice of the outraged revolutionary who cries out for justice and the return of human relationship and fulfillment in work.

Indeed, Thomas Carlyle was a writer of ideas, a didactic writer to be sure, who lashed out violently, uncompromisingly, at his readers. On reading his works, one is astounded at his learning and at his congruity with Nietzsche and Marx, but there were other philosophers whose works he knew well; he corresponded with Ralph Waldo Emerson (q.v.), and he had read Immanuel Kant* and Voltaire.* As summed up in the *Dictionary of Philosophy,* "He [Carlyle] was not in any sense a systematic philosopher but his keen mind gave wide influence to the ideas he advanced in ethics, politics, and economics'' (Runes, 45).

REFERENCES

LaValley, Albert J. *Carlyle and the Idea of the Modern.* New Haven, Conn.: Yale University Press, 1968.
Runes, Dagobert David, ed. *Dictionary of Philosophy.* New York: Philosophical Library, 1983.

CARY, JOYCE. B. December 7, 1888, Londonderry, Ireland. D. March 29, 1957, Oxford, England. British novelist.

Joyce Cary's family lost their property through the Irish Land Acts of the 1880s and went to London as exiles. His youthful poverty had a great effect on young Cary, and other, later negative experiences, such as the Balkan War (1912–1913), only increased his pessimism. From *Aissa*

Saved (1932) on, his central concern was to picture a tragic world. Cary rejected the Victorian concept of freedom. *Mister Johnson* (1939) is the best of his African novels. His other works include *Herself Surprised* (1941), *To Be a Pilgrim* (1942), and *The Horse's Mouth* (1944).

An intellectually demanding writer, Joyce Cary assumes an erudite reading audience, well informed and sensitive to the philosophical and the historical facets of literature.

Influenced by and subsequently disenchanted by Darwinian determinism** Cary rejected Charles Darwin* and chose to believe instead in freedom of choice. Nevertheless, he was convinced that Darwinism** had permeated society and had robbed many of their Christian God.

There is evidence that Cary had read Sigmund Freud's* *Totem and Taboo* as early as 1929 and was also familiar with the work of Carl Jung,* but it is difficult to assess their influence on the author's work. It is difficult to determine to what extent Cary was affected by Platonic thought although he studied the works of both Socrates* and Plato* at Clifton College.

Joyce Cary was generally familiar with the western philosophical tradition, but he was especially interested in and influenced by the works of Søren Kierkegaard,* an interest that can be traced to his friendship with John MacMurray who taught philosophy at Oxford University. Joyce Cary is an important writer who was devoted to the search for truth in the work of Western thinkers from Socrates to Jung, Immanuel Kant,* Baruch Spinoza,* and Kierkegaard.

REFERENCE

Fisher, Barbara. *Joyce Cary: The Writer and His Theme*. Atlantic Highlands, N.J.: Humanities Press, 1980.

CATHER, WILLA. B. December 7, 1873, Winchester, Virginia. D. April 24, 1947, New York City, New York. American poet and novelist.

At the age of nine, Willa Cather moved from Virginia to Red Cloud, Nebraska, where she grew up among the immigrants from Europe who were settling the western frontier. As a student at the University of Nebraska, she exhibited a talent for writing and, on her graduation in 1895, she obtained a position on a Pittsburgh magazine and worked as a music and drama editor for *The Pittsburgh Leader*. She turned to teaching in 1901 but continued her writing, and by 1903 she had published her first book of verse, *April Twilights*. In 1905, she published a collection of short stories, *The Troll Garden,* and at this time assumed the position of managing editor of *McClures*. Her first novel, *Alexander's Bridge,* appeared in 1912, but then she turned to the material that made her famous, her portrayal of the settlers and their frontier life on the American plains, and published the very successful *O, Pioneers* (1913) and *My Antonia* (1918). Cather's two additional popular and enduring novels are *Death Comes to the Archbishop* (1927) and *Shadows on the Rock* (1931). All of her novels are uplifting works that exact the American spirit and the conquest of hardship in the New World.

Although there is evidence that Willa Cather, an enduring writer in American literature, had studied such thinkers as Thomas Carlyle (q.v.), Ralph Waldo Emerson (q.v.), and William James,* according to Loretta Wasserman, she was most significantly influenced by the works of Henri Bergson.* Cather's letters to Elizabeth Sergeant (1911) demonstrate an enthusiasm for Bergson's *Creative Evolution* (1907). Wasserman sums it up this way: "My contention is that Bergson was an important influence on Cather's thinking, and that his philosophical speculations concerning the nature of time and the dynamics of memory are given strikingly parallel expression in Cather's fiction" (Wasserman, 227). Wasserman cites as examples Bergson's stress on intuition as opposed to intellect and his twofold notion of memory—learned and involuntary—"a surging up of lived moments in the past" (Wasserman, 229).

This involuntary memory is very important to writers who in their literary works often allow the past of their characters to emerge and intermingle with the present. An example of this common technique in Cather's *My Antonia,* which Wasserman calls "lived time," occurs when Antonia's children see their own present lives in clear perspective as they contemplate their mother's past. The past remembrances enhance the present, and, with Cather just as with Arthur Miller's *Death of a Salesman,* the present triggers a spark of memory. To quote Wasserman once more, scenes and memory of the past suggest "the power of intuition to go beyond personal memory to include all of human energy and endeavor and to perceive, however dimly, the wholeness of the universe behind the apparent descriptions of change" (Wasserman, 230).

William Curtin cites the influence of William James, whose works influenced so many of Cather's generation roughly from 1890 to 1910. Cather was particularly influenced by James's *The Varieties of Religious Experience* (1902). Curtin traced the religious experiences described in Cather's novels to James's work:

> "A Study of the Fiction of Willa Cather" in light of that great book would
> help to understand the irascible saintliness of Myra Henshawr, the fanatical
> missionary spirit of Enid Rayee Wheeler, the asceticism of Jeanne LeBer,

the saintly compassion of Mrs. Ramsey, the Lutheran scrupulosity of Henry Colbert and the Quaker conscience of his daughter, Mrs. Blake. James' *Varieties* will help to explain the nature of Tom Outland's happiness and the professor's final stoicism''. [**] (Curtin, 123)

REFERENCES

Bohlke, L. Brent. *Willa Cather in Person: Interviews, Speeches and Letters.* Lincoln: University of Nebraska Press, 1986.

Curtin, William M. "Willa Cather and *The Varieties of Religious Experience.*" *Renascence* 27, no. 1 (1975): 115–23.

Murphy, John J. "One of Ours as American Naturalism." *GPQ* 2, no. 4 (Fall 1982): 232–38. (Relationship to naturalism)

O'Brien, Sharon. *Willa Cather: The Emerging Voice.* New York: Oxford University Press, 1987.

Shaw, Patrick W. "*My Antonia:* Emergence and Authorial Revelations." *American Literature* 56, no. 4 (December 1984): 527–40.

Shubik, Valerie Reid. "Willa Cather: An Emersonian Angel of Vision." *DAI* 46, no. 12 (June 1986): 3721A.

Wasserman, Loretta. "The Music of Time: Henri Bergson and Willa Cather." *American Literature* 57, no. 2 (May 1985): 226–39.

Woodress, James. *Willa Cather: A Literary Life.* Lincoln: University of Nebraska Press, 1987.

CHAUCER, GEOFFREY. B. c. 1342/1343, London, England. D. October 25, 1400, London, England. English poet.

Geoffrey Chaucer's father was a successful vintner who could afford to provide his son with a good education. In 1357, Chaucer was placed in the service of the Countess of Ulster, and by 1359 he was serving in the army under Edward III. In 1366 he married Phillipa Pan and at this time was appointed a court official. His first important and successful poem was a narrative love poem called *House of Fame* (c. 1380). From 1380 to 1390 Chaucer suffered political setbacks, but he continued to write and translated Anicius Manlius Severinus Boethius's* *Consolation of Philosophy*. During the 1390s Chaucer regained political favor and established a close relationship with the Earl of Derby, who later became Henry IV. At this time he wrote his greatest and best known work, *The Canterbury Tales* (c. 1387).

The influence of Boethius's *The Consolation of Philosophy* is apparent in much of Chaucer's poetry, for example, the *Knight's Tale*. About Chaucer's *Troilus and Criseyde* Bernard L. Jefferson says:

In the tale . . . he saw a capital example of the sudden reversal of fortune's wheel, and an unusually interesting example of human falseness or lack of steadfastness, of worldly felicity,[**] and of human affairs directed to a predetermined end by a relentless fate; and it will be found that most of the extended passages gathered by Chaucer from sources outside the immediate original, itself influenced somewhat by the *Consolation,* concern these very things.'' (Jefferson, 120)

In *Troilus,* the Boethian concept of fate is important for an understanding of the poem. In the work, the inevitable doom of the hero and heroine is tied in with the destruction of Troy. Fate operates in the *Troilus* exactly as described by Boethius in the *Consolation.* ''Jove of his wise 'Purveyance' grants to the parcae or fates, and to the goddess fortune the execution of the destinal ordinances, just as described in the *Consolation.* Fortune is given a very high rank among the gods, and is honored by Troilus above all others . . . events happen by 'Necessitee' '' (Jefferson, 122).

The influence of Boethius is to be found in many of Chaucer's other works. For example, the poem *Fortune* (c. 1389) sums up all that Boethius said of fortune in the *Consolation.* In the poem *Truth* (c. 1390), ''the influence of Boethius is great, but is an influence of thought rather than one of words'' (Jefferson, 136). In the *House of Fame,* the goddess of fame is a replica of the Boethian conception of fortune. R. M. Kean mentions the fact that Boethius's work and Macrobius's commentary on the *Somnium Scipionis* were the two most important books for Chaucer.

> The importance of these two books to Chaucer, and indeed to the middle ages in general, can hardly be overrated. Between them, they transmitted important aspects of platonic [see Platonism**] and neo-platonic [see Neoplatonism**] thought; but what was perhaps more important was that they are typical representatives of the late Roman blend of philosophical ideas, in which Platonism is combined with Stoicism[**] in a form which was compatible with Christianity. (Kean, 27)

As Joseph Grennen says, in Chaucer's *House of Fame,* ''Plato[*] can be found everywhere'' (Grennen, 237). The work by Plato that influenced Chaucer most was the *Timaeus;* there is no question that the *Timaeus* and the commentary of Chacidius were available to Chaucer. Plato's *Timaeus* could be described as a creation myth which actually ends in a philosophical discourse. *The House of Fame* and the *Timaeus* both concern themselves with an inquiry into the nature of the cosmos.

REFERENCES

Corsa, Helen S. *Chaucer: Poet of Mirth and Morality*. Notre Dame, Ind.: University of Notre Dame Press, 1964.

Grennen, Joseph "Aristotelian Ideas in Chaucer's *Troilus:* A Preliminary Study." *MSH* 14 (1986): 125–38.

————. "Chaucer and Chalcidius: The Platonic Origins of *The House of Fame*." In *Viator: Medieval and Renaissance Studies,* vol. 15, pp. 237–62.

Jefferson, Bernard L. *Chaucer and the "Consolation of Philosophy" of Boethius*. New York: Haskell House, 1965.

Kean, R. M. *Love Vision and Debate*. London: Routledge and Kegan Paul, 1972.

Thomas, Mary Edith. *Medieval Skepticism and Chaucer*. New York: William Frederick Press, 1950.

CHESTERTON, G[ILBERT] K[EITH]. B. May 29, 1874, London, England. D. June 14, 1936, Beaconsfield, Buckinghamshire, England. English critic and author of verse, essays, novels, and short stories.

G. K. Chesterton was educated at St. Paul's School and later studied art at the Slade School and literature at University College, London. For some time he worked as a free-lance journalist during which time he published his first book of poems, *The Wild Knight* (1900). In the early 1900s he published several books on social criticism, including *The Defendant* (1901), *Twelve Types* (1902), *Heretics* (1905), and *What's Wrong with the World* (1910). Chesterton's publications in literary criticism include *Robert Browning* (1903), *Charles Dickens* (1906), *George Bernard Shaw* (q.v.) (1909), *William Blake* (q.v.) (1910), *The Victorian Age of Literature* (1913), and *Robert Louis Stevenson* (1927). Chesterton's theological and religious theories are discussed in *Orthodoxy* (1909), *St. Francis of Assisi* (1923), *St. Thomas Aquinas** (1933), and *Avowals and Denials* (1934). He also wrote fiction, for example, *The Napoleon of Notting Hill* (1904), *The Man Who Was Thursday* (1902), and the famous Father Brown stories (1911–1935).

Chesterton, one of the most celebrated and esteemed figures in modern literature, might be branded by modern literature students as a Catholic apologist, but he was also a successful playwright, novelist, poet, and author of the Father Brown detective stories. Works like *Orthodoxy, The Everlasting Man* (1925), and *St. Thomas Aquinas* show evidence of Chesterton's vast knowledge of Catholic theology and philosophy, but recent scholarship (see John Coates) verifies the fact that he was also very knowledgeable in secular philosophies, especially those of Georg Wilhelm Hegel* and Friedrich Nietzsche.*

Due to the work of Edward Caird and F. H. Bradley, Hegelianism** was well promulgated in the England of Chesterton's youth, but the key ideas of Hegelianism were not acceptable to the young Chesterton. John Coates, in a 1986 article on Chesterton, explains how Hegelianism was supplanted (from c. 1906 to 1913) in England by the philosophy of Nietzsche and Eastern philosophy, both of which became fashionable among intellectuals. Chesterton reacted vigorously against both trends. He saw a danger in the Oriental philosophy that encouraged despotism and the subservience of the individual to the nation. To Nietzschean philosophy, the Catholic Chesterton naturally was antagonistic because of its pessimism and its hostility to religion. Considering both eastern philosophy and Nietzschean philosophy threats to Christian England, Chesterton responded with a prose essay entitled "How I Found Superman." Coates comments on Chesterton's second response, *The Flying Inn:* "The philosophical and religious background of the period in which it was written is of particular importance for adequate assessment of the novel" (Coates, 303). In *The Flying Inn,* Chesterton uses the genre of the novel to satirize both the philosophy of the East and the philosophy of Nietzsche.

REFERENCES

Boyd, Ian. "Chesterton and the Bible." *CRevAS* 11, no. 1 (February 1985): 21–33.
Coates, John. "The Philosophy and Religious Background of *The Flying Inn.*" *The Chesterton Review* 12, no. 3 (August 1986): 303–28.
Corrigan, Maureen. "Gill, Chesterton and Ruskin: Medievalism in the Twentieth Century." *CRevAS* 9, no. 1 (February 1983): 15–30.
Knile, Robert, ed. *As I Was Saying: A Chesterton Reader*. Grand Rapids, Mich.: Eerdmans, 1985.

COLERIDGE, SAMUEL TAYLOR. B. October 21, 1772, Devonshire, England. D. July 25, 1834, Highgate, England. English poet, philosopher, and literary critic.

Samuel Taylor Coleridge received his early education at Hospital School in London. In 1791, he enrolled at Cambridge University but left the college in 1794 without having taken a degree. For a brief period, he gave public lectures and wrote some poetry for *The Morning Post*. He met William Wordsworth (q.v.) in 1795; and in 1797 he published the second edition of *Poems* which included "The Rime of the Ancient Mariner" and "Kubla Khan." His collaboration with Wordsworth on the *Lyrical Ballads* was a landmark in the Romantic movement in England. The year 1799 was spent in study in Germany, where he studied German philosophy. On his return to England he wrote articles for *The Morning Post* and translated Friedrich von Schiller's (q.v.) trilogy *Wallenstein* (1800). In his later years, Coleridge suffered from ill health and an unhappy marriage. He rates high as a literary critic; he earned a reputation as the philosopher of the Romantic movement (see romanticism**); and he is credited with introducing Kantianism** into England.

That philosophy destroyed the poet in Coleridge is a common tale, and Wordsworth, Thomas Carlyle, (q.v.), and Charles Lamb commented on the belief that Coleridge returned to England from Germany with his head full of metaphysics, a frustrated poet. Whether true or not, Coleridge was definitely preoccupied with the philosophy of Immanuel Kant* and Johann Gottlieb Fichte.* Before his study of Kant, the poet had studied the empiricism** of David Hartley,* but Kant helped to rid him of empiricist philosophy. According to the critic philosopher Dorothy M. Emmett, "His quarrel now with the Hartlian sensationalist theory of the compounding of ideas was not that it was empirical but that it was untrue to experience" (Emmett, 164). Earlier, Coleridge had sought in Plato* and the Neoplatonists (see Neoplatonism**) a philosophy that would describe the power of the mind. He never lost his interest in Plato, but it was Kant who showed him "the distinction between the categories and the manifold of sensation; secondly, the distinction between the transcendent and the transcendental; and thirdly, the distinction between understanding and the Reason" (Emmett, 165).

By 1809, Coleridge was immersed in the study of German metaphysics (see metaphysical**), which helped him to develop his own transcendental philosophy (see transcendentalism**). Kant, in the long run, was the most important influence on Coleridge. Having abandoned empiricism, Coleridge's study of Kant provided him with an awareness that empirical knowledge was incomplete and could never tell him the nature of things in themselves. Coleridge found in Kant an active power at work in thinking, which he attempted to apply to art. He had difficulty in saying just what the creative power of the mind was, but he knew that it existed and, as a poet, he could use it to create beautiful works of art. An example of this power is expressed in the following stanza, dedicated to Wordsworth:

> Of the formulations and the building up
> Of a human spirit thou hast dared to tell
> What may be told, to the understanding mind

Revealable; and what within the mind
By vital breathings secret as the soul
Of vernal growth, oft quickens in the heart
Thoughts all too deep for words.

The biography of Coleridge for the National Portrait Gallery describes him as a literary critic, a psychologist, a philosopher, a theologian, and so on. However, as Kathleen Coburn, editor of the 20th Century Views collection of critical essays on Coleridge, states in her introduction, "Coleridge needs a tough-minded, objective, nonallied, nonprofessional philosopher to tolerate and trace his intellectual image, for it is not that of a systematic philosopher" (Coburn, 7). The same opinion was expressed by Lytton Strachey in a 1907 review of Shawcrosses' edition to the *Biographia Literaria:* "The truth is that Coleridge in spite of—one is tempted to say in consequence of—his love of philosophy was not a philosopher. He speculated too much and thought too little" (Coburn, 3).

REFERENCES

Coburn, Kathleen, ed. *Coleridge: A Collection of Critical Essays.* Englewood Cliffs, N.J.: Prentice-Hall, 1967.
DePaolo, Charles. "Kant, Coleridge and the Ethics of War." *WC* 16, no. 1 (Winter 1985): 29–32.
Emmett, Dorothy M. "Coleridge on the Growth of the Mind." In *Coleridge: A Collection of Critical Essays,* edited by Kathleen Coburn. Englewood Cliffs, N.J.: Prentice-Hall, 1967.
Jackson, H. J. "Turning & Turning: Coleridge on our Knowledge of the External World." *PMLA* 101, no. 5 (October 1986): 848–56.
Taylor, Anya. "Coleridge and 'Essential Oneness.' " *WC* 16, no. 1 (Winter 1985): 29–32.

CONRAD, JOSEPH. B. December 3, 1857, Berdyczew, Ukraine. D. August 3, 1924, Kent, England. Naturalized British novelist of Polish background.

Joseph Conrad's youth was tragic; his father was involved in political uprisings, and he was arrested and exiled with his family to Vologda in Russia. As a young man, Conrad became restless with his studies and joined the French merchant navy in 1874. During the next four years he made three voyages to the West Indies. In 1878 he joined an English freighter and, during the next sixteen years, he sailed in British ships. His sailing experiences provided him with material for his first two novels, *Almayer's Folly* (1895) and *An Outcast of the Islands* (1896). Three more books followed: *The Nigger of the "Narcissus"* (1898), *Tales of Unrest* (1898), and *Lord Jim* (1900). Conrad finally settled in Kent, but he was beset with troubles: lack of money, ill health, and an inability to settle his doubts about his creative ability.

The two philosophers whom Conrad had read and followed were Friedrich Nietzsche* and Arthur Schopenhauer.* His letters show Nietzschean disenchantment with the mass man and mass politics in England, and as Friederick Karl points out, both Nietzsche and Conrad felt that "Idealism was simply a disguise for individual failure and a consequent worship of power" (Karl, 227).

> Many aspects of Nietzsche's thought, and particularly his characteristic equation, in *The Twilight of the Idols* (1889) and *The Antichrist* (1895), of altruism, pity, and decadence as the lamentable historical results of Christianity, are present in *The Nigger of the "Narcissus"* (1898). But where Nietzsche writes that "active pity for all the failures and all the weak" is "more harmful than vice," Conrad shows both sides of the problem. On the one hand, the results of the crew's pity for what demonstrates that the increasing sensitivity to the suffering of others which comes with Christianity has made it much more difficult to maintain the cohesion of the social order. . . . On the other hand, whereas Nietzsche proposes as an alternative the proud warrior morality of the superman, Conrad does not. He deprecates the divisions that pity produces in the crew, but he makes Allisoun share their feeling. (Watt, 111)

If readers feel that there is always a dark cloud hovering over Conrad's stories, it is probably the pessimism** of Schopenhauer. In *The Nigger of the "Narcissus,"* it is the pessimism of death that haunts the crew and the ship. At the end, the ship seems lighter, as though relieved of the burden of death itself. This sense of doom has its source in Schopenhauer, but it was also the result of what Karl calls "Polish defeats, a doomed father and doomed causes" (Karl, 194). "If Conrad sees the source of fiction as impressions recollected in maturity, he finds its permanent value as a memorial record in the long chain of human solidarity. This persistent concern is where Conrad most radically diverges, not only from Pater and Schopenhauer, but from Flaubert, Maupassant, and the Symbolists [see symbolism**]" (Watt, 87).

Conrad's pessimism occurs most explicitly in the less known work *Almayer's Folly,* which expresses the lost hopes and dreams of the Nietzschean individual who battles in vain against the will of the world. Actually, Conrad's Promethean** characters (even in his short stories, such as "Youth," 1902) are always set in an antagonistic world, a world of conflict, pain, and suffering, a world without joy, without hope.

Finally, Conrad shared with Sigmund Freud* the awareness of a human existence based on repression and restraint, insecure beyond human control. Hope, they believed, lay in a deeper understanding of man's destructive tendencies and in an awareness of "the modest counter truths on which civilization depends" (Watts, 167).

REFERENCES

Caracciolo, Peter. "Buddhist Teaching Stories and Their Influence on Conrad, Wells and Kipling: The Reception of the Jataka and Allied Genres in Victorian Culture." *Conradiana* 11, no. 1 (May 1986): 24–34.

Karl, Frederick Robert. *Joseph Conrad: The Three Lives*. New York: Farrar, Straus & Giroux, 1979.

Kirschener, Paul. *Conrad: The Psychologist as Artist*. Edinburgh, Scotland: Oliver & Boyd, 1968.

Mergroz, R. L. *Joseph Conrad's Mind and Method: A Study of Personality and Art*. London: Faber, 1931.

Watt, Ian. *Conrad in the Nineteenth Century*. Berkeley: University of California Press, 1979.

D

DAHLBERG, EDWARD. B. July 22, 1900, Boston, Massachusetts. D. February 27, 1977, Santa Barbara, California. American novelist.

Critics praised Edward Dahlberg as a pioneer of proletarian fiction following the publication of his autobiographical novels, *Bottom Dogs* (1929), *From Flushing to Calvary* (1932), and *Those Who Perish* (1934). Dahlberg fell into obscurity after he parted with Theodore Dreiser (q.v.) and the naturalists (see naturalism), but he reemerged in the 1960s when he produced his finest work, *Because I Was Flesh* (1964). He became famous for his attacks on the decline of Western literature and American culture. Dahlberg, a prolific writer of some twenty books which cover a span from the 1920s to the late 1960s, is regarded by the academic community as an intellectual stylist.

In gathering information on Dahlberg, it seemed logical to review his witty and brilliant book of 1971, *The Confessions of Edward Dahlberg*. Here the references to philosophers are so numerous that only some are recorded here. In the *Confessions,* there are fifteen passing references to Aristotle* and ten to Plato,* which indicates Dahlberg's knowledge of these ancient Greek philosophers. Actually, when one reads the entire *Confessions,* one is overwhelmed by the multiplicity of Dahlberg's references to Greek and Roman mythology and to classical writers ranging from Homer to Horace, indicating that Dahlberg's knowledge of antiquity was not superficial.

It is difficult to ascertain the influence of certain philosophers on Dahlberg's writing, but his reading list of the Great Thinkers is endless. He has read René Descartes* and Ralph Waldo Emerson (q.v.). Specific works he read include William James's* *Varieties of Religious Experi-*

ences (1902) and Friedrich Nietzsche's* *The Birth of Tragedy* (1872) and *The Genealogy of Morals* (1887). This great German philosopher definitely made an impact on Dahlberg's thinking because, in the *Confessions* alone, there are at least fifteen in-depth references to Nietzsche. It is interesting to note that when Dahlberg mentions Nietzsche, he customarily recites the exact words of the German philsopher, an indication that his study of Nietzsche was thorough.

One must actually read a book by Dahlberg in order to understand how great is his learning. Reading Dahlberg is like taking a trip through time where one stops periodically to savor a thought from Plotinus* (one of his favorite philosophers) or Socrates* or to meander into the mainstream of art or literature. And yet, with all of the knowledge of the great philosophers stored in his mind, Dahlberg, in his humble way, says, "At nineteen, I was a stranger to myself. At forty I asked 'who am I?' At fifty I concluded I would never know" (Dahlberg, 3).

REFERENCE

Dahlberg, Edward. *The Confessions of Edward Dahlberg.* New York: George
        Braziller, 1971.

DANTE ALIGHIERI. B. May 15, 1265, Florence, Italy. D. September 13/14, 1321, Ravenna, Italy. Italian poet.

Dante attended the University of Bologna and fought in the battle of Campaldino in 1289. He was active in the government of Florence and served on various city councils. In 1301 he went to Rome to negotiate peace between the warring factions of the White Guelphs and the Black Guelphs. The Blacks took over the city and Dante (a White) was sent into exile. He spent the rest of his days wandering from court to court with long sojourns at Verona and at Ravenna. Dante's works include the *Divine Comedy* (1306–1321), *Convivio* (trans. 1903), *Epistolae* (trans. 1920), and *On Monarchy* (trans. 1954).

Dante read the *Nicomachean Ethics* of Aristotle* in conjunction with Saint Thomas Aquinas's* commentary. He was in fact very well read in the philosophers, and Thomas Bergin cites 300 references in his works to Aristotle alone. These references are not those of a slovenly reader; Dante's use of Aristotle's ideas on such important topics as immortality, the nature of the earth, the nobility of soul, and truth exhibits his vast knowledge of the works of Aristotle. "The vision of *Convivio* (c. 1304) which reason revealed to Dante, and which he served as faithfully as he could, may be described as Christianized Aristotelianism. . . . He was firmly grounded in Aristotle—but Aristotle related to the Christian creed and rethought in the light of subsequent cultures'' (Fergusson, 51). In *Convivio* Dante tells us that he discovered that Marcus Tullius Cicero* and Anicius Manlius Severinus Boethius* both played a large role in his works. Dante was also familiar with the *Itinerarium Mentis in Deum* of Saint Bonaventure,* and "his role in the *Paradiso* is certainly as much that of a representative of the extrarational or mystical approach to illumination as it is that of the symbolic Franciscan (Bergin, 65).

Saint Thomas Aquinas is the principal philosopher from whom Dante drew.

> . . . when we consider the cultural impact of Thomism, with its effort to bring the classical ethical system into harmony with revealed truth, its respect for reason, its willingness to give this poor mortal world of ours its due, its all but revolutionary "freedom" in the interpretation of traditional authority, we can see at once that it is of the essence of the *Comedia*. (Bergin, 63)

The influence on Dante of Thomas Aquinas is perceptible throughout Dante's writing. Through the centuries, Thomas Aquinas has been the spokesman for Catholic philosophers and Dante has been the spokesman for Catholic writers. It is true that Dante wrote in an age of one faith, but even today scholars and theologians agree that Dante is soundly Catholic probably because, in dealing with matters of faith, Dante stayed close to the authority of Saint Thomas. Dante's *Divine Comedy* is an astounding work, studded with philosophical and theological gems. At times Dante discusses the question of man's happiness on earth and then Aquinas's ideas on the possibility of miracles. Indeed, no one can read the *Divine Comedy* and doubt that Dante is a great philosophical poet. When one thinks of the great writers of previous ages, the name of Dante surely occurs. Perhaps Dante is an exemplum to modern writers, one that endorses the incorporation of philosophers' ideas into a work of fiction and consequently creates the atmosphere for a great work of literature.

REFERENCES

Bergin, Thomas G. *Dante*. New York: Orion Press, 1965.
Fergusson, Francis. *Dante*. New York: Macmillan, 1966.
Gibson, Étienne. *Dante and Philosophy*. Translated by David Moore (Harper Torchbooks). New York: Harper & Row, 1963.
Limentani, U., ed. *The Mind of Dante*. Cambridge, England: Cambridge University Press, 1965.

Reade, W. H. V. *The Moral System of Dante's Inferno*. Oxford, England: Clarendon Press, 1909.
Stump, Eleanore. "Dante's Hell, Aquinas' Moral Theory, and the Love of God." *CJPhil* 16, no. 2 (June 1986):181–98.

DICKINSON, EMILY. B. December 10, 1830, Amherst, Massachusetts. D. May 15, 1886, Amherst, Massachusetts. American poet.

Emily Dickinson attended both Amherst Academy and Mount Holyoke Female Seminary but apparently did not complete her studies. Around 1848 she became a semirecluse, and her home and garden became her world. Inspired by Ralph Waldo Emerson (q.v.) and Emily Brontë, she began to write poetry in 1850. Her main themes were love, death, and nature, all of which were treated in masterful short lyric poems. Her greatest literary output occurred during the Civil War, but only about seven poems had been published before her death in 1886. Luckily the others were preserved, edited later at Harvard University, and published posthumously. Emily Dickinson is currently considered to be one of the greatest poets in American literature.

Emily Dickinson is a difficult writer to deal with simply because she lived the life of a recluse and so little is known about her life with any certainty. Yet, even here, her biographers (see Clark Griffith and Thomas Ford) have done their work well and have scraped up fragments of her very private existence. In regard to philsophical influences, these scholars have arrived at the conclusion that she was influenced not only by puritanism** but also by Emersonian transcendentalism.** Ford claims that she had definitely read Emerson's essays. One especially gratifying essay was Emerson's "The Divinity School Address," in which the philosopher stated that the church was losing its control of the people. The words of Emerson must have been reassuring to her because she had given up on organized religion.

Emerson's ideas are echoed in many poems of Emily Dickinson, especially the idea of self-sufficiency. In several of her poems she points out that the individual must follow his or her own vision and must grow independently of the society in which he or she lives. Ford explains the influence of transcendentalism in this way: "Emily Dickinson could not fully endorse the ideas of either Puritanism or Transcendentalism, and since she found both unsatisfying, each served to highlight the other. Thus abstract philosophy—whether in the form of Puritanism or Transcendentalism— gave her no satisfactory explanation of man's place in the universe" (Ford, 53). Emily Dickinson turned to the solitary experience of poetry and in the direction of existentialism.** Undoubtedly, she was not aware of the philosophical movement of existentialism, but, as is true with other writers, such as Ernest Hemingway (q.v.) and Franz Kafka (q.v.), her poetry contains the basic elements of existentialism. One example would be the existential "solitariness" which she fostered in her personal life. Other examples would be her preference of the concrete and her never-ending quest to discover the function of death personally "through her own existential experience" (Ford, 89). Søren Kierkegaard* dealt extensively with the subject of despair, and, although she was not aware of his philosophy, she, in her death poems especially, dwells on despair and angst, both of which are characteristic of the existentialist. In attempting to understand the ways of God, death, and so on in her exploratory poetry, Dickinson arrives at an "existential stance" where religion, philosophy, and reason all prove inadequate.

One must agree with Ben Kimpel that Emily Dickinson was her own philosopher and managed to work out her own practical philosophy; however, since this philosophy stressed concrete experience, it is markedly existential in nature.

REFERENCES

Derrick, Paul Scott. "Emily Dickinson, Martin Heidegger, and the Poetry of Dread." *WHR* 40, no. 1 (Spring 1986):27–38.

Ford, Thomas W. *Heaven Beguiles the Tired: Death in the Poetry of Emily Dickinson*. Tuscaloosa: University of Alabama Press, 1966.

Griffith, Clark. *The Long Shadow: Emily Dickinson's Tragic Poetry*. Princeton, N.J.: Princeton University Press, 1964.

Kimpel, Ben. *Emily Dickinson as Philosopher*. New York: The Edwin Mellen Press, 1981.

Kjaer, Niels. "The Poet of the Moment: Emily Dickinson and Søren Kierkegaard." *DicS* 59 (1986):46–49.

Morey, Frederick L. "Dickinson—Kant: The First Critique." *DicS* 60 (1986):1–70.

DINESEN, ISAK (Karen Blixen). B. October 17, 1885, Rungelstedlund, Denmark. D. September 7, 1962, Rungelstedlund, Denmark. Danish novelist and short-story writer.

Isak Dinesen's first work, *Out of Africa* (1937), recorded the seventeen years of living on a farm in Kenya. Her first work of fiction was *Seven Gothic Tales* (1934) which were elaborate tales of fantasy. Her subsequent literary works include *Winter's Tales* (1942), *Anecdotes of Destiny* (1958), and *Ehrengard* (1963). Dinesen is considered to belong as much to English literature as to Danish.

The influence of Søren Kierkegaard* on Isak Dinesen was considerable and helped to mold the ideas of this important Danish writer. She did not consider herself to be an existentialist (see existentialism**) writer and she denied any knowledge of existentialist philosophy, but, as Robert Langbaum states, Romantic writers (see romanticism**) are close to being existentialists because both hold that existence precedes essence and that experience is more important than ideas. In the story "The Dreamers," which is one of the *Seven Gothic Tales,* Dinesen deals with the Don Juan legend, and her material here was derived from Kierkegaard who considered the legend of Don Juan to be Christian. Kierkegaard's explanation of modern isolation also influenced Dinesen's character Lady Flora in the story "The Cardinal's Third Tale." Concerning her work "Country Tale," Langbaum says, "It follows Kierkegaard's statement that individual responsibility is in ancient tragedy only half emerged into consciousness—only half emerged, that is, from the guilt inherited through family and race and passively accepted" (Langbaum, 228–29). Dinesen continued to glean ideas from Kierkegaard and so in the story "The Diver," we meet a young Mohammedan theology student by the name of Saufe, who reaches the absolute as a diver and who has made what Kierkegaard calls in *Fear and Trembling* (trans. Hannay, 1986) "The First Movement of Faith." In one story, however, "Babette's Feast," there is a situation in which Dinesen seems to contradict Kierkegaard. General Loewenheim gives a speech in which he says, "We tremble before making our choice in life," and then goes on to say that the choice does not matter because all roads can lead to salvation. This, of course, contradicts Kierkegaard who insists that one must make a choice. "Isak Dinesen does follow Kierkegaard, however, in her understanding of the mystical way as the triumph of the absurd—in the General's realization that we are granted both what we have chosen and what we have refused" (Langbaum, 254). The final story to discuss, *Ehrengard,* one of Dinesen's finest achievements, is a takeoff from Kierkegaard's "Diary of the Seducer." In this work, the author shows herself to be influenced by Kierkegaard and yet to be an independent thinker because here she does not accept Kierkegaard's evaluation of the esthetic life. In any event, enough examples have been cited here to illustrate two things: first, Dinesen was influenced greatly by Kierkegaard; and second, she was a very religious and philosophical writer who, in dealing with man's destiny, is accustomed to bringing God into question and to showing that our lives are connected with God and His purposes.

REFERENCES

Gress, Elsa. "The Witch Who Dined with Socrates." *ScanR* 74, no. 3 (Autumn 1986):70–73.

Hoyrup, Helene. "The Arabesque of Existence: Existential Focus and Aesthetic Form in Isak Dineson's 'The Roads Round Pise.' " *Scan* 24, no. 2 (November 1985):197–210.

Kierkegaard, Søren. *Fear and Trembling*. Translated by Allistair Hannay. New York: Penguin, 1986.

Langbaum, Robert. *The Gayety of Vision: A Study of Isak Dineson's Art*. New York: Random House, 1964.

Walter, Eugene. "Isak Dineson." *Paris Review,* Autumn 1956, 43–59.

DONNE, JOHN. B. June 19, 1572, London, England. D. March 31, 1631, London, England. English poet.

John Donne studied both at Oxford and Cambridge and had ambitions to enter public service. From 1598 to 1601 he served as secretary to Sir Thomas Egerton. He eventually took Anglican orders and was ordained in 1615. He rose quickly in the Church of England, and in 1621 he became dean of St. Paul's Cathedral. Much of his poetry was written before 1601 and it has marked him as the leading poet of the seventeenth-century metaphysical** school.

As Helen Gardner states in her introduction, opinions of the poet have varied considerably through the years. He was first viewed as a satirist, then as a love poet, and finally as a religious voice. "As early as 1880 he was compared to Hamlet, and Donne the Melancolic, Donne the skeptic, Donne the bitter and sardonic amorist" (Gardner, 4). Donne may be viewed as a religious thinker whose philosophical and theological ideas were influenced chiefly by the writings of Saint Thomas Aquinas* and Saint Augustine.*

"Donne was notoriously, along with Webster and other Jacobeans, 'much possessed by death' " (Carey, 198), but he appeared to be even more possessed by the notion of suicide. Here he turned to Saint Augustine who argued that to wish not to exist is absurd. Since nonexistence is not something but nothing, "you cannot logically make a choice when the object of your choice does not exist" (Carey, 173). Donne's disagreement with Saint Augustine that suicide was "an abominable and damnable crime" (Augustine, *City of God,* i, 17–27) is expounded at some length in *Biathanatos* (1644), a defense of suicide.

There is no question that John Donne read and incorporated theistic (see theism**) concepts into his poetry.

> Elaborate blasphemies are also incorporated into the love poems, as if it were not merely Catholicism but Christianity that Donne had to cure himself of when he proclaims that his love can be expressed only by negatives, or compares the naked girl in "Going to Bed" with "Soules Unbodied,"

he is ingeniously perverting what St. Thomas in the *Summa Theologiae* (1273) had written about God's nature and the joys of the blessed. (Carey, 41)

Another subject which led Donne to Aquinas and Augustine for enlightenment was the resurrection of the human body. Donne was intrigued with the problems raised by cannibals, but he found in Aquinas and Augustine that God, in his omnipotence,** would resolve such problems. In fact, Donne had serious problems with traditional Catholic theology, and it is in his favor that he sought solutions to his theological and philosophical problems in the work of philosophers and theologians. "Of Donne's own admiration for and attachment to Aquinas there can be no question. He couples him with Augustine as an instrument of God in the *Essays in Divinity* (1651), and in the sermons Aquinas is persistently used as a touchstone" (Carey, 232).

REFERENCES

Carey, John. *John Donne: Life, Mind and Art*. New York: Oxford University Press, 1981.
Coffin, C. M. *John Donne and the New Philosophy*. New York: Columbia University Studies, 1937.
Gardner, Helen, ed. *John Donne: A Collection of Critical Essays*. Englewood Cliffs, N.J.: Prentice-Hall, 1962.
Smith, Julia J. "Moments of Being and Not-Being in Donne's Sermons." *PSt* 8, no. 3 (December 1985):3–20.

DOS PASSOS, JOHN. B. January 14, 1896, Chicago, Illinois. D. September 28, 1970, Baltimore, Maryland. American novelist.

The son of a wealthy lawyer, John Dos Passos graduated from Harvard University in 1916 and volunteered as an ambulance driver in World War I. After the war he worked as a news correspondent and travelled widely in Spain and other countries. His first major novel was *Three Soldiers* (1921), a work that came out of his war experiences and was an important contribution to American war literature. *Manhattan Transfer* (1925) and the *U.S.A.* trilogy (1938) expressed the author's criticism of American life. Jean-Paul Sartre* (q.v.) called Dos Passos "the greatest American novelist." He is said to have influenced the German writer Gunter Grass, and Dos Passos's works have been acclaimed in the Soviet Union.

His interest in Thomas Jefferson is expressed in his biography, *The Head and Heart of Thomas Jefferson* (1954), in which he examines the cultural milieu in which Jefferson lived and worked and the political forces with which he had to contend. Although often associated with the left and radical movements, Dos Passos was, in fact, politically conservative; he accepted Jefferson's doctrine of man's perfectability. Like Jefferson, he advocated self-government and minimal political organization and argued that man's self-entrapment in the "isms" he himself created—corporate capitalism, Marxism,** Freudianism (see Freudian**) and so on—obstructed realization of the social realness formulated by Jefferson and other founders of the nation.

For some time, communists in America thought Dos Passos was a convinced fellow traveler, but admitting that he had read Marx incompletely and late, he said, "The Marxist critics are just finding out, with considerable chagrin, that my stuff isn't Marxist" (reported by Ludington, 390). However, his biographer, Townsend Ludington, speaks to the contrary: "[R]eading in *USA* (1938) of the swirl of forces that led to economic collapse in 1929, one might be hard-pressed not to read a Marxist historical imperative into *USA,* despite Dos Passos's claim to the contrary" (Ludington, 390).

Dos Passos never admitted to being a Marxist and often warned his fellow countrymen about the dangers of the Russian experiment, which he considered a failure. He once said, "The history of the political notions of American intellectuals for a better world could blind them to the realities under their noses" (Ludington, 405). In his novels, he attacked totalitarianism** in all of its forms, and in his nonfiction he often warned the American public that the Communist Revolution had turned Russia into a police state where individual freedom had been abolished.

REFERENCES

Aldridge, John W. "Dos Passos: The Energy of Despair." In *After the Lost Generation,* edited by Aldridge. New York: McGraw Hill, 1951.
Butler, Robert James. "The American Quests for Pure Movement in Dos Passos's *U.S.A.*" *TCL* 30, no. 1 (Spring 1984):80–99.
Ludington, Townsend. *John Dos Passos: A Twentieth Century Odyssey.* New York: Dutton, 1980.
Schwartz, Delmore. "John Dos Passos and the Whole Truth." *Southern Review* 4 (October 1938):351–67.

DOSTOEVSKY, FEODOR. B. November 11, 1821, Moscow, Russia. D. February 9, 1881, St. Petersburg, Russia. Russian novelist and essayist.

Feodor Dostoevsky attended the school of Military Engineers in St. Petersburg. In 1849, he was arrested for membership in a utopian society and was sent to Siberia for eight years. On his return, he became very conservative in his politics. In much of his work, he attacked nineteenth-century scientific and rational humanitarian pretensions, and he attempted to justify the necessity of faith and of God as conditions of true freedom. (The Encyclopedia of Philosophy, vol. 2, 411). His important works are *Poor Folk* (1846), *The Double* (1846), *The House of the Dead* (1861), *The Insulted and the Injured* (1861), *Notes from the Underground* (1864), *Crime and Punishment* (1866), *The Idiot* (1868), *The Possessed* (1871), and *The Brothers Karamazov* (1879–1880).

The philosophical complexity of Dostoevsky's work needs no under-lining. His writings reveal a profound awareness of the cultural and intellectual milieu in which he lived as well as the philosophical conjec-tures of major European thinkers. His compelling need, in his early years, to deepen the foundations of his own thinking led to his study of Immanuel Kant,* Georg Wilhelm Hegel,* and Arthur Schopenhauer.* Whether he read the works of Søren Kierkegaard* is uncertain, but his separation of faith from reason conforms to Kierkegaard's acceptance of Hegel's cri-tique of religion.

Although interesting parallels are to be found between Dostoevsky and Schopenhauer, for example, the view that suffering is a fundamental aspect of human existence, Schopenhauer argues that the will rather than the intellect is the controlling force responsible for the evil condition of life as we find it. Dostoevsky argues that it is through intellect that man comes to an awareness of the inevitability of death and that this revelation is the immediate cause of his torment, of his spiritual suffering. Thus Dostoevsky's characters are in a state of constant suffering. Dostoevsky, like Schopenhauer, seeks escape from suffering. Rejecting Schopen-hauer's solution in the negation of will, Dostoevsky more optimistically "contemplates the disappearance of duality in the world. Without duality there will be no suffering, and man's ideal existence will be attained" (Pachmuss, xv).

Dostoevsky, always a seeker of truth, searched desperately for an answer to the mystery of existence. Concerning his theories of human suffering, it should finally be said that Dostoevsky did not accept the pessimism of Schopenhauer, but he arrived in his search for truth at a religious and spiritual solution to the suffering of man. He believed finally that only eternal life could give meaning and purpose to man's suffering existence. And so he proclaimed: "Immortality, which promises eternal life binds man to earth all the more. Only through faith in immortality can man perceive the whole reasonable purpose of life on earth" (Pach-muss, 113).

REFERENCES

Bruss, Neal. "The Sons Karamazov: Dostoevsky's Characters as Freudian Transformation." *MR* 27, no. 1 (Spring 1986):40–67.

Frank, Joseph. *Dostoevsky: The Stir of Liberation, 1860–1865*. Princeton, N.J.: Princeton University Press, 1986.

Milosz, Czeslaw. "Dostojewski i Sartre." *KulturaP* 2 (February 1983):19–32.

Pachmuss, Temira. *F. M. Dostoevsky: Dualism and Synthesis of the Human Soul*. Edwardsville: Southern Illinois University Press, 1963.

DREISER, THEODORE. B. August 27, 1871, Terre Haute, Indiana. D. December 28, 1945, Los Angeles, California. American novelist.

Theodore Dreiser, the son of a poor German immigrant, spent a restless childhood in the American midwest. His first novel *Sister Carrie* (1900) was suppressed because of its strong realism. His most important work, *An American Tragedy* (1925), was based on a murder that was committed in upper New York State in 1906. In his later years, he turned to political activities and became a member of the American Communist party. Dreiser's works portray a naturalistic view of human nature and society (see naturalism**).

Although most literary historians marked Dreiser as a naturalistic novelist, the critic Roger Asselineau believes that he was a transcendentalist (see transcendentalism**). If this sounds like a contradiction, one must remember that Dreiser's mind thrived on contradictions. As he writes in *A Traveller at Forty* (1913), "I cannot view life or human nature save as an expression of contraries" (p. 34). Thus Dreiser constantly swayed between two positions, the external materialistic experience and the hidden mysterious elements that lie beyond reality.

If one delves into his lesser known poetry, one will see his transcendentalism expressed forcibly in a collection of poems entitled *Moods* (1914–1926). Some examples will prove this point. In "Wood Note," he describes a "mysterious spiritual presence in the woods" (Asselineau, 100) and, as a true follower of American transcendentalists, he sees God in all things, in a bootblack shining his shoes and in the birds flying over a river. In these poems, he searches constantly for the underlying mystery and often expresses the lack of purpose and meaning in a puzzling universe. Asselineau points out the pessimism** in such poems as "The Passing Freight" and "Ephermeron," in which Dreiser's depression is far removed from the optimism of Ralph Waldo Emerson (q.v.). Although Dreiser's poems often border on the mystical (see mysticism**), his statements in *A Traveller at Forty* express doubt and disillusionment in his quest for truth:

> For myself, I accept now no creeds. I do not know what truth is, what beauty is, what love is, what hope is. . . . I indict nature here and now . . . as being aimless, pointless, unfair, unjust. I see in the whole thing no scheme, but an accidental one—no justice save accidental justice. (pp. 4, 42)

Despite this statment, which smacks of nihilism,** Asselineau still maintains Dreiser's transcendentalism, reminding us that even Emerson had his periods of doubt. And, despite these doubts, Dreiser said fervently in one poem, "Yet I must pray."

And so, in his poetry, we see that Dreiser was mystical, that he worshipped life and sought beauty beneath the ugly reality which he described in such books as *Sister Carrie*. Perhaps he was a true transcendentalist.

REFERENCES

Asselineau, Roger. *The Transcendentalist Constant in American Literature*. New York: New York University Press, 1980.

Epstein, Joseph. "The Mystery of Theodore Dreiser." *NewC* 5, no. 3 (November 1986):33–43.

Snell, George. "Theodore Dreiser: Philosopher." In *The Shapers of American Fiction, 1798–1947*, edited by Snell. New York: Dutton, 1947.

Whalen, Terry. "Dreiser: Tragic Sense: The Mind as 'Poor Ego.' " *ON* 11, no. 2 (Spring–Summer 1985):61–80. (Sources in Freud)

DRYDEN, JOHN. B. August 19, 1631, Northamptonshire, England. D. May 1, 1700, London, England. English poet, dramatist and critic.

John Dryden was educated at Trinity College, Cambridge. Supported comfortably by the legacy of his father's estate, Dryden moved to London and took up the profession of letters. His first works appeared in 1659, with an elegy on the death of Oliver Cromwell. In 1672 he began to write for the newly reopened London theatres. His dramas include *The Conquest of Granada* (1670–1671), *The Wild Gallant* (1664), and *Marriage a la Mode* (1672). His greatest nondramatic poem is *Absalom and Achitophel* (1681), a long, witty piece in the heroic manner. He is also remembered for *Religio Laici* (1682), a verse apologia for the Anglican position in theology. Dryden's importance in English literature is confirmed by the designation of the Restoration period as "The Age of Dryden," which set the tone of English poetry for nearly a century.

John Dryden wrote in the preface to *Religio Laici* that he was "naturally inclined to scepticism in philosophy'' (reported by Van Doren, 16), and, although he never really arrived at a system of philosophy, major figures, for example, Thomas Hobbes,* made deep and permanent impressions on his thinking. As Van Doren says, "It was Hobbes who inspired his deep distrust of human beings in the mass and his lifelong intolerance of movements that threatened to disturb the peace" (Van Doren, 16).

Religio Laici is a philosophical poem which deals with the scope and limits of human reason and makes specific references to Stoicism** and Epicureanism.** Dryden had a strong interest in the atomistic theory of Epicurus*; here he was in good company because Hobbes, with the publication in 1651 of *Leviathan,* became the champion of atomism.**

> He [Hobbes] was soon reinforced by an abler, more subtle mind—that of [Baruch] Spinoza[*] whose *Tractatus Theologico—Politicus* was published in 1670. . . . James Tyrell, who was lawyer, historian, and personal friend of John Locke[*] placed Spinoza and Hobbes in the same tub: both sages maintained that man's actions and thoughts are bound up in an inexorable chain of determinism,[**] which obliterates the power of choice and, therefore, the human distinction between good and evil. (Hooker, 133)

In *Religio Laici,* Dryden took the position of a philosophical sceptic, but Dryden was not a philosopher. He was a playwright and poet who was attempting to examine all the abuses of reason. He wrote against the atomist because the theories of atomism threatened Dryden's value system. T. S. Eliot (q.v.), in his short book on Dryden, says that the writer found the English speechless and gave them speech. With this, Eliot would agree that, in such a work as *Religio Laici,* if the modern reader finds fault with Dryden's philosophy, he at least must acknowledge Dryden's contribution to the refinement and enrichment of the English language.

Dryden never remained indifferent to the political and religious upheavals of his age. He immersed himself in the philosophical thought of his time, in the theories of Hobbes and Spinoza, but also he educated himself in the philosophies of Aristotle* and Epicurus.

REFERENCES

Bredvold, Louis I. *The Intellectual Milieu of John Dryden*. Ann Arbor: University of Michigan Press, 1962.
Hooker, Edward N. "Dryden and the Atoms of Epicurus." In *Twentieth Century Views,* edited by Bernard N. Schilling. Englewood Cliffs, N.J.: Prentice-Hall, 1963.
Van Doren, Mark. *John Dryden: A Story of His Poetry*. Bloomington: Indiana University Press, 1963.

E

ELIOT, GEORGE (MARY ANN EVANS). B. November 22, 1819, Chilvers Coton, Warwickshire, England. D. December 22, 1880, London, England. English novelist.

In 1841 Mary Ann Evans disavowed orthodox Christianity. Her first literary endeavor was the translation of a major German religious work *The Life of Jesus* (1846). At the same time, she began work in journalism and became subeditor of the influential *Westminster Review*. As George Eliot, she wrote *Adam Bede* (1859), *The Mill on the Floss* (1860), and *Silas Marner* (1861). Her masterpieces, however, are considered to be *Middlemarch* (1871–1872) and *Daniel Deronda* (1876).

It would be a mistake to brand George Eliot as just a writer of fiction because, as editor of the *Westminster Review,* she was involved in politics, history, religion, and philosophy. Under her editorship, there were contributions by John Stuart Mill*; John Oxenfold's pioneer essay on Arthur Schopenhauer,* which "formed the foundation of Schopenhauer's fame" (Haight, 97); and four important articles by the philosopher Herbert Spencer* outlining his theory of evolution. George Combe recorded his impression of Miss Evans when he met her on August 29, 1851: "She showed great analytic power and an instinctive soundness of judgment . . . and her conversation on religion, economics, and political events persuaded Combe that with the exception perhaps of Lucretia Mott, she appeared to me the ablest woman whom I have seen" (Haight, 101).

Mary Ann Evans met Herbert Spencer in August 1851, and they became romantically involved. To assume that the philosopher suitor influenced the lady would ordinarily be a mistake, but when one considers her intellectual quality one must assume that Spencer must have piqued her philosophical curiosity. It was an intellectual friendship, in which, as Haight says, a vacation on the seashore meant "picking up shells, gathering wild flowers, discussing Aristotle's[*] view of the chief good and his [Spencer's] own (plan of the *Psychology*), for which he was reading the copy of Mills *Logic* (1843) that Mary Ann lent him" (Haight, 114–115). While editor of the *Westminster Review,* Mary Ann Evans became acquainted with the positivist (see positivism**) science of Auguste Comte.* In January 1851, she wrote a review entitled "The Progress of the Intellect," which demonstrated that she was an independent thinker who did not hesitate to disagree with the ideas of great philosophers. Her review began by pointing out that, although the positivist science of Comte offers the only hope of extending man's knowledge and happiness, it was a serious mistake to suppose that the study of the past and the labors of criticism have no important bearing on the present. "It is an impressive article, written with distinction, firm in its critical tone, revealing for the first time the extraordinary grasp of her massive intellect" (Haight, 80). Eliot's biographer, Gordon Haight, claims that "the extent of George Eliot's concern with positivism has been greatly exaggerated" (Haight, 301).

Mary Ann Evans had a lifelong association with famous philosophers and their works. In 1854, she translated Ludwig Feuerbach's* *Das Wesen des Christenthums* (The Essence of Christianity). "The powerful appeal the book had for her sprang, not from its bold humanism, but from Feuerbach's daring conception of love . . . she agreed wholeheartedly with Feuerbach's distinction between 'self-interested love' and 'the true human love,' which 'impels the sacrifice of self to another' " (Haight, 137). Although it is difficult to say to what extent Feuerbach's ideas influenced her own writing, the humanism** that the philosopher taught is certainly to be found in the novels of George Eliot. If she is not ordinarily thought of as a philosophical writer, it may be because her readers do not readily perceive the influence of Comte, Feuerbach, Charles Darwin,* Baruch Spinoza,* and Ralph Waldo Emerson (q.v.), among others, in her fiction.

REFERENCES

Bennett, Joan. *George Eliot: Her Mind and Her Art*. Cambridge, England: Cambridge University Press, 1948.
Haight, Gordon S. *George Eliot*. Oxford, England: Oxford University Press, 1968.
Paris, Bernard J. *Experiments in Life: George Eliot's Quest for Values*. Detroit, Mich.: Wayne State University Press, 1965.
Paxton, Nancy L. "Feminism and Positivism in George Eliot's *Romola*." In

19th Century Women Writers of the English Speaking World, edited by
Rhoda B. Nathan. Westport, Conn.: Greenwood Press, 1986. (Sources
in positivism, especially of Auguste Comte)

ELIOT, T[HOMAS] S[TEARNES]. B. September 26, 1888, St. Louis,
Missouri. Naturalized British citizen, 1927. D. January 4, 1965, London,
England. American/British poet and critic.

T. S. Eliot was educated at Harvard University. His first important
poem was "The Love Song of J. Alfred Prufrock" (1917). This work
and *The Waste Land* (1922) established Eliot as an important twentieth-
century poet, and both remain as central texts of modernism. In 1927,
Eliot became a British subject and formally joined the Church of England.
"Ash Wednesday" appeared in 1930 followed by the *Four Quartets*
(1935–1942), a long poem which explores the question of time and the
incarnation. In the 1930s, Eliot published two important poetic dramas,
Murder in the Cathedral (1935) and *The Family Reunion* (1939). T. S.
Eliot is also highly regarded as a literary critic.

The complexity of Eliot has been a subject of considerable controversy
and frustration for students and critics of his work from the beginning.
For example, Harriet Monroe, editor of *Poetry,* refused to accept "The
Love Song of J. Alfred Prufrock" because it was "too difficult"; however, Rajnath makes a telling point: "Eliot is difficult not because he
knows so much or the age is so complex, but because he is a special sort
of poet, a philosophical poet in an age of unbelief" (Rajnath, 160). Eliot
makes demands on his readers which, too often, they cannot satisfy and
are therefore left to ponder. His undergraduate and graduate work in
philosophy provided him with the metaphysical** perspective, the conceptual foundation, which he required to keep the poet in himself alive.

It is probably surprising to some that in Eliot's Christian poem the
Four Quartets he uses material taken from Heraclitus,* a pre-Christian
philosopher from 500 B.C. whose ideas of the four elements and the
intersection of time and eternity are interspersed throughout the poem.

> The Heraclitean flux[**] does not admit of a "still point" where there is
> neither arrest nor movement. We must add that the Heraclitean flux as far
> as it goes is very much present in the *Four Quartets.* "You cannot step
> twice into the same river," writes Heraclitus, "for fresh waters are flowing
> in upon you." (reported by Rajnath, 160)

Critics have been accustomed to attribute, as the philosophical sources
of Eliot's poetry, the philosophy of Henri Bergson* and Francis Bradley,*
but there is yet another influence—Saint Augustine.* Rajnath claims that

the Augustinian notion of time operating on three levels, the past and future having their roots in the present, occurs in *The Waste Land* and in *Four Quartets*, in which Eliot concludes that "All time is unredeemable" ("Burnt Norton," line 5). "The concept of time as the eternal present including both past and future time is both Augustinian and Bergsonian and also Bradleyan. In fact, there are striking similarities between the Augustinian, the Bergsonian and the Bradleyan concepts of time" (Rajnath, 162).

Eliot was a serious student of philosophy from his earliest literate years. In 1913, T. S. Eliot was reading Émile Durkheim and Francis Bradley, among others. In 1914, he participated in the Lowell Lectures at Harvard, where he attended Bertrand Russell's* course on symbolic logic**. In a letter, Russell called Eliot an interesting and able student. Two years later Eliot's doctoral dissertation at Harvard, "Experience and the Objects of Knowledge in the Philosophy of F. H. Bradley" (1916), was called the work of an expert by the renowned philosopher Josiah Royce.*

Eliot's dissertation demonstrated to the academic world that he was a philosophically self-conscious poet who worked within a carefully structured conceptual framework, a fact reflected in his early critical work (*Selected Essays*), as well as in his poetry.

REFERENCES

Bollier, E. P. "T. S. Eliot and F. H. Bradley: A Question of Influence." *Tulane Studies in English* 12 (1962): 87–111.
Keetzer, J. M. "T. S. Eliot and the Problem of Will." *MLQ* 45, no. 4 (December 1984): 373–94. (Sources in Francis Bradley and Arthur Schopenhauer)
Le Brun, Philip. "T. S. Eliot and Henri Bergson." *The Review of English Studies,* New Series, 18 (1967): 149–61, 274–86.
Rajnath. *T. S. Eliot's Theory of Poetry*. Atlantic Highlands, N.J.: Humanities Press, 1980.
Thompson, Eric. *T. S. Eliot. The Metaphysical Perspective*. Carbondale: Southern Illinois University Press, 1963.

EMERSON, RALPH WALDO. B. May 25, 1803, Boston, Massachusetts. D. April 27, 1882, Concord, Massachusetts. American poet, lecturer, and essayist.

Ralph Waldo Emerson entered Harvard College at the age of fourteen in 1817. He was ordained in 1829 to the Unitarian ministry but resigned in 1832. He travelled to Europe and met the English Romantic Thomas Carlyle (q.v.), Samuel Taylor Coleridge (q.v.), and William Wordsworth (q.v.), encounters that inspired him to develop his personal version of transcendentalism.** A successful lecturer, Emerson became the spokesman for romantic individualism, and he was a central figure in the Concord literary circle that included Henry David Thoreau (q.v.) and Nathaniel Hawthorne (q.v.). His best known works include *Nature* (1836), ''The American Scholar'' (1837), the ''Divinity School Address'' (1838), and volumes of *Essays* (1841 and 1844), a collection that made him famous in Europe and in the United States.

There is no question of the importance of Platonism** as a molding power in Emerson's thinking; his introduction to Platonic concepts, through Thomas Taylor's translation, produced an intellectual framework from which Emerson never escaped. Taylor's committed acceptance of the Neoplatonic speculations (see Neoplatonism**), a la Plotinus* and Proclus in particular, resulted in a translation of the dialogues which differs significantly from the body of philosophical doctrine expressed in Benjamin Jowett's translation, which is more generally accepted as an accurate expression of Plato's* work.

Through Taylor, Emerson was led to an extensive study of translations of Neoplatonist views. He read prodigiously in classical philosophy, but he was drawn always to those thinkers who spoke to that mystical system (see mysticism**) that arose out of the Neoplatonist interpretations of Plato's idealistic philosophy (see idealism**).

Emerson's acquaintance with Coleridge added a facet to him which further refracted his interpretation of Plato's doctrine. His introduction to Francis Bacon* by Coleridge led to his adoption of the idea that all philosophical inquiry must consider the correlation of matter and mind. Emerson's eclectic** predilection resulted then in a view which could hardly be described as a Platonic system. His work suggests a loose synthesis of the mysticism of Plotinus and the Neoplatonists, the pre-Socratics, and finally the philosophy of natural law, which he learned from Bacon through Coleridge. Emerson was also familiar with the works of Immanuel Kant,* Johann Gottlieb Fichte,* Friedrich Schelling,* and Georg Wilhelm Hegel,* whom he saw as improvisations of the earliest Greek inquirers.

REFERENCES

Gura, Philip F. ''Emerson, Thoreau, and Transcendentalism. *AmLS* (1984): 3–26.

Harrison, John. *The Teachers of Emerson*. New York: Haskell House, 1966.

Leary, Lewis. *Ralph Waldo Emerson: An Interpretative Essay*. Boston: Twayne, 1980.

Proclus. *The Six Books of Proclus on the Theology of Plato*. Translated from the Greek by Thomas Taylor. 2 vols. London: n.p., 1816.

Shimkin, David. "Emerson, Playful Habit of Mind." *ATQ* 62 (December 1986): 3–16.

Tebeaux, Elizabeth. "Skepticism and Dialectic in Emerson's 'Experience.' " *ESQ* 32, no. 1 (1st quart. 1986): 28–35.

F

FAULKNER, WILLIAM. B. September 25, 1897, New Albany, Mississippi. D. July 6, 1962, Oxford, Mississippi. American novelist and short-story writer.

Although William Faulkner expressed his interest in being a writer, he exhibited little interest in formal education. He dropped out of high school after the tenth grade and spent only one year at the University of Mississippi as a special student. Denied admission into the U.S. Air Force in 1918, he joined the Canadian Royal Air Force, but World War I ended before he had completed his training. He worked at a variety of menial jobs for several years and attempted at the same time to establish himself as a writer. His first book, *The Marble Faun* (1924), a collection of poems, did little to establish his reputation as a writer. Although *Soldier's Pay,* published with the support of Sherwood Anderson, was not a success in the market, it initiated his career as a novelist, and it was followed by his first successful novel, *The Sound and the Fury* (1929), and then *As I Lay Dying,* in 1930. It was not until 1931, with *Sanctuary,* that Faulkner achieved the status of a major novelist. There followed a succession of great novels including *Light in August* (1932), *Absalom, Absalom!* (1936), *Go Down Moses and Other Stories* (1942), *Intruder in the Dust* (1948), *Requiem for a Nun* (1951), *A Fable* (1954), *The Town* (1957), *The Mansion* (1959), and *The Reivers* (1962). In 1949, Faulkner was awarded the Nobel Prize for Literature and, in 1955, the Pulitzer Prize.

Considerable critical attention has been paid to Faulkner's philosophical indebtedness, particularly with respect to his concepts of God and time (see Abel, Callen, and Hutchinson). Mick Gidley, in "One Continuous Force," tells us that Faulkner admitted his indebtedness to Henri Bergson* in an interview with Loic Bouvard.

The precise nature of Bergsonian influence on Faulkner's notion of God is, at best, uncertain and conjectural. Although Gidley's conjectures are feasible, his use of "seem" and "apparent" highlights the difficulty one confronts in any attempt to extrude a clear idea of Faulkner's notion of God or to discover any precise linkages that lead to that notion. One thing, however, is clear; Faulkner was not a systematic philosophical thinker. His thoughts were "complex, contradictory, troublesome, and rich" (Gidley, 383). Whether objective entity, force, or process, Faulkner's concept of God is humanistic (see humanism**)—"the will to prevail" as expressed in the major figures who people "Yoknapatawpha County."

Note must be made of an article by Darlene Unrue, in which she finds Augustinian elements (see Saint Augustine*) in Faulkner's fiction, most explicitly in the Easter Sunday Sermon in *The Sound and the Fury*. Unrue argues convincingly that the sermon "is a study in faith and timelessness, and it is incidently a masterful exemplification of Augustinian Theology" (Unrue, 5).

REFERENCES

Abel, Darrel. "Frozen Moment in *Light in August*." *Boston University Studies in English* 3 (Spring 1957): 32–44.

Bouvard, Loic. *Interview with William Faulkner*. Translated from French by H. D. Piper. In *Lion in the Garden*, edited by James P. Meriwether and Michael Milgate. Lincoln: University of Nebraska Press, 1980.

Brooks, Cleanth. *Toward Yoknapatawpha and Beyond*. New Haven, Conn.: Yale University Press, 1979.

Callen, Shirley. *Bergsonian Dynamism in the Writings of William Faulkner*. Ann Arbor, Mich.: University MicroFilms, 1962.

Gidley, Mick. "One Continuous Force: Notes on Faulkner's Extra-Literary Reading." In Wagner, Linda W. *William Faulkner: Four Decades of Criticism*. East Lansing: Michigan State University Press, 1973, pp. 55–68.

Hutchinson, James P. "Time, the Fourth Dimension in Faulkner." *South Dakota Review* 6 (Autumn 1980): 91–103.

Unrue, Darlene Harbour. "Saint Augustine and the Easter Sunday Sermon in William Faulkner's *The Sound and the Fury*." *Wascana Review* 19, no. 2 (Fall 1984): 3–16.

FORSTER, E[DWARD] M[ORGAN]. B. January 1, 1879, London, England. D. June 8, 1970, Coventry, Warwickshire, England. British novelist.

The son of an architect, E. M. Forster was educated at Tonbridge School and King's College, Cambridge. After taking his degree, he turned to writing as a career. Forster wrote two collections of essays: *Abinger Harvest* (1936) and *Two Cheers for Democracy* (1951). It is difficult to label these essays, but they do exhibit a mistrust of institutional religion and an acknowledgement of the weakness of the liberal position. His major novel, *A Passage to India* (1924), was the culmination of two earlier novels: *The Longest Journey* (1907) and *A Room with a View* (1908).

There is, undeniably, an explicit philosophical facet to E. M. Forster's fiction, but whether it was the result of formal study—of G. E. Moore, for example—or whether he arrived at his philosophical posture through the influence of Hugh Meredith—from whom he learned about G. E. Moore—is controversial. It is conceivable that Forster's refutation of George Berkeley's* idealism** formed its way into *The Longest Journey* through his acceptance of Moore's philosophical realism** and Moore's projection, with Bertrand Russell,* of idealism, a central issue in the opening discussion of the reality of objects in the first chapter of the novel.

In *The Longest Journey*, Forster adapted Moore's philosophical realism, which establishes the philosophical framework of the novel. The central thesis of the novel, the rejection of idealism for realism, transposes it into a novel of ideas. The opening philosophical discussion in *The Longest Journey* about the existence of objects—whether or not they exist independently of the perceiver and therefore whether reality is subjective or objective—is clearly Forster's rendition of Moore's refutation of idealism. Readers of *The Longest Journey* cannot but see Forster's philosophical focus since the characters in the novel discuss the value of philosophy and whether it reveals what is good and true. In the novel, Ansell reveals himself as a philosophical realist. There is probably no other modern novelist who has expressed a stronger or more explicit philosophical posture in his works than has E. M. Forster. Perhaps some readers object to his novels of ideas, maintaining that fiction is for entertainment and escape. However, one must admit that Forster, in this vein, is merely following the lead of such great philosophical writers as Dante Alighieri (q.v.) and, in modern times, T. S. Eliot (q.v.) and Thomas Mann (q.v.). By posing ethical and metaphysical** questions, Forster has added a dimension to his fiction that makes it more interesting and enlightening.

REFERENCES

E. M. Forster. *A Human Exploration*. New York: New York University Press, 1979.

Henke, Suzette A. *"Howards End:* E. M. Forster without Marx or Sartre."
    MSpr 80, no. 2 (1986): 116–20.
Kumar, Shiv K. *Bergson and the Stream of Consciousness Novel.* London:
    Blackie, 1962.
Lamont, Corliss. *Humanism as a Philosophy.* London: Watts, 1952.

FOWLES, JOHN. B. March 31, 1926, Leigh-on-Sea, Essex, England.
English novelist.

John Fowles attended Bedford School from 1940 to 1944, then studied
at the University of Edinburgh for six months. In 1945–1946, he served
as a lieutenant in the Royal Marines. From 1947 to 1950 he studied
French at New College, Oxford University, and received his BA degree.
From 1950 to 1952 he taught English at the University of Poitiers in
France and then at Anargyrios College in Spetsai, Greece. Returning to
London in 1953, he spent the next ten years at various teaching posts in
and around the English capital. His first novel *The Collector* was published
in 1963; *The Aristos* followed in 1964 and *The Magus* in 1965. *The
French Lieutenant's Woman,* his most popular work, was published in
1969 and won for Fowles the Silver Pen Award from the English Center
of the International P.E.N. By 1973 he had published a collection of
Poems and in the following year *The Ebony Tower.* Heterosexual love
and the nature of freedom are the major themes of all of Fowles's works.

John Fowles, an Oxford-trained English teacher, is one of the most
learned modern novelists. In *The Aristos: A Self-Portrait in Ideas,* Fowles
exhibits an interest in and a knowledge of philosophical thought from the
ancient Greeks to the present, from Socrates* and Heraclitus* to Søren
Kierkegaard,* Jean-Paul Sartre* (q.v.), and Albert Camus (q.v.). Indeed,
Fowles's familiarity with philosophers and the philosophical tradition
enables him to incorporate philosophical thought into fiction with ease
and skill. This is especially true of his use of existentialist thought (see
existentialism**) in *The French Lieutenant's Woman.*

Fowles's fiction is thoroughly saturated with existentialist thoughts—
"with the problems of self-definition, of individuality, of freedom, of
choice, and of revolt" (Palmer, 7). In *The Collector,* the character of
Miranda is portrayed as one who is concerned with human experience
and human dignity (she is degraded by Clegg who rapes her with his
camera). In *The Magus,* the theme of freedom, another major concern
for the existentialist, is exploited. Indeed, in each of his novels, John
Fowles, the novelist-philosopher, creates a fictitious world in which man
creates his own values and in which the existentialist values of commitment, freedom, and intensity of experience rule. Barry Olshen sums up

the philosophical concerns to be found in Fowles's fiction and nonfiction: "While *The Aristos* presents the issues, the novels are predicated on the supposition of individual free will and the ideal of self-realization. Their conceptual focus remains on the nature and limits of human freedom, the power and responsibility that freedom entails, and the cruelty and necessity of conscious choice" (Olshen, 11).

REFERENCES

Olshen, Barry N. *John Fowles*. New York: Frederick Ungar, 1978.
Palmer, William J. *The Fiction of John Fowles: Tradition, Art, and the Loneliness of Selfhood*. Columbia: University of Missouri Press, 1974.
Pifer, Ellen, ed. *Critical Essays on John Fowles*. Boston: G. K. Hall, 1986.

FRISCH, MAX. B. May 15, 1911, Zurich, Switzerland. Swiss novelist and dramatist.

In 1933 Max Frisch withdrew from the University of Zurich and became a newspaper correspondent, but in 1936 he returned to the university and studied architecture. Frisch ran his own architectural practice from 1942 to 1954, but, after the success of his novel *I Am Not Stiller* (1954), he decided to write full time. Two more successful novels followed: *Homo Faber* (1957) and *Wilderness of Mirrors* (1964). Frisch's international fame rests on two parable plays, *The Fireraisers* (1961) and *Andorra* (1961). His plays attack the prevalence of bourgeois hypocrisy after the manner of Bertolt Brecht (q.v.) and Thornton Wilder (q.v.).

No one writing in the German language today attracts more critical attention than the contemporary Swiss writer Max Frisch. The central theme of such works as *Stiller* and *Gantenbein* (1964) is the search for identity and the impossibility of escaping from the roles we assign to each other. Frisch probably derived this philosophical premise from Søren Kierkegaard* who argues that man cannot escape from himself and must learn to accept himself. Self-acceptance is the necessary complement of the search for identity. In the novel *Gantenbein,* the hero hides behind his black glasses and creates different self-portraits as he plays out different roles. Kierkegaard calls this aesthetic (see aesthetics**) existence "[a] way of life which rejects choice and commitment in favor of role-playing and constant change" (Butler, 18).

Hans Banzinger claims a relationship between Frisch and Kierkegaard:

> The connection with Kierkegaard is complicated. On the one hand Frisch's understandable restraints hinder him from openly acknowledging this religious writer. Formally, for example in regard to the relationship between life and work, the similarity is evident. It has been claimed that there is

hardly a written work into which the author's own life story has been amalgamated to such an extent as in that of the Dane. (Probst and Bodine, 52)

"In the novels *Jurg Reinhard* (1984) and *Die Schwierigen* (1943), Frisch gives an epic account of the same existential [see existentialism**] dialogue with himself. The literary genre may have changed his control; his central occupation, however, has remained the same: Frisch's subject continues to be the art of self-reflection" (Jurgensen, 4). This is why Michael Butler and Banzinger attempt to link Frisch with the existentialism of Kierkegaard. Banzinger says that there is a direct path from Kierkegaard to Frisch. The renowned Swiss writer Friedrich Durrenmatt said that Frisch's novels are existential: "The undertaking with no regard other than to portray himself, to mean himself, could annoyingly only be dated in the form of an admission, a confession, related to the new personal background of religion; a religion back drop suspends the private aspect, as in the case of [Saint] Augustine[*] and Kierkegaard" (Probst and Bodine, 42–43).

REFERENCES

Butler, Michael. *The Plays of Max Frisch*. New York: St. Martin's Press, 1985.
Haberl, Franz P. "Death and Transcendence in Max Frisch's *Tripych* and *Man in the Holocene*." *WLT* 60, no. 4 (Autumn 1986): 580–85.
Ivask, Ivar. "Max Frisch: Sensitive Explorer of the Boundaries of Self and the World." *WLT* 60, no. 4 (Autumn 1986): 540–43.
Jurgensen, Manfred. "The Drama of Frisch." In *Perspectives on Max Frisch*, edited by Gerhard F. Probst and Jay F. Bodine. Lexington: The University Press of Kentucky, 1982.
Kieser, Rolf. "From Utopia to Eschatology: The Road of the Thinker Max Frisch." *WLT* 60, no. 4 (Autumn 1986): 561–65.
Kristiansen, Borge. "Max Frisch und Friedrich Nietzsche." *T&K* 16(Suppl.) (1983): 164–205.
Probst, Gerhard F., and Jay F. Bodine, eds. *Perspectives on Max Frisch*. Lexington: The University Press of Kentucky, 1982.

FROST, ROBERT. B. March 26, 1874, San Francisco, California. D. January 29, 1963, Boston, Massachusetts. American poet.

When Robert Frost was only eleven years old, his father died, and his mother, a schoolteacher, moved the family to New England. His interest in poetry began in his school years and continued while he was a student at Harvard. Illness forced him to give up his university studies, and he turned first to farming (1899–1906) and then to teaching (1906–1912). At this point in his life, he made an important decision. He moved with his family to England and successfully tried his hand at writing. In 1913, his collection of lyric poems, *A Boy's Will,* was published and in 1914 his narrative poems, *North of Boston.* Both works brought him fame; on returning to the United States, he received a series of appointments to several prestigious colleges and universities. Frost was awarded the Pulitzer Prize for poetry in 1924, 1931, 1937, and 1943.

So much has been written about Robert Frost, so many statements about his poetic theory have been made, that his life and poetry are usually well known to students of literature. However, the poetry of New England's "Farmer Poet" often appears to many as simplistic nature poetry and Frost himself as a man of common sense but not as a man of uncommon intellectual accomplishments. His correspondence to John Bartlett, Sidney Cox, and Louis Untermeyer reveals a mind well read both in literature and philosophy. As early as 1913, he wrote to Bartlett that he was more Aristotelian** than Platonic (see Platonism**), although his interest in Aristotle* seems to have been limited to literary things as expressed in *The Poetics,* particularly Aristotle's dictum on the use of colloquial language and on the way language imitates nature.

Much has been written concerning the connection of Ralph Waldo Emerson (q.v.) and Robert Frost including works by Reginald Cook, G. R. Eliott, and Yvor Winters, but the most revealing discussion on Frost's relationship with Emerson is probably found in Alvan S. Ryan's article "Frost and Emerson: Voices and Vision," which appeared in *The Massachusetts Review* in October 1959. Ryan argues that Frost is Emersonian, but with a difference: Frost apparently rejected Emerson's emphasis on mysticism,** accepted Emerson's views of evil and suffering among men, and like Emerson "made plain to them [countrymen] the terrible things of human life" (reported by Ryan in *Critical Essays on Robert Frost,* 130, 131). Although it cannot be proven that Frost learned from Emerson that the most intrinsic religious experience is found in the contemplation of nature, in his poetry, Frost does attempt to teach his reader to attune himself to spiritual meaning in the contemplation of nature.

Finally, two other philosophical influences on Robert Frost are discussed by John Sears. Frost had read William James* while a student at Harvard and had called James "my greatest inspiration." The two works of James that he had read were the *Pragmatism* and the *Psychology.* The other philosopher was Henri Bergson,* whose work *Creative Evolution* Frost read with enthusiasm in 1911. Sears sums up the influence of James and Bergson on Frost: "Along with Emerson, particularly the Emerson of 'fate,' they [James and Bergson] provided Frost with a source of suggestive metaphors for the connection between spiritual fact and natural fact, between mind and event, feeling and process, which he could adapt to his own philosophical or poetic needs" (Sears, 343).

REFERENCES

Bell, Barbara Currier. "Frost on Humanity in Nature." *ArQ* 42, no. 3 (Autumn 1986): 223–38.
Cook, Reginald. *Robert Frost: A Living Voice*. Amherst: University of Massachusetts Press, 1974.
Gerber, Philip L., ed. *Critical Essays on Robert Frost*. Boston: G. K. Hall, 1982.
O'Brien, Timothy D. "Archetypal Encounter in 'Mending Wall.' " *American Notes and Queries* 24, nos. 9–10 (May–June 1986): 147–51.
Rogers, William E. "Mysteries in Frost." *FurmS* 32 (December 1986): 53–64.
Ryan, Alvan S. "Frost and Emerson: Voice and Vision." In *Critical Essays on Robert Frost*, edited by Philip L. Gerber. Boston: G. K. Hall, 1982.
Sears, John. "William James, Henri Bergson and The Poetics of Robert Frost." *New England Quarterly* 48 (1975): 341–61.

G

GARDNER, JOHN. B. Batavia, New York, July 21, 1933. D. Binghamton, New York, September 14, 1982. American novelist.

Although Gardner was an established scholar on the age of Chaucer, he is best known for his original and well-crafted works of fiction. His novel *Grendel* (1971) retells the Beowulf legend from the monster's point of view. His other works include a short-story collection, *The King's Indian* (1974), and the novels *The Wreckage of Agathon* (1970), *The Sunlight Dialogues* (1972), *Nickel Mountain* (1973), and *October Light* (1976), which won the 1977 National Book Critics Circle Award for Fiction. Two of his works were published posthumously: *On Becoming a Novelist* (1983) and *The Art of Fiction* (1984).

Gardner's knowledge of philosophy is revealed in *Grendel* in which he summarizes the major ideas of Western civilization. As David Cowart, his biographer, says concerning this work,

> Gardner manages to scan major social and economic ideas like chivalry, feudalism, and mercantilism; theology from primitive animism to [Søren] Kierkegaard,[*] with side glances at oriental religions; metaphysics from [David] Hume[*] to [Jean-Paul] Sartre[*] [q.v.] and from [Martin] Heidegger[*] to Whitehead; and political philosophy—the origins, legitimacy, and accountability of the state—from Plato[*] to [John] Locke[*] and [Thomas] Hobbes,[*] and from Machiavelli to [Karl] Marx[*] and Georges Sorel. (Cowart, 43)

When Cowart says that "the Existentialism[**] of Sartre provides a point of reference for Gardner's plan in *Grendel*," the comments of another biographer, Gregory Morris, must be considered. Morris explains that the work is actually an attack on Sartre's existentialism. In the work, *Jean-Paul Sartre,* Gardner's "philosophical bogy" is dominant. Gardner's long-standing feud with Sartre has been documented; in interviews, Gardner has consistently attacked the "whiny despair" of the existentialist position. *Grendel,* as a critique of the existentialist position, has been studied by numerous critics, and there can be no doubt that one of Gardner's intellectual targets is this dominant philosophical school, a philosophy that runs counter to everything Gardner attempts in his writing.

Friedrich Nietzsche,* another philosopher who appears in the works of John Gardner, is one whose teaching certainly has made an impact on the mind of the American author. The philosopher appears in the work *Mickelsson's Ghosts* (1982). "Standing opposed to these powers are the philosophical figures of [Martin] Luther and Nietzsche, Mickelsson's metaphysical and ethical bogies. . . . Mickelsson comes round to the ways of thought of Luther and Nietzsche, uses their peculiar disdain to his moral advantage, and acts finally from the darkest of his furious instincts" (Morris, 217, 218). Actually, Mickelsson's final stage is life as lived by the *ubermensch* (superman**) of Nietzsche. Like Nietzsche he lives alone and, as Cowart mentions, "where Nietzsche went literally insane, possibly from syphilis, Mickelsson arrives at a state of benign Lunacy, the necessary condition, as Gardner often suggests in his fiction, for responding to the world positively" (Morris, 225).

And so we see in the fiction of John Gardner explicit references to such philosophers as Nietzsche, Sartre, and Immanuel Kant,* in *The Resurrection* (1979)—references that verify Gardner's knowledge and concern with philosophy.

REFERENCES

Cowart, David. *Arches and Light: The Fiction of John Gardner.* Carbondale: Southern Illinois University Press, 1983.

Henderson, Jeff. "John Gardner's Jason and Medea: The Resurrection of a Genre." *PLL* 22, no. 1 (Winter 1986): 76–95.

Morris, Gregory L. *A World of Order and Light: The Fiction of John Gardner.* Athens: The University of Georgia Press, 1984.

Simmons, Kenith L. "The Fit Will Survive: Freddy's Book and Natural Selection." *MSE* 10, no. 1 (Spring 1985): 46–58.

Strehle, Susan. "John Gardner's Novels: Affirmation and the Alien." *Critique* 18, no. 2 (1977): 86–96.

GENET, JEAN. B. December 19, 1910, Paris, France. French novelist and dramatist.

Jean Genet was in prison in 1942 when he wrote his novel *Our Lady* *of the Flowers,* a shocking work that glorifies crime and homosexuality. His plays were more successful, and it is in his plays where his literary reputation lies. The most successful plays were *The Maids* (1947), *The Balcony* (1956), and *The Blacks* (1958). Genet's career and popularity were enhanced in 1953 by Jean-Paul Sartre's* (q.v.) *Saint Genet: Actor and Martyr,* in which Sartre exalts Genet as an existentialist (see existentialism**) rebel and hero. Genet's novels and plays are nihilistic (see nihilism**), and in his plays he successfully displays avant-garde theatrical devices. Until the 1960s, Genet's works were banned in Great Britain and in the United States.

Existential absurdity** to nihilism characterize Genet's work concepts. Since Genet's characters exist on the fringe of society (see *Deathwatch*) and are outcasts who pride themselves on being outcasts from normal society, they never move from alienation to reconciliation, but they are driven to a state of nothingness. "Despising the present, he [Genet and his characters] yearns for a future void of sound and motion, of space and time—a future which, the goal of all human endeavor, is nothingness" (Jacobsen and Mueller, 129). In *Deathwatch* (1949) and *The Maids,* the protagonists seek to change their status, but as we see in the case of La Ranc (*Deathwatch*) such efforts are in vain and end in defeat. In these plays nihilism is tied in with a strong sense of determinism.** For example, in *Deathwatch,* the viewer and the reader are clearly apprised of the fact that green eyes did not choose his crime. It was his destiny to murder; he was driven by illogical forces that eventually drove him to crime. This element of fatalism is linked with the absurdity of the human condition. Fate drives Genet's people to commit crimes and to alienate themselves from society. "Green eyes *had* to commit the murder. He was not man acting but man acted upon by those mysterious, invisible powers that play their game of chess with human counters" (Jacobsen and Mueller, 133).

Much has been said of the Sartre-Genet relationship, especially since 1952 and the publication of Sartre's book *Saint Genet: Actor and Martyr.* It is possible that, after 1952, Genet saw himself in the Sartrean image, but with Genet's tendency to portray a deterministic situation in his dreams, it seems impossible to label him an existentialist. The existentialist believes in man's freedom and that he makes his own world through free acts of the will. And yet, in reference to a passage in *Funeral Rite's* (1968), in which Pierret inadvertently puts a maggot in his mouth, Sartre says, "He found himself caught between fainting with nausea and dominating his situation by willing it. He willed it. He made his tongue and palate artfully and patiently feel the loathsome contact. The act of willing was his first poetic attitude governed by pride'' (Sartre, 66–67). Perhaps the greatest philosophical influence on Genet did come from Sartre.

Jean Genet is a modern writer who, like Marcel Proust and James Joyce (q.v.), examines the mask of reality. His is an absurd universe, a nihilistic domain, where all the so-called normal values of family, religion, and heterosexuality are questioned.

REFERENCES

Clark, Eleanor. "The World of Jean Genet." *Partisan Review* 16 (April 1949): 442, 448.
Coe, Richard. *The Vision of Jean Genet.* New York: Grove Press, 1968.
Jacobsen, Josephine, and William R. Mueller. *Ionesco and Genet: Playwrights of Silence.* Hill and Wang, 1969.
Sartre, Jean-Paul. *Saint Genet: Actor and Martyr.* Translated by Bernard Frechtman. New York: Braziller, 1963.
Stewart, H. E. "You Are What You Wear: Appearance and Being in Jean Genet's Work." *Francofonia* 10 (Spring 1986): 31–40.

GIDE, ANDRÉ. B. November 22, 1869, Paris, France. D. February 19, 1951, Paris, France. French novelist, essayist, dramatist, and critic.

André Gide's early years were marked by a puritanical upbringing (see puritanism**) and an early interest in learning especially science and art. His first novel, completed at the early age of twenty-two, was entitled *The Notebooks of André Walter* (1891). The novel concerns the conflict between the Bible and science. In the same year he also published *The Treatise of the Narcissus,* a work which reflects his initiation into the symbolist movement (see symbolism**) and his association with Paul Valéry and Stéphane Mallarmé. In 1893, threatened with tuberculosis, he went to North Africa. *The Return of the Prodigal Son* (1897) is a touching story that treats the need of the young to break away from the protective care of the family. Gide's two most famous and important dramas are *Bathsheba* (1912) and *Oedipus* (1931); however, his crowning work was *The Counterfeiters* (1926), which includes his thoughts about life's problems with a discussion of what a novel should be. Gide won the Nobel Prize for Literature in 1947.

In September 1894, Gide began a serious study of the German philosopher Gottfried Leibniz.* The work in question was *Nouveaux Essais* (1765), a refutation of John Locke's* *Essay Concerning Human Understanding* (1690). In his work, Leibniz accepted what Locke condemned, the existence of innate ideas.

> Despite his insistence upon innate ideas, or rather, upon ideas which are of the understanding alone—Leibniz recognizes the catalytic effect that the senses have upon the understanding. He thereby acknowledges, unlike [René] Descartes,[*] the role of the outside world and of the body in the learning process. . . . Through Leibniz, Gide discovered the philosophical justification of sense-experience in the formation of ideas. Absolute truth concerning man and his condition, which was Gide's main objective during his Symbolist Period, is beyond the Ken of Man. (Rossi, 107)

Gide learned much from Leibniz about man and his capabilities, and the ideas that he gleaned from Leibniz's *Nouveaux Essais* were set down in a pamphlet entitled *The Treatise of the Narcissus.* "The pamphlet is the statement of a point of view, of a way of seeing the world and its inhabitants and the artist's role in it" (Rossi, 109).

Gide claimed that his real initiation into philosophy came through his reading and rereading of Arthur Schopenhauer* whose influence on his thinking he acknowledges in his memoirs. In Book III of Schopenhauer's *The World As Will and Idea* (1819), the philosopher discusses art forms and genres and their relationship to reality, and of course this was of great interest to the artist Gide. His biographer, Vinio Rossi, hints that Gide possibly had trouble absorbing Schopenhauer's ideas for he says, "Gide had withdrawn to Annecy to create a frame of mind facilitating the contemplation described by Schopenhauer and so necessary for a felicitous creative act. But, alone in his ivory tower, Gide proved able to contemplate only himself and his self-engendered emotions" (Rossi, 24).

> When he read Schopenhauer during his eighteenth year, Gide found formulated many of the ideas he had been nurturing. The German philosopher's insistence upon a true reality of the idea and the gift of genius to perceive and express it encouraged Gide along his aesthetic and mystical path [see aesthetics** and mysticism**]. Furthermore, in distinguishing history from poetry, the behavior of men from that of a single man, Schopenhauer encouraged Gide's self-scrutiny. (Rossi, 41–42)

After reading Friedrich Nietzsche's* *The Birth of Tragedy* (1872), Gide wrote that it summed up Nietzsche's whole philosophy. Eventually Gide's interest in Nietzsche would result in his masterpiece *The Immoralist* (1902), a work which was directly influenced by Nietzsche. But when Gide drew on Nietzsche's writing he made the new literary work his own. Finally, it should be mentioned that, in December 1899, Gide wrote a critical essay on Nietzsche.

One can assume that Leibniz and Schopenhauer led Gide to a deeper understanding of the human condition and also to an understanding of his role as an artist. An awareness of these philosophical influences might lead to a clearer understanding of the masterpieces of this French writer who, as Rossi says, "offers by far the greatest resistance to codification, to labels of any kind, to the one-word or one-phrase descriptions that fill manuals of literature" (Rossi, 159).

REFERENCES

Fayer, H. M. *Gide, Freedom and Dostoievsky*. Burlington, Vt.: Lane Press, 1946.
Rossi, Vinio. *André Gide: The Evolution of an Aesthetic*. New Brunswick, N.J.: Rutgers University Press, 1967.
Stary, Sonja C. "The Ironic Pursuit of Freedom in Gide's *Les Caves du Vatican*." *RR* 77, no. 4 (November 1986):368–75.
Thierry, Jean-Jacques. *André Gide*. Paris: Hachette, 1986.

GOETHE, JOHANN WOLFGANG VON. B. August 28, 1749, Frankfurt, Germany. D. March 22, 1832, Weimar, Germany. German poet and playwright.

The greatest of all German poets and an outstanding figure of world literature since the Renaissance, Goethe, a precocious child, was sent to the University of Leipzig at the age of sixteen, but serious illness forced him to return home. In 1770 he received his law degree at Strassburg. *Götz von Berlichingen* (1773) established Goethe as a leader of the German preromantic storm and stress movement. His most successful and important early work was *The Sorrows of Young Werther* (1774). An important phase of his life had begun by mid–1771 when Goethe became Duke Karl August's friend and adviser. What followed were the so-called Weimar years, the most productive literary period of Goethe's life. Two of his major works during this period were *Hermann and Dorothea* (1797), a love story set against the background of the French Revolution, and *Wilhelm Meister* (1829). Goethe's major contribution to world literature is *Faust* (1832), a monumental tragedy and his masterpiece.

Goethe was a scholar of considerable depth, and, in his early years, had read the *Phaedo* of Plato* as well as the *Timaeus,* the *Symposium,* and the *Apologia*. Later in his work *Farbenlehre* (1810), Goethe praised "the holy awe" with which Plato approaches nature. He learned of the Platonism** of the eighteenth century and the world of the Greeks through the writings of Anthony Ashley Cooper, 3rd Earl of Shaftesbury, and Johann Winkelmann, but the German poet was not always in agreement with Plato. "Goethe's view that idea and phenomenon are one in the outward form would alone bring him in an unbridgeable opposition to Plato. What unifies the Greek and the German is the setting of the problem itself and the way in which they approach nature" (Vietor, 62).

Goethe was also familiar with the works of Plotinus,* and in his *Wanderjahre* (1829) he translated some of the passages of the *Enneads*. In Goethe's *Farbenlehre,* he called Plotinus an "early witness to the old truth that like can only be known by its like" (Vietor, 63). Goethe was an independent thinker, and here again we find him disagreeing with the Neoplatonist (see Neoplatonism**) Plotinus on the subject of the begetter and the begotten. Goethe said, in opposition to the philosopher, "The Begotten is not less than the Begetter; indeed, it is the advantage of living procreation that the Begotten can be more excellent than the Begetter" (Goethe, 35:318).

In his autobiography, Goethe speaks at length and with approval of Baruch Spinoza.* His acceptance of Spinoza's pantheism** (as early as 1770, Goethe began to read about pantheism in the works of Giordano Bruno*)—that God and the world are one and that God is in all of his works, in the flowers, the ocean, in everything—led Goethe to a happy and beautiful unity with God and nature. Spinoza strengthened for him the conviction that events do not occur by chance but are regulated by law. Goethe's biographer, Karl Vietor, points out some differences between the thought of Spinoza and Goethe:

> Goethe emphasizes the point, in opposition to Spinoza, that every existing thing has its existence in itself and cannot be measured by anything which is outside it; that no organism is put together out of parts but that each is an integral whole, and as such is an image of the universe. (Vietor, 67)

Goethe's reading of Immanuel Kant,* Friedrich Schelling,* and Georg Wilhelm Hegel* resulted in an essay entitled "Einwirkung der Neueren Philosophie" (Influence of Recent Philosophy). He rejected Kant's concept of duty as did Friedrich von Schiller (q.v.), but he accepted Kant's limits of pure reason with reservations. In fact, it was probably Kant's notion of the limits of the human mind that inspired the magnificent ode *Grenzen der Menschheit* (1789) which begins, "For against Gods let no man ever measure himself." Finally, in regard to his reading of Kant, Goethe violently disagreed with the philosopher's doctrine of evil in human nature. Goethe was more in agreement with the ideas of Schelling, and what strongly attracted him was Schelling's doctrine of one reality, which is spirit from within.

Goethe read Hegel but admitted that he rejected Hegel's philosophy: "[T]he fundament of his [Hegel's] doctrine lay outside the sphere of my vision . . . but I have always drawn a genuine spiritual advantage from it" (Goethe's letter to Varnhagen von Ense, January 5, 1832).

REFERENCES

Goethe, Johann Wolfgang von. *Collected Works*. Cambridge, Mass.: Suhrkamp/Insel, 1983.

Lovejoy, A. O. *The Great Chain of Being*. Cambridge, Mass.: Harvard University Press, 1936.

Nisbet, H. B. "Lucretius in 18th Century Germany: With a Commentary on Goethe's 'Metamorphose der Tiere.' " *MLR* 81, no. 1 (January, 1986): 97–115.

Vietor, Karl. *Goethe the Thinker*. Cambridge, Mass.: Harvard University Press, 1950.

Wilkenson, E. M. and L. A. Willoughby. *Goethe, Poet and Thinker*. New York: Barnes and Noble, 1962.

GRAVES, ROBERT. B. July 24, 1895, London, England. D. December 7, 1985, Deya, Majorca, Spain. British poet.

Robert Graves fought in World War I and recorded his war experiences in his autobiography *Goodbye to All That* (1929). He was severely wounded in 1916 and remained deeply troubled for a decade after the war. He was treated by Dr. W. H. R. Rivers, a pioneer British psychoanalyst who encouraged Graves to write poetry as a form of therapy. Graves's mental problems were exacerbated by an increasingly unhappy marriage which ended in divorce. He wrote two historical novels: *I, Claudius* (1934) and *Claudius the God* (1934). In his poetry he is satiric and concerns himself primarily with failure in love and a search for identity. He is thought of as a love poet. Since the publication of the first collection of his poems in 1927, there have been five successive editions of *Collected Poems* (1938–1975).

Graves began his career in poetry under the influence of Rivers, a Freudian** psychologist. Early in his career, he was convinced that the writing of poetry would be psychologically therapeutic.

> Graves was convinced then, at least, of the relevance of dreams to poetic creativity and the psychologically therapeutic function of poetry in working out emotional conflicts. Not only did he later reject his former psychological views, he vehemently repudiated all psychological explanations of myth. Yet, the strength of his denial of Freudian and Jungian[**] contributions to myth appears to be directly correlated to their relevance to himself. (Snipes, 190–91)

While living in England in the 1920s, Graves met Bertrand Russell,*
and it is coincidental that, at this time, his philosophical interests surfaced.
Neither Katherine Snipes, his biographer, nor Douglas Day attribute this
interest to Russell but to a Hindu friend, Basanto Mallik, who was studying philosophy at Oxford. "Mallik was for some months a constant visitor
at the Islip cottage, and Graves' new fascination with philosophical speculation threatened for a time almost to replace poetry as his vocation"
(Day, 64). This never happened, however, and in 1924 Graves published
Mock Beggar Hall (1924), a collection of fifteen new and intellectually
demanding poems. Several of these poems, especially "Knowledge of
God," reflect his philosophical studies at that time. "In 'Knowledge of
God' there is an echo of the Pythagorean[**] belief in eternal recurrence,
with perhaps overtones of Eastern theology derived from the poet's con-
versations with Mallik" (Day, 65).

Although Graves never showed much interest in existentialism,** there
is evidence that, in *My Head! My Head* (1925), he uses the existential
principle that "existence precedes essence" and argues that it applies to
gods as well as man. Snipes sees a similarity between Graves and Jean-
Paul Sartre* (q.v.), who claims that human beings choose God's nature.
What Graves seems to be suggesting in addition is that a god, at any
stage of its development, is a real source of magical power for his priest
or prophet (Snipes, 95).

When one reads the Clark lectures, which Graves delivered at Cambridge University in 1954, and the lectures given at Oxford in the 1960s,
when he held the chair of poetry there, one is overwhelmed by his
comprehensive learning and erudition. In these lectures he moves easily
from Carl Jung's* collected works to multiple references ranging from
Hebrew mythology to modern philosophy and literature. He refers to a
number of philosophers in these lectures; and one is easily convinced
that Robert Graves was one of the most philosophically sophisticated
poets in English literature. There is little evidence that he incorporated
any particular philosopher's doctrines in his poetry, but there is evidence
that he had read the works of the world's greatest thinkers.

REFERENCES

Cohen, J. M. *Robert Graves*. New York: Grove Press, 1960.
Day, Douglas. *Swifter Than Reason: The Poetry and Criticism of Robert Graves*.
    Chapel Hill: The University of North Carolina Press, 1963.
Graves, Robert. *On Poetry: Collected Talks and Essays*. New York: Doubleday,
    1969.
Kirkham, Michael. *The Poetry of Robert Graves*. New York: Oxford University
    Press, 1969.

Snipes, Katherine. *Robert Graves*. New York: Frederick Ungar, 1979.
Stade, George. *Robert Graves*. New York: Columbia University Press, 1967.

GREENE, GRAHAM. B. October 2, 1904, Berkhampstead, Herts, England. British novelist.

After abandoning a brief journalistic career, Graham Greene began writing fiction and published his first novel, *The Man Within* (1929), a thriller with a historical setting. His first real success was *Stamboul Train* (1932), which was also a thriller but with political themes. Greene called these novels "entertainments," and he was so successful with this type that he produced two more: *A Gun for Sale* (1936) and *The Confidential Agent* (1939). His novels took a turn to morality with *Brighton Rock* (1938); then, in 1940, his writings became "Catholic" with the publication of *The Power and the Glory* (1940), *The Heart of the Matter* (1948), and *The End of the Affair* (1951). In these novels, Greene's protagonists are filled with a sense of sin rather than grace, and humanistic values are juxtaposed with religious ones. Greene has also achieved success as a writer of plays, screenplays, essays, and travel books.

Graham Greene's fiction may be characterized, at least in part, as a somewhat less than traditional expression of certain aspects of Roman Catholic doctrine. Although he cautions his readers not to consider himself a theologian, several of his works, including *Brighton Rock* and *The End of the Affair,* focus heavily on sin and man's relationship to God from a Catholic perspective. It is true that the picture of Catholicism which Greene paints is not always brightly optimistic and that his presentation of Catholic doctrine is often somewhat unorthodox, facts which no doubt annoy traditional Catholic readers. He borders on heresy for example in *The Heart of the Matter,* when he suggests that a suicide may find salvation.

In his fiction, in spite of often vehement criticism from his readers, Greene continued throughout his productive years to present difficult moral problems, and he responded with equal vehemence to his critics quoting Unamuno: "Those who believe that they believe in God, but without passion in their heart, without anguish of mind, without uncertainty, without doubt, without an element of despair even in their consolation, believe only in the God idea, not in God himself" (reported by Sharrock, 23).

One of Greene's more interesting achievements is his successful attempt to preserve the role of the protagonist sinner in fiction, a role exploited by Feodor Dostoevsky (q.v.) and by Henry James (q.v.), whom Greene admired and saluted "as the only writer of his time who knew about evil."

REFERENCES

Hynes, Samuel L. *Graham Greene: A Collection of Critical Essays*. Englewood
    Cliffs, N.J.: Prentice-Hall, 1973.
Kulshrestha, J. P. *Graham Greene: The Novelist*. Madras: Macmillan Co. of
    India, 1977.
Sharrock, Roger. *Saints, Sinners and Comedians: The Novels of Graham Greene*.
    Notre Dame, Ind.: University of Notre Dame Press, 1984.
Stratford, Philip. *Faith and Reason: Creative Process in Greene and Mauriac*.
    Notre Dame, Ind.: University of Notre Dame Press, 1964.

H

HARDY, THOMAS. B. June 2, 1840, Dorset, England. D. January 11, 1928, Dorchester, England. English novelist and poet.

Thomas Hardy was the son of a builder and master mason and for some time followed his father's profession. Between 1862 and 1867, however, he began to write seriously, and one of the results of this period was a fine poem called "Neutral Tones." *Desperate Remedies* (1871), his first published novel, was followed by his famous *The Return of the Native* (1878), *The Mayor of Casterbridge* (1886), *Tess of the d'Urbervilles* (1891), and *Jude the Obscure* (1895). The outraged public reaction to Hardy's treatment of adultery in *Jude the Obscure* disgusted the author, and he rejected the novel in favor of poetry. *Wessex Poems* appeared in 1898, followed in 1901 by *Poems of the Past and the Present*.

Thomas Hardy was, in an interesting way, a victim of the intellectual ferment that characterized English literature and thought in the 1860s. His reading of John Stuart Mill,* Herbert Spencer,* Aldous Huxley (q.v.), Auguste Comte,* and later Algernon Charles Swinburne and Charles Darwin* led to a deterministic metaphysics (see determinism** and metaphysical**), which found expression in the angry fatalism** that characterized much of his work from *The Poor Man and the Lady* (1867–1868) to *Tess of the d'Urbervilles* and finally *Jude the Obscure*.

However, possibly no single work had a greater impact on Hardy than Darwin's *The Origin of Species* (1858). Although Hardy's views were influenced by other scientists and philosophers, they did not change fundamentally after 1865, a few years after he first read Darwin. Hardy accepted the Darwinian notion (see Darwinism**) that we live in a world of imperfection, struggle, and cruelty, where events impinge on us and proceed by the laws of nature and where personal choice is determined by the limitations of chance hereditary characteristics and external circumstances. Later, in *The Woodlanders* (1887), Hardy expresses his acceptance of the deterministic view and presents glimpses of the outer Darwinian world that reinforce his perception of the tragedy of the human condition.

At the end of his writing career, Hardy became obsessed with Darwin's theories on heredity; in fact, in the poem "Heredity" (1889), Hardy expresses his conviction that his life had been preconditioned by his ancestors. In *Tess* he places the heroine at the exhausted end of a long family line, a tragic situation from which there can be no escape. She is trapped by her heredity and environment. But Tess's aggressive energy in the face of the pressures of the Darwinian world asserts Hardy's conviction of the value of individual life and his belief in human progress. *Tess* is, finally, a deeply felt response to the intellectual and emotional crisis so evident in nineteenth-century thought and letters from Alfred Lord Tennyson to Hardy.

REFERENCE

Page, Norman, ed. *Thomas Hardy: The Writer and His Background*. New York: St. Martins Press, 1980.

HAWTHORNE, NATHANIEL. B. July 4, 1804, Salem, Massachusetts. D. May 19, 1864, Plymouth, New Hampshire. American novelist and short-story writer.

The son of a sea captain, who died when Hawthorne was still a boy, Nathaniel Hawthorne was raised in the home of his maternal grandfather where, because of a lameness that resulted from a foot injury, he was forced to eschew the normal play of his peers and acquired the habit of reading. He graduated from Bowdoin College in 1825 and began writing stories which were published anonymously. Hawthorne's first successful book, *Twice Told Tales* (1837), praised by Henry Wadsworth Longfellow, was well received by a small audience of readers. Publication of *The Scarlet Letter* (1850) brought him a considerable amount of fame and provided him with a reasonable level of financial independence. During the following two years, he published *The House of the Seven Gables* (1851), *The Blithedale Romance* (1852), and several, perhaps less significant, works. His friendship with Franklin Pierce, for whom he wrote a campaign biography, won him an appointment as counsul to Liverpool and Manchester, which afforded him the opportunity to travel in Europe.

He began writing the *Marble Faun* (1860) in Italy and completed it in England two years later. Hawthorne was buried in Concord, Massachusetts, in Sleepy Hollow cemetery.

The name of Hawthorne in American literature usually evokes thoughts of puritanism,** Salem, witchcraft, and Gothic fiction. For example, the very popular and heavily anthologized story "Young Goodman Brown," set in Salem, is a tale of evil and devil worship. However, as Arlin Turner points out in his analysis of Hawthorne's works, "His characters and his stories may assume the entire sweep of the New England colonists' beliefs, including witchcraft, but the appearance of those beliefs in his works does not mean that he necessarily held with the early Puritans in any of them, including witchcraft" (Turner, 20). Turner goes on to state that the Puritan views on morality, elements of Puritan dogma, are simply the trappings, the externals that manifest human problems. In short, Hawthorne found the people and events in early Puritan America that were suitable for the presentation of his ideas. In accordance with his sense of fair play, Hawthorne presented both the Puritans who were champions of religious freedom and those who used the stocks and whipping post.

Although one finds general agreement among his critics that Hawthorne's major theme was the unpardonable sin, there continues to be considerable controversy concerning the ethical dimension in his work, seen by his critics at once as didactic and purposely vague and ambiguous. According to James K. Folsom, "The moral dimension of Hawthorne's art . . . becomes an aesthetic [see aesthetics**] means to suggest the multiplicity of motives and explanations inherent in any human action." The apparent (or real) ethical ambiguity in Hawthorne's fiction is deliberate and expresses his view that the moral dilemmas with which his characters are confronted and the decisions which result suggest multiple interpretations. The moral decisions made by his fictional characters are not necessarily meant by Hawthorne to represent his own moral position. The ambiguity, which is always there in his fiction, teases the reader, addresses the complexity of human behavior, and forces the inevitable conclusion that there is no right choice available to man in this, the sense world. There is, however, in Hawthorne's fiction the suggestion of an ideal world, a Platonic world (see Platonism**) of ideal form, of essences, a transcendence beyond human awareness, a perfect morality. Moral behavior, like art (see Folsom), is an imitation of an Ideal, never completely realized by mankind but always the object of human endeavor. The absence of a conclusive moral (or aesthetic) statement in Hawthorne's work speaks to a qualified Platonism which may, or may not, help to clarify the mysterious, the unexplained incidents and conclusions in Hawthorne's fiction.

REFERENCES

Baym, Nina. *The Shape of Hawthorne's Career*. Ithaca, N.Y.: Cornell University Press, 1976.
Folsom, James K. *Man's Accidents and God's Purposes*. New Haven, Conn.: College and University Press, 1963.
Turner, Arlin. *Nathaniel Hawthorne: An Introduction and Interpretation*. New York: Barnes and Noble, 1961.
Wagenknecht, Edward. *Nathaniel Hawthorne: Man and Writer*. New York: Oxford University Press, 1961.
Young, Philip. *Hawthorne's Secret: An Untold Tale*. Boston: David R. Goding, 1984.

HEMINGWAY, ERNEST. B. July 21, 1898, Oak Park, Illinois. D. July 2, 1961, Ketchum, Idaho. American novelist.

After graduating from high school, Ernest Hemingway became a reporter for the *Kansas City Star*. He served in World War I with the ambulance corps and was wounded. After the war, he spent some time in Paris attempting to establish himself as a writer and here was befriended by Gertrude Stein. During his lifetime, Hemingway became quite a celebrity whose exploits of African safaris and deep-sea fishing adventures spilled over into his novels to the point where his readers had difficulty distinguishing between fiction and real-life adventures. In 1925 Hemingway published a collection of short stories entitled *In Our Time* and introduced himself as a new stylist of short, concise sentences and understated dialogue. This was followed in 1926 with a novel, *The Sun Also Rises,* which depicted the so-called lost generation in Paris after World War I. *A Farewell to Arms,* a novel of love and war, was published in 1929. Hemingway, having established himself as an important American writer, published two more noteworthy novels: *For Whom the Bell Tolls* (1940) and *The Old Man and the Sea* (1952). He was awarded the Nobel Prize for Literature and the Pulitzer Prize for fiction in 1952.

A careful review of Hemingway's major works reveals that the author passed from one philosophical stage to another. *The Sun Also Rises,* for example, and the short story "A Clean, Well Lighted Place" reveal elements of existentialism.** Life here is absurd and meaningless; man is nothing, and he is extremely alienated from society. The nihilistic (see nihilism**) life that these characters live seemed to be untenable for Hemingway, so he moved on to hedonism** and Epicureanism** where physical pleasure and material activities are of prime importance. This, too, did not suffice, so Hemingway created tough, stoical characters who believed in self-control and followed "The Code." This form of Stoicism** was its own reward.

As far as we know, Hemingway never expressed a debt to the Stoics, but a close reading of Hemingway's major works will show that some basic Stoic tenets occur implicitly, again and again, in the American novelist's short stories and novels. In Hemingway's work, the Stoic accepts life with dignified resignation (things happen and he cannot change them); he controls his attitudes and emotions toward events and accepts them; and he faces death with courage. In Stoicism, "The virtuous man finds happiness in himself and is independent of the external world which he has succeeded in overcoming by mastering himself, his passions and emotions" (Runes, 301).

Numerous examples in Hemingway's works show his heroes to be stoical and to accept events calmly and with dignity. Ole Anderson in "The Killers" turns over in his bed and patiently awaits the assassin. Macomber accepts his wife Margot's infidelity, and one of the most memorable scenes in the conclusion of A Farewell to Arms is the one in which Frederich Henry placidly walks out into the rain after the death of Catherine. As for facing death bravely, think of just about every Hemingway hero. They all, from Robert Jordon in For Whom the Bell Tolls to Santiago in The Old Man and the Sea, and even Macomber, face death bravely. In short, the Hemingway hero is always the true Stoic. He is never a complainer, never a coward; he accepts everything, even death, because he knows he cannot change the course of human events.

Hemingway, one of the most influential writers in American literature, is usually not regarded as a philosphical writer. However, in an attempt to prove that Hemingway is an existentialist, John Killinger argued that certain characteristics, like Hemingway's treatment of violence, the constant presence of death, and the reduction of life to its simplist terms, put Hemingway in the company of such existentialists as Jean-Paul Sartre* (q.v.) and Albert Camus (q.v.). No one, not even Killinger, attempts to show that the existentialist philosophers had a direct influence on the American novelist. "Rather, such similarities have arisen because Hemingway and the existentialists are products of the same milieu—The Catastrophic, war-ridden world of the twentieth century" (Killinger, book jacket).

REFERENCES

Asselineau, Roger. *The Transcendentalist Constant in American Literature*. New York: New York University Press, 1986.

Burnam, Tom. "Primitivism and Masculinity in the Work of Ernest Heming-
    way." *Modern Fiction Studies,* August 1955, 20–24.
Cargill, Oscar. *Intellectual America: Ideas on the March.* New York: Macmillan,
    1941.
Killinger, John. *Hemingway and the Dead Gods: A Story in Existentialism.*
    Lexington: University of Kentucky Press, 1960.
My, Qiang. "A Preliminary Exploration of Hemingway's Aesthetic Views."
    Foreign Lit. Studies (China) 34, no. 4 (December 1986): 21–37.
Runes, Dagobert David, ed. *Dictionary of Philosophy.* New York: Philosophical
    Library, 1983.
Stumpf, Samuel Enoch. *Philosophy—History and Problems.* New York:
    McGraw-Hill, 1971.
Wenley, Robert M. *Stoicism and Its Influences.* New York: Cooper Square, 1963.

HESSE, HERMANN. B. July 2, 1877, Calw, Baden-Württemberg,
Germany. Naturalized Swiss citizen, 1923. D. August 9, 1962, Montagnola, Ticino, Switzerland. German/Swiss novelist and poet.

Born on the edge of the Black Forest, at an early age and at the behest
of his father, Hermann Hesse entered the Maulbronn Seminary. After a
year there, he ran away, and his dejection was so suicidal that his father
removed him from the seminary. After this experience, Hesse proved
that he could not adapt to secular schools, and he was apprenticed in a
Calw tower clock factory and later to a Tubingen bookstore. Hereafter,
Hesse, self-educated, became a free-lance writer and began to write novels. During World War I, Hesse lived in neutral Switzerland, wrote
denunciations of militarism and nationalism, and edited a journal for
German war prisoners. He became a permanent resident of Switzerland,
became a Swiss citizen in 1923, and settled in Montagnola. Hesse's first
novel *Demian* (1919), a great success, was published under a pseudonym.
His next novel, *Siddhartha* (1922), was a poetic life of Buddha. Bud-
dhistic (see Buddhism**) ideas were to be found also in *Steppenwolf*
(1927), but in this novel Hesse colored the work with the psychology of
Carl Jung.* His final novel in the pre–World War II years was *Narziss
und Goldmund* (1930), a work that depicts two contrasting types of men.
In 1943 Hesse's works were put on the Nazi blacklist. Consequently,
The Glass Bead Game was published instead in Zurich in that year. In
this work, Hesse raised the question of whether practical action should
dictate one's political and social life. In 1946, Hesse received the Nobel
Prize for Literature.

Herman Hesse's psychoanalysis as a patient of the Jungian** psychiatrist Joseph Bilang and his experience as a student of Jung led him to

a study of Jungian psychology and, most important, to a familiarity with Jung's notion of myth and archetype. Hesse's study of Jung's works affected his personal life and led him to a conceptual framework based on Jungian psychoanalysis, a framework which resulted in the acquisition of a rationale for social and psychological insights which became the formative structures in his novels. Ralph Freedman claims that psychoanalysis made a decisive change in Hesse's style: He was not able "to portray inner experience in pictorial and dramatic terms" (Freedman, 188). Hesse also learned about Jung's anima,** which supplies creativity, and the animus, which gave masculine control to his writing.

In 1896, Hesse read Friedrich Nietzsche's* *Ecce Homo* (1888), and at this time wrote to Karl Isenburg that his favorite thinkers were Johann Wolfgang von Goethe (q.v.) and Nietzsche. When he moved to Basel, Switzerland, in 1900, he arrived with the works of Nietzsche and a framed reproduction of Arnold Bocklin's "Island of the Dead" in his luggage. According to Freedman, *Peter Camenzind,* which appeared in serial form in *die Neue Rundschau* in 1903, had grown out of his studies of Nietzsche, "a philosopher who views man's relations with the world in terms of dual inner impulses of passion and order" (Freedman, 111).

Demian represented dreams and the inner life in the terms of his newly found insights based on readings of Sigmund Freud* and Jung. Demian, in a story imbued with Nietzsche's anti-Christian teachings, advises Sinclair to follow his inner voice, not the teachings of Christianity, in determining what is good or evil. The Nietzschean hero is awakened in solitude, in the isolation of the soul from the herd. In fact, throughout the story, Nietzsche's doctrine of herd morality is implicit. This theme, which occurs in other works of Hesse, is similar to the isolation of the artist in Thomas Mann's (q.v.) works. Projecting the world within has always been the mark of Hesse's mysticism,** which, by his own admission, evolved partly from his reading of Novalis and his studies of Nietzsche. Finally, in 1919, "in three intense days and nights Hesse completed the Nietzschean parable for the first world war, *Zarathustra's Return,* in which the great sage castigates the Germans for finding fault with their fate rather than with their hubris of elevating war, and their enthusiasm for war, to a higher level" (Freedman, 198).

1922 was a fruitful year for Hesse; in this year, he completed one of his most important works, *Siddhartha,* a testimony to Hesse's involvement in eastern philosophy, especially Buddhism. Hesse was busy lecturing during this time, and the main content of these lectures presented his own convictions of "Buddha's way to salvation," which he explained was "not just learning and knowing, but spiritual experience that can be earned only through strict discipline in a selfless life" (Hesse, I, 145–48).

Hesse has been criticized: "His thought has been called secondhand" (Bullock and Woodings, 324). The fact is that Hesse, like many other great writers of fiction, felt that it was important to incorporate philosophical ideas of great thinkers into his works. Indeed, this is not a weakness in Hesse's writings because the teachings of Nietzsche and Jung only strengthened his novels and gave them a depth they would not otherwise have.

REFERENCES

Andrews, R. C. "The Poetry of Hermann Hesse." *German Life and Letters* 6 (1952–1953): 117–27.
Boulby, Mark. *Hermann Hesse, His Mind and Art.* Ithaca, N.Y.: Cornell University Press, 1967.
Bullock, Alan, and R. B. Woodings, eds. *20th Century Culture.* New York: Harper & Row, 1983.
Fickert, Kurt J. "The Development of the Outside Concept in Hesse's Novels." *Monatshefte* 52 (1960): 171–78.
Freedman, Ralph. *Hermann Hesse: Pilgrim of Crisis: A Biography.* New York: Pantheon, 1938.
Hesse, Hermann. *Siddhartha.* Translated by Hilda Rosher. New York: Bantam, 1951.

HÖLDERLIN, FRIEDRICH. B. March 20, 1770, Lauffen, Germany. D. June 7, 1843, Tübingen, Germany. German poet.

At a young age, Friedrich Hölderlin trained for the Lutheran ministry, but he did not take orders. He earned his living primarily as a tutor for well-to-do families in Germany, Switzerland, and France. While acting as tutor in the household of a Frankfurt banker, he fell in love with Suzette Gontard, his employer's wife, and she returned his affection. This incident was an important occurrence in his life, for after he had left Frankfurt and was attempting without success to earn his living as a writer, he learned of Suzette's death. Distraught, he set out for home on foot and arrived completely destitute and mentally deranged. He never made a complete recovery, and in his last years he was transferred to a Tübingen clinic, but was then moved to a carpenter's house where he died. Hölderlin is highly ranked in German literature as a poet who naturalized the forms of Greek poetry in German. His major works include the novel *Hyperion* (1797), *The Death of Empedocles* (a dramatic fragment), and a series of lyric poems, including "Brot und Wein," "Der Rhein," and "Heidelberg."

There is no better example of a German writer who was imbued with love of ancient Greece than the poet Hölderlin. He saw the ancients as exemplar of a humanistic and artistic people to be admired and modeled. Among the Greek philosophers, Plato* impressed him the most, as can be seen in Hölderlin's major work *Hyperion,* in which he immortalizes his mistress, Suzette Gontard, as Diotima, Plato's priestess of love in *The Symposium.*

> The justification for bringing Plato into the discussion [in *Hyperion*] is given by Hyperion himself when, in the first book, he and Alabanda read Plato together. . . . Plato distinguishes between the age of Kronos and the age of Zeus. In the former, a timeless golden age prevails and man is born in full maturity from Mother Earth, grows young, reenters the earth and continues the cycle; in the age of Zeus, man is born of parents as child and grows old, then to die. (O'Frye, 152)

Although Hölderlin continuously tried to recreate the world of ancient Greece, he was nevertheless taken up with the contemporary world of German idealistic philosophy (see idealism**) which, as Stephen Tonsor says, "[i]mpinged so dramatically on the personality of Hölderlin in the form of his youthful friendship with [Georg Wilhelm] Hegel[*] and [Friedrich] Schelling[*]" (Tonsor, 57). German idealism stressed the spiritual in man's interpretation of experience and held that reality exists essentially in one's consciousness rather than in sensory things. This appealed to Hölderlin's romantic nature. Tonsor argues that Hölderlin was convinced that he was living at "a decisive moment in history . . . that a new age was at hand." (Tonsor, 59, 60). In concert with Friedrich Nietzsche,* Hölderlin believed that "the new age was to be an age under the sign of Dionysius" (see Dionysian**) (Tonsor, 61).

REFERENCES

Baker, John Milton, Jr. "Myth and Poetic Statement: The Myth as Function of Discursive Temporality in Texts of Hölderlin, Keats and Wordsworth." *DAI* 46, no. 10 (April 1982): 3024A.
George, Emery, ed. *Friedrich Hölderlin: An Early Modern.* Ann Arbor: University of Michigan Press, 1972.
Most, Glenn W. "Hölderlin and the Poetry of History." *GR* 61, no. 4 (Fall 1986): 154–67.
O'Frye, Lawrence. "Seasonal and Psychic Time in the Structuring of Hölderlin's

Hyperion.'' In *Friedrich Hölderlin: An Early Modern,* edited by Emery George. Ann Arbor: University of Michigan Press, 1972.

Tonsor, Stephen. "Hölderlin and the Modern Sensibility." In *Friedrich Hölderlin: An Early Modern,* edited by Emery George. Ann Arbor: University of Michigan Press, 1972.

HOPKINS, GERARD MANLEY. B. July 28, 1844, Stratford, Essex, England. D. June 8, 1889, Dublin, Ireland. British poet.

A student at Balliol College, Oxford, in 1863, Gerard Manley Hopkins studied with Walter Pater and graduated with first-class honors in classics. He converted from High Anglicanism to Catholicism and abandoned poetry. In 1875, however, after becoming a Jesuit priest, he resumed his poetical efforts and produced his most memorable poem, "The Wreck of the *Deutschland,''* a poem commemorating its loss. Although Hopkins's poems were not published until 1918, twenty-nine years after his death, he is admired for his technical devices, unusual diction, and imagery; and he is ranked as a first-class modern poet. The "Terrible Sonnets," which describe a process of spiritual desolation, written during the last years of his life, are considered his greatest achievement.

Since Hopkins was Jesuit trained, one can assume that he was educated in the classics and in the tradition of Thomism.** In biographies of Hopkins (for example, by John Pick), one finds evidence that he was well read in classic philosophy, particularly Artistotle* and Plato.* The philosopher, however, whom he loved and admired the most and who exerted the deepest influence on his thinking was John Duns Scotus.*

In his biography of Hopkins, John Pick is so convinced of the influence that Duns Scotus had on the development of Hopkins's thought and art that he includes an appendix entitled "Duns Scotus and Hopkins." To begin with, it should be stated directly that Hopkins found in the writing of Duns Scotus a justification for his analysis of beauty. Duns Scotus's insistence on the particularity of the individual—of the singularity of inner form expressed in its unity with matter—appealed to Hopkins who saw beauty as form revealed through the substance which was its expression.

Hopkins leaned toward the philosophy of Duns Scotus for other reasons. The poet had the blessing of Duns Scotus in emphasizing the operations of the will. Again, Duns Scotus's ideas may have had an influence on the sacramentalism** expressed in Hopkins's poetry.

Hopkins was never comfortable with his dual role of Jesuit priest and poet. He felt that writing poetry was unprofessional because his main obligation was his spiritual growth as a Jesuit priest. A trained classicist, as well as a committed Jesuit, Hopkins's discomfort with his writing of "The Wreck of the *Deutschland*," which he considered to be unprofessional and unpriestly, can come as no surprise to the readers.

REFERENCES

Cotter, James Finn. *Inscape: The Christology and Poetry of Gerard Manley Hopkins*. Pittsburgh, Pa.: University of Pittsburgh Press, 1972.
Downes, David A. *Gerard Manley Hopkins: A Study of His Ignatian Spirit*. London: Vision Press, 1960.
Pick, John. *Gerard Manley Hopkins: Priest and Poet*. New York: Oxford University Press, 1966.
Pilecki, Gerard A. "Hopkin's 'Spring & Fall' and Modes of Knowing." *VP* 24, no. 1 (Spring 1986): 88–91.

HUXLEY, ALDOUS. B. July 26, 1894, Goldaming, Surrey, England. D. November 22, 1963, Hollywood, California. British novelist and writer.

Aldous Huxley was an intellectual and a versatile writer of novels, essays, and travel books. In the 1920s he published *Crome Yellow* (1921), *Antic Hay* (1923), and *Those Barren Leaves* (1925), all of which are characterized by witty, cynical dialogue. His first real success was *Point Counter Point* (1928), but his masterpiece, which rocked the literary world, was *Brave New World* (1932). By 1936 Huxley had abandoned himself to his disgust with humanity, and he turned to mystical idealism.** His experiences with mysticism,** drugs, and so on are related in *The Perennial Philosophy* (1945).

Huxley, an erudite and accomplished scholar, published a broad range of works from novels like *Brave New World* to philosophical essays. His readings included the works of many western thinkers, such as Saint Augustine* and Søren Kierkegaard,* as well as eastern theology and philosophy. Huxley's early work *Antic Hay* deals with the philosophy of nothingness, but he soon moved away from this position to Oriental religious views and the idea of an impersonal God. In fact, he admires Buddha (see Buddhism**) as the most powerful of religious leaders, one who was advanced in moving beyond the concept of a personal god.

Huxley was familiar with Carl Jung* whom he considered the most illuminating and inspired psycholgist, but he regarded Sigmund Freud* as monomaniacal. In concluding his estimation of Freud, Huxley, although he himself was constantly searching for a satisfactory system of philosophy, once said, "The greater part of the world's philosophy and theology is merely an intellectual justification for the wishes and the day dreams of philosophers and theologians'' (reported by Holmes, 48).

In many of his novels, Huxley alternates on the themes of sex, love, politics, and death, but his search for truth and philosophical certainty is obvious. And, although the philosophical aspect is always there, it often comes off as an analysis of modern culture. Nevertheless, it is evident in works like *Do What You Will* that Huxley is a well read and learned man who is as at ease in referring to William Wordsworth (q.v.), Jonathan Swift (q.v.), Percy Bysshe Shelley (q.v.), and Charles Baudelaire as he is with Kierkegaard and the Oriental thinkers. An example of this wide learning is found in his familiarity with Blaise Pascal* whom he admired but blamed for trying to convert man to the worship of death. These many references to the world's greatest thinkers mark Huxley as a truly philosophical writer. One will remember the scene from *Brave New World* in which the controller not only takes the Bible from the safe where the forbidden books are kept, but also brings out William James's* *Varieties of Religious Experiences* (1902). The author Huxley has Mustpha make fun of Francis Bradley.* Finally, concerning his most famous work, *Brave New World,* Holmes says, "It is an exploration in the most significant existentialist tradition [see existentialism**] of the relationship between the self and contemporary culture" (Holmes, 89).

We see in the works of Huxley the influence of many philosophers and theologians and a mixture of philosophy, theology, and sociology. Huxley is an example of a well-educated and learned writer who had gleaned ideas from the greatest thinkers and wove them into his novels and essays. If his works are read 100 years from now, it will probably not be the plots that attract readers, but the inherent philosophical ideas that are an integral part of his works.

REFERENCES

Holmes, Charles M. *Aldous Huxley and The Way to Reality*. Westport, Conn.: Greenwood Press, 1978.

Joad, Cyril E. M. *Return to Philosophy*. London: Faber and Faber, 1935.

Quina, James H. "The Philosophical Phases of Aldous Huxley." *College English* 28 (May 1962): 636–41.

Schall, J. V. "Buber and Huxley: Recent Developments in Philosophy." *Month* 19 (February 1958): 97–102.

Wilson, Colin. "Existential Criticism and the Work of Aldous Huxley." *London Magazine* 5 (September 1958): 46–59.

I

IBSEN, HENRIK. B. March 20, 1828, Skien, Norway. D. May 23, 1906, Christiana, Norway. Norwegian poet and playwright.

After an impoverished childhood caused by his father's bankruptcy, Henrik Ibsen went to Christiana where he studied from 1850 to 1851. In Christiana he gained practical experience in the theatre which led to a producer's job in Berlin. From 1857 to 1862, he served as artistic director in the Norwegian Theatre. His first successful verse drama was *Brand* (1866). Other important works include *Peer Gynt* (1867), *A Doll's House* (1879), *Ghosts* (1881), and *Hedda Gabler* (1890). Ibsen is regarded in literary history as one of the great dramatists of all time.

Ibsen read the works of Søren Kierkegaard* at an early age and through them became aware of the intellectual currents of the time. Some of the features that attracted the young Ibsen in Kierkegaard were the insistence on freedom and the emphasis on individualism which appealed to the radicalism in Ibsen's nature. There was also an influence of Georg Wilhelm Hegel.* Halvdan Koht describes this period of Ibsen's life and the influence of both philosophers:

> Ibsen did not become a philosopher. He never mastered the abstract language of philosophy and never constructed a philosophical system of his beliefs; he probably never resolved for himself the disagreement between Hegel's objectivity and Kierkegaard's impassioned subjectivity. He simply took what he needed from each and thus parted company with both. (Koht, 62)

Love's Comedy (1900) is the work that was most influenced by the philosophy of Kierkegaard.

> It is possible that Ibsen was not himself aware of any direct influence from Kierkegaard, for it had been many years since he read anything by the philosopher. But the ideas must have sunk deep into his mind, and there are unmistakable similarities between *Love's Comedy* and at least two of Kierkegaard's writings, ''The Seducer's Diary'' in *Either-Or* (1843) and more importantly *Repetition* (1843). The psychological conflicts that the philosopher dramatized in these narratives must have remained in his memory. (Koht, 144–45)

Hans Heiburg also states that it is clear that *Love's Comedy* was influenced by Kierkegaard; the critic further states that ''Søren Kierkegaard was undoubtedly one of the godparents of the fundamental ideas behind *Brand*. . . . Brand* became the drama of vocation and responsibility, as being wholly oneself, in contrast to everyday half-measures'' (Heiburg, 125). Under the influence of Kierkegaard, Ibsen turned *Brand* into an intense inner dialogue with himself, and he depicted the priest Brand as a vivacious hero who demands everything of himself and of others. Under Kierkegaard's guidance, Ibsen made *Brand* a significant breakthrough for individualism in society, a heroic voice who cries with Kierkegaard that, though the times are wicked, ''I complain because they are trivial for they are without passion, the thoughts in their heart are too petty to be sinful—Brand would proclaim the need for truth in one's personal life, the need for courage and strength in the very accents of Kierkegaard'' (Koht, 196).

Friedrich Nietzsche's* influence on Ibsen's philosophy is evident in at least one play, *John Gabriel Borkman* (1896), in which the protagonist is ''a superman who believes he has the right to exploit everyone on behalf of the great things he wants to accomplish'' (Koht, 443).

REFERENCES

Downs, Brian W. *Ibsen: The Intellectual Background*. New York: Macmillan, 1946.

Heiberg, Hans. *Ibsen: A Portrait of the Artist*. Coral Gables, Fla.: University of Miami Press, 1967.

Knight, G. Wilson. *Henrik Ibsen*. New York: Grove Press, 1962.

Koht, Halvdan. *Life of Ibsen*. New York: Benjamin Bloom, 1971.

Westphal, Merold. ''Ibsen, Hegel and Nietzsche.'' *ClioI* 14, no. 4 (Summer 1985): 395–406.

ISHERWOOD, CHRISTOPHER. B. August 26, 1904, Highlane, Cheshire, England. Naturalized U.S. citizen, 1946. D. January 4, 1986, Santa Monica, California. English/American writer.

Christopher Isherwood was born in England at the turn of the century, attended the Repton School, and then enrolled in Corpus Christi, Cambridge. He worked as a private tutor and free-lance journalist at first and was a student of medicine. He later joined W. H. Auden (q.v.) in Germany and devoted himself to writing, gaining initial recognition with *All the Conspirators* (1928) and *The Memoria* (1932). *Goodbye to Berlin* (1939), a collection of stories based on his experiences in Germany, was dramatized by John Van Druten and produced on Broadway as *I Am a Camera*. He collaborated with Auden on three verse dramas: *The Dog Beneath the Skin* (1935), *The Ascent of Fog* (1936), and *On the Frontier* (1938), after which he emigrated to the United States and began a successful career as a film writer. His successful novels include *The World in the Evening* (1954), *Down There on a Visit* (1962), and *A Single Man* (1964), a highly regarded novel which describes the loneliness of an intellectual homosexual.

Isherwood, a a member of the literary circle that included Auden, Stephen Spender, and Aldous Huxley (q.v.), settled finally in Santa Monica, California, where he came under the influence of Swami Prabhavananda, a Hindu monk from Calcutta. The depth of Isherwood's involvement in Vedantic thought, which stresses human evolution, meditation, and the notion that the individual is bound to the physical world, is expressed in *An Approach to Vedanta* (1963). Isherwood published two other books on Vedanta, *Ramakrishna and His Disciples* (1965) and *Essentials of Vedanta* (1969).

Although Isherwood had a classical education at Cambridge, there is little evidence of the influence of traditional western philosophy on his fiction. However, in the 1960s, he worked with Charles Laughton on a theatrical version of the dialogues of Plato based on the life of Socrates.

Isherwood is a western writer of English origin and education who, like Ezra Pound (q.v.) and Hermann Hesse (q.v.), incorporates eastern philosophy into his writings.

REFERENCES

Elick, Catherine Lilly. ''Isherwood and His Critics: A Historical Reading of *Goodbye to Berlin*.'' *DAI* 47, no. 4 (October 1986): 1317A.

Finney, Brian. *Christopher Isherwood: A Critical Biography*. New York: Oxford University Press, 1979.

IVANOV, VYACHESLAV. B. February 16, 1866, Moscow, Russia. D. July 16, 1949, Rome, Italy. Russian philosopher, classical scholar, and a leading poet of the Russian symbolist movement.

Ivanov's father, a land surveyor, died when Ivanov was five, and he was raised by a devoted mother who provided him with a religious education. He began the study of ancient Greek at the age of twelve, and this was the beginning of a lifelong devotion to classicism. Recognizing his promise as a scholar, Ivanov's teachers arranged for him to study in Berlin in 1886. In 1891 Ivanov went to Paris for a year and then left for Rome where he prepared his doctoral dissertation. In 1903, at the age of thirty-seven, he published his first collection of poems, *Pilot Star*. His second collection of verse, *Translucency,* followed in 1904. By 1909, when he returned to Russia, he was already well known and was accepted as a leading poet of the Russian symbolists (see symbolism**). His prose works include a collection of philosophical, aesthetic, and critical essays, entitled *By the Stars* (1909), and another collection of verse, *Cor Ardens* (1911). From 1920, Ivanov held the university chair of classical philosophy at Baku. In 1926 he joined the Catholic Church.

During his Berlin years as a student of the great historian Theodor Mommsen, Ivanov came under the spell of Friedrich Nietzsche,* as did all of Europe in the 1880s. When he went to Paris in 1891, Ivanov took with him a volume of Nietzsche's writing.

He understood the essence of Nietzsche's Dionysianism (see Dionysian**), but after a struggle, Ivanov freed himself of the charm of Nietzsche's philosophy, and he turned instead to the Hebrew and the Hellenic religions as the precursors of Christianity. Actually, Ivanov rejected Nietzsche's mythic conception of Dionysius and accepted him as "the suffering god" (Jackson and Nelson, 302).

But there was another German philosopher who made his presence felt in the life and intellectual development of Ivanov: Immanuel Kant* and the new Kantianism.** As James West says,

> Ivanov is himself a post-Kantian thinker whose philosophy incorporates directly or indirectly more of the heritage of Kant than is immediately apparent; many of his ideas, while unquestionably a part of his own coherent philosophical scheme, display a tantalizing proximity to those of the sage of Konigsberg, once the reader is accustomed to the idiosyncratic language of both philosophers. (West, 313)

Ivanov, along with Kant, gives primacy to poetry, and here in the field of aesthetics Ivanov even approaches the same terminology used by Kant.

In short, Ivanov extended the Kantian system and formulated his own theory of knowledge.

Robert Jackson sums up the achievement of Ivanov with the following:

> When the mists lift entirely from the period now known as the silver age of Russian literature and culture, they will reveal a landscape slightly changed from the one historians have marked out on the maps; the most notable difference will be the vastly increased stature of the poet, philosopher and rhetorician of the Russian symbolist movement, Vyacheslav Ivanov. (Jackson and Nelson, 1)

REFERENCES

Jackson, Robert Louis, and Lowry Nelson, Jr., eds. *Vyacheslav Ivanov: Poet, Critic, and Philosopher*. New Haven, Conn.: Yale Center for International and Area Studies, 1986.

Mueller, Patricia Ann Vollmer. "Dionysius Reborn: Vyacheslav Ivanov's Theory of Symbolism." *DAI* 46, no. 1 (July 1985): 166A.

Mureddy, Donata. "Petrarch and Vyacheslav Ivanov." *SSI* 30 (1984): 73–101.

West, James. "Kant and Neo-Kantianism." In *Vyacheslav Ivanov: Poet, Critic, and Philosopher,* edited by Robert Louis Jackson and Lowry Nelson, Jr. New Haven, Conn.: Yale Center for International and Area Studies, 1986.

J

JAMES, HENRY. B. April 15, 1843, New York City, New York. Naturalized British citizen, 1915. D. February 28, 1916, London, England. American/British novelist.

Henry James's father was a well-known Swedenborgian (see Swedenborgianism**), and his brother, William James,* was a renowned American philosopher. In 1876, James settled in London, where he was to spend most of his life. His masterpieces were *The Europeans* (1878), *Washington Square* (1881), *The Portrait of a Lady* (1881), and *Daisy Miller* (1879), which describe the clash of American and European cultures. In the *Bostonians* (1886), he explores sexual roles and feminism in America. His later novels, which focus on cultural change and the conflict of generations, include *The Tragic Muse* (1890) and *The Awkward Age* (1899). Among the great novels of the final phase of his life are *The Wings of the Dove* (1902), *The Ambassadors* (1903), and *The Golden Bowl* (1904).

Henry James's youth was spent in the home environment of an intellectual father, whose friends and house guests included Ralph Waldo Emerson (q.v.) and where the names of Emanuel Swedenborg* and Charles Fourier* were household words.

> In Swedenborg Henry James, Sr. had found the new heaven. Now in Charles Fourier he found the ''scientific insight'' for the new life on earth. . . . Fourier's practical social science could in a sense be read as complementing the doctrine of Swedenborg. Man made in the image of God had

God-given instincts. To inhibit them, as civilization did, was to violate
the will and the intention of God. (Edel, 34)

This was the intellectual atmosphere in which Henry James, Jr., was
raised, an atmosphere created by his father and his gifted friends who
contributed significantly to his philosophical as well as his literary
development.

Much has been written concerning the influence of Emerson and his
philosophy on Henry James, especially in the *Spoils of Poynton* (1897)
(see Kaston). In this work, James transfers the basis of nature in transcendentalism** to society and depicts characters whose powers of imagination create another world, apart from this one. In his 1967 dissertation
entitled "The Influence of Emerson on the Fiction of Henry James,"
Richard Baldwin sees James's characters of consciousness as Emersonian
because they are aware of themselves as the centers of their world through
the activity of consciousness. Baldwin associates consciousness with self-
reliance and therefore with isolation and the inability to achieve satisfying
relations in both Emerson and James" (Kaston, 98). In spite of strong
sibling friction between Henry James and his philosopher brother, William, who was one of the severest critics of Henry's literary works, Henry
read and was influenced by the philosophical writings of his brother.

REFERENCES

Cohen, Paula Marantz. "Freud's Dora and James's *Turn of the Screw:* Two
     Treatments of the Female 'Case.' " *Criticism* 28, no. 1 (Winter 1986):
     73–87.
Edel, Leon. *Henry James: The Untried Years*. New York: Lippincott, 1953.
Gide, André. "Henry James." *YR* 75, no. 2 (Winter 1986): 239–41.
Kaston, Carren. "Emersonian Consciousness and *The Spoils of Poynton.*" *ESQ*
     26 (1980): 88–99.
Krook, Dorothea. *The Ordeal of Consciousness in Henry James*. London, Eng-
     land: Cambridge at the University Press, 1963.
Ward, J. A. *The Imagination of Disaster: Evil in the Fiction of Henry James*.
     Lincoln: University of Nebraska Press, 1961.

JEFFERS, ROBINSON. B. January 10, 1887, Pittsburgh, Pennsylvania. D. January 20, 1962, Carmel, California. American poet.

Robinson Jeffers did not achieve fame until he published his third book
of poetry entitled *Tamar and Other Poems* (1924), which included a verse
play, "The Tower beyond Tragedy," considered to be his best work. In
short lyrics, Jeffers celebrated the splendor of the Pacific coast's scenery
near Carmel, California. In 1946 he wrote a dramatic adaptation of Eu-

ripides' *Medea,* which became Jeffers's most popular success. Although the object of profound attack by his critics, Jeffers has maintained his place in literature as a major American poet.

The touchstone to Jeffers's poetry is German idealism.** His poetry attempts a grand synthesis of idealism and pragmatism.** The strongest influence on Jeffers's poetry is undoubtedly Friedrich Nietzsche.* Jeffers himself has confessed his indebtedness to Nietzsche: "To this may be added his earlier statement made in reference to *The Women at Point Sur* (1924) to the effect that the individual can in his own mind escape racial introversion by 'transvaluing values' " (Squires, 43). The phrase "transvaluing values" occurs in *Thus Spake Zarathustra* (1883–1884). "In a more general way others have remarked that misanthropy, distrust of the city, and an aristocratic rejection of the crowd are common to Nietzsche and Jeffers" (Squires, 46). But there are major differences between them. For example, Jeffers believed that a strict morality makes for a vigorous culture and that religion stimulates the morality of society. Nietzsche, on the other hand, expressed a strong contempt for conventional morals and a horror of any religion. Another major difference is that Jeffers believed a breaking away from humanity means a turning to the contemplation of God. Nietzsche, however, rejected the contemplation of God in favor of the contemplation of man.

Nietzsche's ongoing battle with Christianity necessarily implied scorn for the notion of Christian pity. Zarathustra mocks all pity, and Nietzsche wrote further, "Thus be warned of pity: from there a heavy cloud will yet come to man" (Kaufman, 202). Although Jeffers at times appeared heartless, he wrote in the poem "The World's Wonders," I have hardened my heart only a little: I have learned that happiness is important." It is significant here that Jeffers considered happiness important, for here again he opposed Nietzsche who, with Arthur Schopenhauer,* considered pain the culmination of life. Jeffers was in accord with Schopenhauer that pain is inevitable, but he believed that the substitution of great suffering for a lesser ill allowed a discovery of God. Radcliffe Squires sums up the influence of Nietzsche and Schopenhauer on Jeffers in these words: "The tortured God of Nietzsche and the Schopenhauerian concept of 'life as pain' combines with Jeffers instinctive religious intensity. The pessimism[**] of Schopenhauer and the strong, paradoxical skepticism[**] of Nietzsche inspired Oswald Spengler[*] and reinforced Jeffers's own Spenglerean ideas" (Squires, 55). The reference here is to Jeffers's verse "The Fall of an Age," an idea popularized by Spengler's classic *Decline of the West* (1926–1928). In a 1941 address to a Harvard audience, Jeffers spoke of the patterned rise and decline of one civilization after another.

In this speech he revealed his vast knowledge of the subject. He told his audience that his ideas of ''culture-cycles'' actually came from his reading of Sir Flinders Petrie's *The Revolution of Civilization* (1911) and from Giambattista Vico's book published in 1725. Squires speaks of a possible influence of Petrie and Spengler on the early poetry of Jeffers:

> Although it is clear from the youthful poetry that Petrie and Spengler did not create Jeffers's endemic fatalism, I think it likely that they confirmed him in a set of dualisms intellectually related to that fatalism[**]: a dualism between Nature and history, a dualism between Nature and man, a dualism between culture and civilization. (Squires, 57).

Jeffers's poetry describes a society which is about to enter its final stage; like Spengler, he sees the present as the final period of culture. This final greatness of an age is expressed in ''The Broken Balance'' (1928): ''When you stand on the peak of time, it is time to begin to perish'' (Hunt, 374).

In summation, it can be said that Robinson Jeffers gleaned many of his ideas from Nietzsche, yet he disagreed with Nietzsche's views of morality and religion. It must also be said that much of Jeffers's poetry expresses the extreme pessimism of Schopenhauer and Spengler.

REFERENCES

Bennet, Melba Berry. *The Stone Mason of Tor House: The Life and Works of Robinson Jeffers*. Los Angeles, Calif.: Ward Ritchie Press, 1966.

Hunt, Tim, ed. *The Collected Poetry of Robinson Jeffers*. Stanford, Calif.: Stanford University Press, 1988.

Morris, David Copland. ''Literature and Environment: The Inhumanist Perspective and the Poetry of Robinson Jeffers.'' *DAI* 46, no. 9 (March 1986): 2694A.

Squires, Radcliffe. *The Loyalties of Robinson Jeffers*. Ann Arbor: University of Michigan Press, 1963.

Sterling, George. *Robinson Jeffers, The Man and the Artist*. New York: Boni and Liveright, 1926.

Van Wyck, William. *Robinson Jeffers*. Los Angeles: Ward Ritchie Press, 1938.

Walter Kaufmann, ed. and trans. *The Portable Nietzsche*. New York: Penguin, 1954.

JOYCE, JAMES. B. February 2, 1882, Dublin, Ireland. D. January 13, 1941, Zurich, Switzerland. Irish novelist.

James Joyce was educated at Clonowes Wood College, Belvedere College, and University College. In 1904 he met Nora Barnacle, whom he finally married in 1936, and the two left Ireland in that year and settled in Trieste where he taught English and worked in a bank. He chose voluntary exile from his homeland because he felt that the free development of art was threatened in Ireland. In 1916 his *A Portrait of the Artist as a Young Man* appeared. It is the story of Stephen Dedalus, who frees himself from the restraints of family, race, and church. His masterpiece, *Ulysses,* was published in Paris in 1922 and earned him international reputation. His final work, which was very complex in content and style, was *Finnigan's Wake* (1939). Joyce had established himself as one of the major literary figures of the twentieth century.

As early as 1903, while in Paris, Joyce read Victor Cousin's translation of Aristotle's* *De Anima, Metaphysics,* and *Poetics.* The manner and the topics of Aristotle greatly interested him, especially the philosopher's theories of tragedy and comedy in the *Poetics.* In his notebook, Joyce argued that comedy was superior to tragedy because it produces joy whereas tragedy produces sorrow.

Much has been written concerning the possible influence of Sigmund Freud* on James Joyce, but one thing is explicit: Joyce denied that he borrowed the interior monologue from Freud. Joyce was knowledgeable about philosophy and psychoanalysis, having read Freud and Carl Jung* in 1913, and he once remarked to Paolo Cuzzi, a pupil of his, that Freud had been anticipated by Vico. His profound interest in dreams has led some of his critics and biographers to see a strong Freudian** element in his work, but, as his biographer Richard Ellmann notes, Joyce actually had a distaste for Freud (Ellmann, 1982, 546). Ellmann quotes Joyce as saying, "I don't believe in any science, but my imagination grows when I read Vico as it doesn't when I read Freud and Jung" (Ellmann, 1977, 546). Joyce's interest in Italian philosophers is reflected in his student studies of Giordano Bruno,* the clerical villain who was burned at the stake in 1600. A voracious reader, Joyce read deeply in occultism** and Eastern philosophy as evidenced by his possession of a copy of H. S. Olcott's *A Buddhist Catechism,* dated May 7, 1901.

Ellmann further reports that Joyce was significantly influenced by Friedrich Nietzsche whom Joyce read in 1903: "[I]t was probably upon Nietzsche that Joyce drew when he expounded to his friends a neopaganism that glorified selfishness, licentiousness, and pitilessness, and denounced gratitude and other domestic virtues" (Ellmann, 1982, 142).

Except for Aristotle, Joyce was never impressed by the Greek philosophers; he distrusted Plato,* and he once remarked that Hellenism** was the "European appendicitis" (Ellmann, 1982, 103). Nor did Immanuel Kant* or Arthur Schopenhauer* impress him; in 1913, he attempted to discourage one of his pupils, Boris Furlan, from his studies of these two philosophers. He told Furlan at the time that the greatest philosopher was Saint Thomas Aquinas.* He had begun his own studies of Thomas Aquinas in 1898, while a student at University College. Ellmann speaks of this period:

> Joyce had looked into Thomas Aquinas enough to know Thomas's doctrine that those things are beautiful which, when seen, please us and had hit upon the idea of isolating this dictum from Thomas's theory of final causes and using it as the basis for excluding instruction from among the purposes of art. (Ellmann, 60)

REFERENCES

Bloom, Harold, ed. *James Joyce*. New York: Chelsea, 1986.
Ellmann, Richard. *James Joyce*. Oxford: Oxford University Press, 1982.
———. *The Conscience of Joyce*. New York: Oxford University Press, 1977.
Res, Joanna E. "A Few Observations on Plutarch and Rabelais in *A Portrait*." *JJQ* 28, no. 3 (Spring 1986): 357–59.
Riquelme, John Paul. *Teller and Tale in Joyce's Fiction*. London: The Johns Hopkins University Press, 1983.

K

KAFKA, FRANZ. B. July 3, 1883, Prague, Bohemia, Austria-Hungary. D. June 3, 1924, Kierling, Austria. Austrian novelist.

As a child and adult, Franz Kafka was dominated by his father. In fact, in a famous letter "To My Father," he states that all of his writings were about his father. He studied law at the University of Prague and later worked for an insurance company. Kafka published little during his lifetime, and, when he was dying of tuberculosis, he instructed his close friend Max Brod to burn his writings. Brod instead published Kafka's writings after his death and Kafka became world famous. Kafka's first publication was a short work entitled "Das Urteil" (1916, trans. E. Muir and W. Muir, "The Judgment," 1949). His most famous novels were "Die Verwandlung" (1915, trans. E. Muir and W. Muir, *The Metamorphosis and Other Stories,* 1925, trans. E. Muir and W. Muir); *The Trial* (1937, trans. E. Muir and W. Muir); *Das Schloss* (1926, trans. E. Muir and W. Muir, *The Castle,* 1930); and *Amerika* (1927, trans. E. Muir and W. Muir, 1938). Kafka has become so famous in literary circles that the word "Kafkaesque" has been coined in English to mean "one is placed in an irrational situation."

Franz Kafka is often linked with existentialism** because his characters are, as John Killinger calls them, "Pilgrims without a place to rest" (Killinger, 12). The typical Kafka character is an outsider, the true individual dear to the heart of Søren Kierkegaard* and especially Karl Jaspers,* who abhors the *Masse-Mensch,* the conformist. In 1923, forced to abandon his writing because of a prolonged, severe illness, Kafka devoted much of his time to the study of Kierkegaard.

During the writing of *The Castle,* Kafka was again studying Kierkegaard. One of the main elements that he incorporated into the novel was the prevailing theme of uncertainty and insecurity. Kierkegaard would call Joseph K.'s condition angst,** and Kierkegaard regarded anxiety as a necessary road to true faith. The feeling of angst is also prominent in *The Trial,* in which the hero is led into strange surroundings where rationality does not exist.

Gregor Samsa and Joseph K. are social outsiders. Gregor is a stranger even to his immediate family. The characters in Kafka's world do not fit into the mainstream of society; alienated and isolated, they are feared and treated in a hostile manner by the conformists in the world around them. Kafka sees no hope of social redemption for these individuals. They struggle through life as strangers, and, in practically all of his stories, they simply die. Kafka presents us with a world without hope, but the true existentialist would claim with Jean-Paul Sartre* (q.v.) that they lived in "good faith" and they died "free."

Kafka read deeply in Friedrich Nietzsche* and Baruch Spinoza* as well in his groping search for an acceptable way of life and a key to the riddle of existence.

Many writers have treated the works of Kafka from a Freudian** point of view. As early as 1959, Frederick Hoffman recognized the Freudian implications of Kafka's relationship to his father as found in such stories as "The Metamorphosis" and "The Judgment." That Kafka could have read Freud was quite probable; there is scarcely any question that Kafka was knowledgeable about psychoanalysis.

REFERENCES

Grunfelo, Frederic B. *Prophets without Honour: A Background to Freud, Kafka, Einstein and Their World.* London: Holt, Rinehart & Winston, 1979.
Heidsleck, Arnold. "Logic and Ontology in Kafka's Fiction." *GR* 61, no. 1 (Winter 1986): 11–17. (Role of philosophy)
Killinger, John. *Hemingway and the Dead Gods: A Study in Existentialism.* Lexington: University of Kentucky Press, 1960.
Pawel, Ernst. *The Nightmare of Reason. A Life of Franz Kafka.* New York: Farrar, Straus & Giroux, 1984.
Taubeneek, Stephen. "Kafka and Kant." *JKSA* 8, nos. 1–2 (June–December 1984): 20–27.

KEATS, JOHN. B. October 31, 1795, London, England. D. February 23, 1821, London, England. English poet.

John Keats was well advanced toward a medical career when, at the age of twenty-one, he was influenced by his mother and friends to devote himself exclusively to poetry. In the beginning, he was not successful, and his first important sonnets, "O Solitude" and "On First Looking into Chapman's Homer" (October 1816), went unnoticed. His long poem *Endymion* also received strong criticism. In 1819 he wrote "La Belle Dame Sans Merci" and the great odes "On Melancholy," "To a Nightingale," "On a Grecian Urn," and "To Psyche." Today, Keats is recognized as one of the greatest of the nineteenth-century English lyric poets.

It was Percy Bysshe Shelley (q.v.) who awakened Keats's interest in philosophy, but it was William Hazlitt's philosophical essays that enlightened him to the tenets of empiricism.** "Just as Shelley helped him to interpret the Neoplatonism[**] of [Herbert] Spencer [*], Shakespeare, and [Michael] Drayton, so Hazlitt, who was an empiricist, assisted him in interpreting [William] Wordsworth's [q.v.] Empiricism, especially the principles of sensation and associations" (Finney, 300). In order to understand Keats's philosophy of beauty, one must understand that he fused contemporary empiricism with the Neoplatonism of the Renaissance.**

> He accepted, first of all, the platonic distinction between the world of matter and the world of ideas. The material world, he believed, is an unreal, imperfect, everchanging reproduction of the ideal world, which is real, perfect, and unchanging. Man can ascend to a fellowship with essence—that is, to a communion with the ideal world—by means of the chain of beauty which binds all things together from the highest forms of spirit to the lowest forms of matter. (Finney, 301)

From the empirical principles, Keats denied the existence of innate ideas and was convinced that the bases of mental activity are sensations. From this point, he concluded that the sensations produce strong emotions which "induce a state of ecstasy in which the imagination apprehends or intuits truth in the form of beauty" (Finney, 301). It is possible that he learned this principle from Hazlitt's essays or Wordsworth's poems for, in "Tintern Abbey," Wordsworth said: "What the imagination seizes as beauty must be truth. . . ."

The fact remains that Keats apparently learned little philosophy through direct sources; instead, he collected his philosophical ideas from associations and readings of literary figures. Finally, it would seem that he was on questionable philosophical ground when he arrived at the conclusion that the imagination is the only faculty by which one can apprehend truth. He once exclaimed, "O for a life of sensations rather than of thoughts" (reported by Finney, 302).

REFERENCES

Evert, Walter H. *Aesthetic and Myth in the Poetry of Keats*. Princeton, N.J.: Princeton University Press, 1936.
Finney, Claude Lee. *The Evolution of Keats's Poetry*. Vol. 1. New York: Russell and Russell, 1963.
Little, G. L. " 'Do I Wake or Sleep?' Keats's 'Ode to a Nightingale.' " *SSEng* 11 (1985–1986): 40–50.
Sperry, Stuart M. "Keats's Skepticism and Voltaire." *KSJ* 12 (1963): 75–93.

KLEIST, HEINRICH VON. B. October 18, 1777, Frankfurt an der Oder, Germany. D. November 21, 1811, Wannsee, Germany. German playwright and poet.

Heinrich von Kleist grew up in military surroundings that were distasteful to him. He resigned his commission and studied law, mathematics, and philosophy. It is said that his study of Immanuel Kant* destroyed his faith in the value of knowledge. After abandoning his studies, Kleist settled in Switzerland, and here he wrote his first tragedy *Die Familie Schroffenstein* (1803). Between 1803 and 1809, Kleist, in Dresden, Germany, became a member of a large circle of writers and painters, and with the political philosopher Adam Muller, he published a distinguished periodical, *Phobus*. Kleist's adaptation of Molière's *Amphitryon* (1807) attracted some attention, and this was followed by *Penthesilia* (1808), a work which received little acclaim at the time but has come to be held as one of Kleist's most powerful works. In March 1808, Kleist's one-act comedy in verse, *Der Zerbrochene Krug* (*The Broken Pitcher*) was unsuccessfully produced by Johann Wolfgang von Goethe (q.v.) in Weimar, Germany. Kleist also wrote eight masterly novellas including *Michael Kohlhaus* and *Die Marquis Von O* (1810–1811). His last drama, which is also his most famous work, was *Prinz Friedrich von Homburg* (published posthumously in 1821 by Johann Ludwig Tieck).

Kleist was a very emotional and unstable artist, and so, when he read Jean-Jacques Rousseau (q.v.), he naively accepted the French thinker's ideas without question. Rousseau suddenly became the master in Kleist's discovery of feeling and emotion. And as Kleist matured and began to write the plays that have come to be regarded in German literature as masterpieces of drama, he incorporated Rousseau's teaching into his works.

Nature and love became the vehicles of morality, the example was given by people in the loneliness of the mountains and their valleys; the natural man was good, the man in society was bad. State and church, in *Earthquake in Chile* (1810–11), were wicked; the rejects of society, Josephe and Jeronimo were good. (Hohoff, 29)

Rousseau not only affected Kleist's writing but also his life and life-style. In the German Catholic city of Würzburg, Kleist developed a terrible hatred of the Catholic church, and in Paris, where he stayed only briefly, he could not bear the city life because, in his mind, it was a product of corrupt civilization.

According to Rousseau, the fall of man comes about because he leaves nature when he establishes society and concludes the *contrat social*. In Émile's education, a rational motive, usefulness, takes the lead. Kleist still does not feel the contradiction; he emphatically adopts the human being who is by nature good, pure, noble and harmonious. (Hohoff, 30)

Kleist had also studied Kant, or we should say misread Kant, and had concluded that the philosopher told him that he could not decide whether truth was really truth. Actually, Kant did not doubt all principles but merely questioned the assumptions of one's experience. It was Kleist's misreading of Kant that led to his contention in *Die Familie Schroffenstein* that reality deceives us as to the true character of existence.

And so we see in Kleist the man an unstable person who was often confused about his own position in the universe, a man of doubts who mistrusted himself and everyone and everything he came in contact with. It is obvious that his life and his art were influenced by such thinkers as Rousseau and Kant, but unfortunately their philosophy was not always clearly understood by Kleist, and he saw what he wanted to see in their teachings, whatever fit his personality and temperament.

REFERENCES

Anon. "Heinrich von Kleist." *The Times Literary Supplement,* 21 August 1953, pp. 529–30.

Bennett, E. K. "The Metaphysical Novelle-Kleist." In *A History of the German "Novelle"*, edited by H. M. Waidson. Cambridge, England: University Press, 1961.

Hohoff, Curt. *Heinrich von Kleist.* Bonn, West Germany: Inter Nationes, 1977.

Maass, Joachim. *Kleist: A Biography.* New York: Farrar, Straus & Giroux, 1983.

KRAUS, KARL. B. April 28, 1874, Bohemia, Czechoslovakia. D. June 12, 1936, Vienna, Austria. Austrian critic and satirist.

In 1899, Karl Kraus founded and edited *die Fackel* (The Torch), a literary and satirical journal. During World War I he was an outspoken critic of the military establishment. In 1922, he completed his masterpiece *The Last Days of Mankind* and in 1934 wrote a harsh criticism of Nazism in *The Third Walpurgis Night*.

Karl Kraus, one of the most reputable and prolific satirists of twentieth-century literature, was an active member of the Vienna circle which dominated the intellectual life of Europe in the early 1900s. The group consisted of such famous writers, artists, and scientists as Arnold Schönberg, Alfred Adler, Gustav Mahler, Hugo von Hofmannsthal, and Sigmund Freud.* Kraus met Freud in 1904, and Freud expressed his pleasure at finding his name mentioned repeatedly in *die Fackel,* the literary journal edited and published by Karl Kraus. Freud read *die Fackel* regularly and evidently admired Kraus's work. It is difficult to ascertain, however, to what extent Kraus was knowledgeable about Freud's work. It is a matter of record that in 1907 Kraus was attending lectures of Freud on "Dreams," and it is quite possible that Kraus had read *The Interpretation of Dreams* (1899). Through the years Kraus had acquired the reputation of being anti-Freudian, but his biographer Timms refutes this opinion: "Both authors see erotic experiences as quite distinct from the mechanism of reproduction which it may set in motion. It is this non-reproductive emphasis which leads Kraus and Freud to defend the homosexual and espouse the emancipation of women" (Timms, 96). Researchers who investigate the Kraus archives will find that he always praises Freud and his work, and that in *die Fackel* there are absolutely no hostile references to Freud.

Just as it is difficult to prove the influence of Freud on the writings of Karl Kraus, so it is with that of Friedrich Nietzsche,* a philosopher whose name and writings appeared constantly during Kraus's terms as editor of *die Fackel*. In his biography of Kraus, Timms cautions readers that Kraus was not, like so many German writers of that age, under the spell of Nietzsche, and he states that the numerous references to Nietzsche in *die Fackel* were made by other contributors. Nevertheless, since our task in this sourcebook is to point out possible philosophical influences, we would maintain that Kraus, simply through his association with the Vienna Circle and *die Fackel,* had to be familiar with Nietzschean doctrines. Finally, there is documented evidence that in 1902 Kraus was reading *Thus Spake Zarathustra* (1883).

Kraus as a satirist is a controversial figure in German letters, but one thing is evident from his writings; he was an intellectual writer whose daily association with other intellectuals of his day leads one to the conclusion that he possessed at least a superficial knowledge of philosophy, especially that of Nietzsche.

REFERENCES

Heller, Erich. "Karl Kraus." In *The Disinherited Mind,* edited by Erich Heller. London: Bowes and Bowes, 1952.

Iggers, Wilma. *Karl Kraus: A Viennese Critic of the 20th Century.* New York: M. S. Rosenberg, 1967.

Timms, Edward. *Karl Kraus: Apocalyptic Satirist: Culture and Catastrophe in Hapsburg Vienna.* New Haven, Conn.: Yale University Press, 1986.

Zehn, Harry. *Karl Kraus.* New York: Twayne World Authors, 1971.

L

___

LAWRENCE, D[AVID] H[ERBERT]. B. September 11, 1885, East-wood, Nottinghamshire, England. D. March 2, 1930, Vence, France. British writer.

D. H. Lawrence began to write poetry in 1904 and fiction in 1906, when he went to Nottingham University College. He worked as a schoolteacher in Croydon, England, between 1908 and 1911, but he abandoned teaching after a severe illness and went to Germany and Italy in 1912 with Frieda Weekley, whom he married in 1914. His first major novel was the autobiographical *Sons and Lovers* (1913). His next novel, *The Rainbow* (1915), which charted sexual and social change in a Midlands family, was banned as immoral. His other major works were *Women in Love* (1920), *Aaron's Rod* (1922), and *The Plumed Serpent* (1926). For a writer who died at the age of forty-four, Lawrence's output was immense: 12 novels, 60 stories, travel books, plays, and over 900 poems.

As a young man, Lawrence read and annotated Arthur Schopenhauer's* *The World as Will and Idea* (1819). The pessimism did not affect Lawrence, but the chapter ''The Metaphysics of Love,'' especially the remarks on mismating and discord, impressed him because it reminded him of his parents. ''Schopenhauer's concept of the will to live, of which the mind and knowledge are merely servants, rationalizing our instincts, suggests the most central possible influence'' (Tedlock, 8).

A greater philosophical influence on Lawrence was Friedrich Nietzsche,* for here the similarity between Lawrence's values and the philosopher's ideas is much clearer. As Tedlock states, ''He is closer to

Nietzsche in expressing the notion of a slave morality engendered by exaltation of the lowly and inherited in Judaic-Christian culture, broached by Nietzsche in the *Genealogy of Morals* (1887)'' (Tedlock, 9). Lawrence wrote two essays, ''Aristocracy'' and ''Blessed Are the Powerful,'' which express attitudes similar to Nietzsche's. In the second essay, he reversed the Christian beatitudes, which would have pleased Nietzsche. Lawrence continued to show his familiarity with Nietzschean philosophy. In his second novel, *The Trespasser* (1912), Helena and Siegmund read Nietzsche and mouth anti-Christian values in Nietzschean fashion. In this novel, Lawrence expresses a belief in the need for a new aristocracy that would integrate the concept of a higher life—a concept similar to the superman** theory of Nietzsche and George Bernard Shaw (q.v.). In fact, Lawrence was moved more and more by the idea of submission to the superior individual, and this Nietzschean concept became an increasingly important theme in Lawrence's works. Tedlock comments on the ''power urge'' as found in Lawrence's novel *Aaron's Rod:*

> If the power-urge seems dangerous, it need not be the Nietzschean will to power, but a dark, living fructifying power, not seeking any fixed state, but urging the displacement of the old and the inception of the new. Since there must be ''someone who urges and someone who is compelled,'' there must be ''submission'' but this need not be a slave's submission to foolish and arbitrary power, but a deep, rich submission by women and men to the power-soul in the individual man. (Tedlock, 154)

D. H. Lawrence is often perceived as presenting a totally nihilistic (see nihilism**), Dionysiac (see Dionysian**) view of the human condition, focusing on the destructive power of the soul which, when not checked, culminates in cruelty and sadism, for example, in ''The Prussian Officer'' (1914). Although he is most popularly recognized as a forerunner of sexual freedom, the crucial key to an understanding of Lawrence is, according to Kingsley Widmer, an awareness of the negation and nihilism which pervade the corpus of his work. Self-destructing and self-annihilating, Lawrence's heroes, especially his heroines, driven by the dark forces of the soul, at once reject and attack conventional middle-class values, for example, domesticity and fixed love.

Lawrence's nihilism is complemented by his Satanism.** Several of his major characters—Romeo in ''The Princess,'' the gypsy in ''The Virgin and the Gypsy,'' and Mellors in *Lady Chatterley's Lover* (1928)— are demon lovers, aliens, outsiders who people his dark world where chaos, passion, and emotional violence are common.

REFERENCES

Ansari, A. A. "Women in Love: Search for Integrate Being." AJES 10, no. 2 (1985): 156–177.
Bloom, Harold, ed. *D. H. Lawrence*. New York: Chelsea, 1986.
Froeman, Mary. *D. H. Lawrence: A Basic Study of His Ideas*. Gainsville: University of Florida Press, 1955.
Tedlock, E. W. *D. H. Lawrence: Artist & Rebel*. Albuquerque: University of New Mexico Press, 1963.
Widmer, Kingsley. *The Art of Perversity: D. H. Lawrence's Shorter Fiction*. Seattle: University of Washington Press, 1962.

LESSING, DORIS. B. October 22, 1919, Kermanshah, Iran. British author.

Doris Lessing grew up in Southern Rhodesia, a setting described in *Martha Quest* (1952). In 1949, before the publication of her first novel, *The Grass Is Singing* (1950), Lessing settled in London. In her early adult years she was an active Communist. Her other novels include *A Ripple from the Storm* (1958), *The Four-Gated City* (1969), *Briefing for a Descent into Hell* (1971), *The Summer before the Dark* (1973), and *The Memoirs of a Survivor* (1975). In her early novels, Lessing is critical of colonial attitudes toward race, politics, and the role of women in society. In the 1980s Doris Lessing has written *The Good Terrorist* (1985).

Since, in her novels, she is primarily concerned with the element of place and its effect on the lives of her characters, Lessing's novels may be characterized as existentialist (see existentialism**). The concept of place and human consciousness deals with the degree to which a person associates himself with place and leads to either "existential insideness" or "existential outsideness."

Existential outsideness refers to a state of alienation in which one feels one is homeless and does not belong. This alienation, common with such existentialist writers as Franz Kafka (q.v.) and Albert Camus (q.v.), is also found in such works as *In Pursuit of the English* (1960). Her newcomers arrive in a foreign environment, and they experience a feeling of unreality and a sense of environmental oppression. In *Pursuit*, "the London landscapes and buildings project an atmosphere of isolation, threat and frustration" (Seaman, 87).

The unreality of place experienced by Lessing's characters often leads to a sense of confusion and disorder. Since the newcomer is unable to adapt to a new environment, he or she develops a sense of distrust for the place and also for the people who live there. Lethargy sets in and, like the characters in a Marcel Proust novel, the newcomer feels set adrift in a world of places. An essential existential element that Lessing concentrates on is the quest for identity: One must find out who one is.

Although it is difficult to establish whether Doris Lessing read such existentialist writers as Søren Kierkegaard,* the existential angst** and dread are certainly experienced by the characters in her novels. And so, our conclusion is that the philosophy most evident in her literary works is existentialism.

REFERENCES

Bloom, Harold, ed. *Doris Lessing*. New York: Chelsea, 1986.
Marchind, Lois. "The Search for Self in the Novels of Doris Lessing." *Studies in the Novel* 4 (1972): 252–61.
Rubenstein, Roberta. *The Novelistic Vision of Doris Lessing Breaking the Forms of Consciousness*. Urbana: University of Illinois Press, 1979.
Seaman, David. *The Human Experience of Space and Place*. New York: St. Martin's Press, 1980.

LESSING, GOTTHOLD EPHRAIM. B. January 22, 1729, Kamenz, Germany. D. February 15, 1781, Braunschweig, Germany. German playwright, critic, and philosopher.

The son of a pastor, Gotthold Ephraim Lessing studied theology for a time and later medicine at Leipzig, Germany, but his interest in the theatre led to his writing several comedies. In 1748, he moved to Berlin where he earned a living as a translator of history and philosophy. Here in Berlin he made a name for himself as a critic. From 1751 to 1752 he studied in Wittenberg, Germany, where he took his degree in medicine. Between 1753 and 1755 he published a six-volume collection of his works, which included the first German domestic tragedy, *Miss Sarah Sampson* (1755). In Berlin he became friends with the philosopher Moses Mendelssohn, on whom he based the leading character of his drama *Nathan der Weise* (1779). Between 1760 and 1765, Lessing was secretary to the military governor of Breslau, Germany, and during this period he produced his famous comedy *Minna von Barnhelm* (1767) and another major work entitled *Laokoön* (1766). In addition to his plays, Lessing wrote a series of brilliant essays which attacked the tradition of French theatre and, in particular, the dramas of Pierre Corneille and Voltaire.

Although Lessing was trained in the Greek and Roman classics, his interest in philosophy seems to have been restricted to contemporary philosophers, especially Baruch Spinoza* and Gottfried Leibniz.* "In the draft of a letter to Mendelssohn, he compares Leibniz and Spinoza.

Here he lays particular emphasis on the identity of body and soul in Spinoza's philosophy and implies his preference of this identity to Leibniz's conception of body and soul as distinct'' (Garland, 171).

In 1773, Lessing published an essay on Leibniz, *Leibniz von den ewigen Strafen* (Leibnitz on Eternal Punishment). In this work he supports the belief that hell is eternal and that the torments of hell are symbolically the natural result of sin.

In a conversation with Lessing, recorded in 1780 by F. H. Jacobi, "Lessing openly acknowledged his adherence to the philosophy of Spinoza 'There is no other philosophy than that of Spinoza' '' (reported by Garland, 174). One of the areas in which Spinoza's influence on Lessing is evident is the subject of free will. Spinoza was a determinist (see determinism**) and so was Lessing, who told Jacobi, "I desire no freewill. . . . I thank the creator that I am not free" (reported by Garland, 174).

Lessing believed with Spinoza in the progress of man, which he felt would take place despite the errors of man. And, although Lessing often steered away from the tenets of orthodox religion, he was convinced that "The various religions and their various phases are stages in an attempt to reach the truth. And even though they are false and true in equal degree, yet they contribute as much as what is false as by what is true to the progress of man" (Garland, 175).

In German literature, Lessing's stature as a dramatist and critic is gigantic. As a critic, he tore German drama from the influence of the French; and in his refutation of French literary critics, he displayed a thorough knowledge of Aristotle* and the *Poetics*. His essays on literature, education, and religion show him to be one of the best educated men of his day, and it is evident that the doctrines of such philosophers as Leibniz and Spinoza provided a strong basis for this education.

REFERENCES

Garland, H. B. *Lessing*. Cambridge, England: Bowes and Bowes, 1949.
Quinn, Timothy Sean. "Aesthetics and History: A Study of Lessing, Rousseau, Kant and Schiller." *DAI* 46, no. 5 (November 1985): 1302A.
Ugrinsky, Alexei, ed. *Lessing and the Enlightenment*. Westport, Conn.: Greenwood Press, 1986.
Wessell, Leonard P., Jr. "Lessing as an Aesthetic Thinker. An Essay on the Systematic Structure of Lessing's *Aesthetics,* the Philosophical Background." *LY* 15 (1983): 177–211.

LEWIS, C(LIVE) S(TAPLES). B. November 28, 1898, Belfast, Northern Ireland. D. November 22, 1963, Oxford, England. British author and satirist.

C. S. Lewis was educated privately and attended Malvern College for one year. He served in the Somerset light infantry in France during World War I, and in 1918 he went to University College, Oxford where he excelled as a classics scholar. From 1925 to 1954, he was fellow and tutor of Magdalene College, Oxford; from 1954 to 1963, he was professor of Medieval and Renaissance English at Cambridge University.

Lewis's first work to gain recognition was *The Pilgrim's Regress: An Allegorical Apology for Christianity, Reason and Romanticism* (1933). In 1936 he published a work considered by some to be his greatest work, *The Allegory of Love; A Study in Medieval Tradition;* however, his best-selling and most popular work was *The Screwtape Letters* (1942). Lewis also excelled in writing stories for children; the first of a series of seven tales about the land of Narnia was *The Lion, the Witch and the Wardrobe* (1950). Lewis recounts his early life in *Surprised by Joy: The Shape of My Early Life* (1955).

C. S. Lewis was a prodigious writer whose literary output ranges from novels, science fiction, and children's books to literary criticism and religious books. In the 1920s he studied Latin and Greek literature, philosophy, and ancient history. Later he taught philosophy for one year; during this time, his biographer Chad Walsh claims "that he reached the point of believing in 'the God of the philosophers' which he still insisted was not 'the God of popular religion' " (Walsh, 7).

Being a staunch Christian (he wrote several books explaining and defending Christianity including an apology for Christianity), Lewis naturally leaned toward such Christian thinkers as Saint Thomas Aquinas* and Saint Augustine*; at one point in *The Four Loves* (1960), Lewis actually contradicted Augustine's advice about giving one's heart to anyone but God. As Walsh points out, Lewis was a trained philosopher, familiar with the ideas of such pre-Christian philosophers as Socrates,* Plato,* and Aristotle.* "Another source of power is Lewis's ability to use Aristotle's tools to maximum effect" (Walsh, 247).

That Lewis was familiar with Plato's works, especially *The Republic, Phaedo,* and *The Laws,* is revealed in such works as *The Magician's Nephew.* However, his understanding of Plato was significantly influenced by Augustine and the Neoplatonists (see Neoplatonism**). William Johnson and Marcia Houtman sum up Lewis's Platonism** thus: "Lewis' own Platonism is highly selective and highly diffused, and although he was quite familiar with the corpus of Plato's writings, the application of Plato's ideas is through Lewis' Platonized Christianity" (Johnson and Houtman, 76).

C. S. Lewis's philosophical concerns are expressed in his science fiction as well as in his more serious works. Walsh tells us that "what interested Lewis and ultimately set his imagination to work was the kind of tale that uses space adventures as the medium for metaphysical, philosophical, religious and psychological themes" (Walsh, 82).

Since Lewis's nonfiction invariably addresses religious subjects, it comes as no surprise that, in *The Abolition of Man* (1943), he attacks logical positivism,** which prevailed in British philosophy at the turn of the century, and takes naturalism** to task in *Miracles* (1947).

REFERENCES

Johnson, William C., and Marcia K. Houtman. "Platonic Shadows in C. S. Lewis' Narnia *Chronicles.*" *MFS* 32, no. 1 (Spring 1986): 75–87.
Patterson, Nancy-Lou. "Letters from Hell: The Symbolism of Evil in 'The Screwtape Letters.' " *Mythlore* 12, no. 1 (Autumn 1985): 47–57.
Tetreault, James. "Parallel Lines: C. S. Lewis and T. S. Eliot." *Renascence* 38, no. 4 (Summer 1986): 256–69.
Walsh, Chad. *The Literary Legacy of C. S. Lewis.* New York: Harcourt Brace Jovanovich, 1979.
Wood, Doreen Anderson. "Of Time and Eternity: C. S. Lewis and Charles Williams." *CSL Bulletin* 17, no. 5 (March 1986): 1–7.

LEWIS, WYNDHAM. B. November 18, 1882, Amherst, Nova Scotia. D. March 7, 1957, London, England. English artist and writer.

In about 1893, Wyndham Lewis moved to London with his mother, and at the age of sixteen he won a scholarship to London's Slade School of Art. He left three years later without completing the course, and he went to Paris where he practiced his painting and attended lectures at the Sorbonne. On his return to London in 1909, he began to write stories and to exhibit his paintings. In 1914, Lewis's writings appeared in *Blast,* a vorticist review (see vorticism**), which showed the influence of imagist poetry. In World War I Lewis served at the front as an artillery officer. After his first novel *Tarr* (1918) was published, he went into seclusion until 1926, when a series of his books began to appear: *The Art of Being Ruled* (1926), a book on political theory, and *Time and Western Man,* an attack on subjectivity in modern art. Lewis continued to write and paint in the 1930s and published *Revenge for Love* (1937) but received scant recognition from fellow artists and the community. At this time, Lewis was deeply in debt and had suffered the results of two successful libel suits against him. This and his articles championing fascism lost him many friends and publishers. During World War II, Lewis fell on hard times and spent three years in a dilapidated hotel in Toronto, Canada, in extreme poverty. His 1954 novel *Self-Condemned* is a fictionalized account of these years. After the war, he returned to London as art critic for *The Listener,* and a year before his death he was honored with an exhibition at London's Tate Gallery.

Wyndham Lewis, an apparently forgotten writer in the 1980s, reveals in his novels, political essays, and philosophical tracts qualities which continue to deserve attention.

Classically trained at Rugby, Lewis showed an early interest in philosophy which led finally to a rejection of British philosophers in favor of German thinkers, especially Arthur Schopenhauer* and Friedrich Nietzsche.* E. W. F. Tomlin states that Lewis considered Schopenhauer and Nietzsche to be the first major Western thinkers to challenge "the values that had animated Western man over many centuries" (Tomlin, 30).

Schopenhauer's influence is evident in *Time and Western Man* in which Lewis expresses the view that Schopenhauer's conception of the will as the principle behind all things marked Schopenhauer as a "Time-Philosopher" (see Tomlin, 35, 36). Closer, and perhaps more interesting, parallels between Lewis and Schopenhauer can be seen in their common sense of disillusionment with the human condition, their pessimistic view of life and the world (see pessimism**).

Nietzsche's influence on Lewis's thinking is apparent in *The Human Age* (1928) and in *Tarr.* Lewis did, however, approach Nietzsche with considerable caution. Stoical and restrained himself, Lewis was repelled by the exuberant fanaticism he saw in Nietzsche, finding a more sympathetic and agreeable soul in Schopenhauer. Of Nietzsche, Lewis wrote, "Nietzsche was a death snob and he was also a madness-snob. This is a very ancient form of snob; but *formerly* the madness-snob never dreamt of going mad himself in his enthusiasm" (Tomlin, 40).

REFERENCES

Kirk, Russell. "An Enemy of Cant and Delusion." *CRevAS* 11, no. 1 (February 1985): 61–65.

Meyers, Jeffrey, ed. *Wyndham Lewis: A Reevaluation.* Montreal, Canada: McGill-Queen's University Press, 1980.

Tomlin, E. W. F. "The Philosophical Influences." In *Wyndham Lewis: A Reevaluation,* edited by Jeffrey Meyers. Montreal, Canada: McGill-Queen's University Press, 1980.

LONDON, JACK. B. January 12, 1876, San Francisco, California. D. November 22, 1916, Glen Ellen, California. American novelist.

As a young man, Jack London travelled around the United States and worked as a sailor and laborer. In *The Call of the Wild* (1903), he dramatized Darwinian (see Darwinism**) themes. London later became a committed Socialist; his work *The Iron Heel* (1907) was one of the most influential pieces of Socialist propaganda produced in the United States. The strong Nietzschean element in London's work distinguishes his brand of socialism from the more temperate socialist attitudes dominant in the America of his day.

Generally recognized as a writer of adventure stories, Jack London did not succeed in convincing his readers of the accuracy of his self-image as an intellectual and thinker. It is not difficult to understand why, given his desultory reading in philosophy and social literature, he might assume that posture. Self-educated, untrained in the disciplines of scholarship, he read, at an early age, Charles Darwin,* Karl Marx,* Ernst Heinrich Haeckel,* Herbert Spencer,* and Immanuel Kant,* among others. His study of Marx led him to believe that he had the makings of a Socialist (Labor, 20).

However, Friedrich Nietzsche* was apparently a major influence in his fiction. Wolf Larsen in *The Sea Wolf* (1904), for example, is modelled on Nietzsche's *Uebermensch,* even though London claimed that the novel was meant as an attack of rather than an acceptance of Nietzsche and his concept of the superman.** It is interesting to note that London's critics did not see the novel as an attack on Nietzsche.

The influence of Darwin and Marx, as well as Nietzsche, is apparent in London's work—a view which is expressed by Charles Watson in his analysis of *The Iron Heel* which he claims "is not only framed by the Marxist dialect but also persuaded by the apocalyptic[**] vision of Christianity and naturalistic imagery [see naturalism**] of social Darwinism" (Watson, 119).

London's reputation as an author of adventure stories for boys is at least inaccurate, perhaps unjust. His work represents an attempt, admittedly eclectic** and unsystematic, to express a worldview garnered from his reading in philosophical literature.

REFERENCES

Beauchamp, Gorman. "What to See in London." *CRevAS* 17, no. 1 (Spring 1986): 9–80.

Labor, Earle. *Jack London*. New York: Twayne, 1974.

Mitchell, Lee Clark. " 'Keeping His Head': Repetition and Responsibility in London's 'To Build a Fire.' " *JML* 13, no. 1 (March 1986): 76–96. (Relationship to naturalism)

Moreland, David A. "The Quest That Failed: Jack London's Last Tales of the

South Seas." *Pacific Studies* 8, no. 1 (Fall 1984): 48–70. (Sources in Carl Jung*)

Watson, Charles N. *The Novels of Jack London: A Reappraisal*. Madison: University of Wisconsin Press, 1983.

LOWELL, ROBERT. B. March 1, 1917, Boston, Massachusetts. D. September 12, 1977, New York City, New York. American poet.

Robert Lowell, a great-grandson of James Russell Lowell, was born into a distinguished New England family. He began studies at Harvard but came under the influence of the southern formalist school of poetry and transferred to Kenyon College where he was a student of John Crowe Ransom (q.v.). He graduated in 1940, married the novelist Jean Stafford, and converted to Catholicism. He was a conscientious objector during World War II and refused service in the armed forces. Because of this, he was sentenced to one year in prison, of which he served five months at the Federal Penitentiary at Danbury, Connecticut. "In the Cage" tells of his experience in prison. In 1946 he published *Lord Weary's Castle,* a collection of poems that won the Pulitzer Prize. In 1948, he was divorced, and he later married writer and critic Elizabeth Hardwick. After a few years abroad, Lowell settled in Boston in 1954. In 1959, his *Life Studies* appeared and won the National Book Award for poetry. In the 1960s, Lowell was engaged in civil rights and antiwar activities, and three volumes of poetry came out of this period: *For the Union Dead* (1964), *Near the Ocean* (1967), and *Notebook 1967–68* (1969). His other works include *The Old Glory* (1965), *Phaedra* (1963), and *Prometheus Bound* (1969). He won a Pulitzer Prize in 1974 for *The Dolphin*.

It was early in his career as a student at Kenyon College when Robert Lowell was introduced to Aristotle* and the Greek classics which continued to interest him throughout his troubled life. Anthony Manousos says: "No major American poet after World War II was more deeply involved with the classics than Robert Lowell" (Manousos, 16). In the classics, he saw a feeling for humanity that is often lacking in modern poetry, but he saw also an element of the irrational, which is the subject of E. F. Dodds's study, *The Greeks and the Irrational*. Such early poems as "Falling Asleep over the Aeneid" demonstrate not classical restraint but irrational elements as portrayed by the neurotic Aeneas, to what Manousos explains as a Freudian** influence on Lowell's classical writing. It is known that, in 1953, the poet seriously read the works of Sigmund Freud* and then, in a letter to Elizabeth Hardwick, exclaimed, "I am a slavish convert of Freud" (reported by Manousos, 17). Jeffrey Meyers, one of Lowell's biographers, whose book on the poet is significantly called *Manic Power,* elaborates further the linkage between Freud and Lowell:

> Jarrell, Berryman and Lowell had mental breakdowns and extensive therapy, and used their psychological insight to write poems about Freud. All accepted the value of his teaching—which illuminated the connection between the conscious and unconscious mind, and helped to explain the origins of creativity—and employed him [Freud] for their own poetic, personal or political end. (Meyers, 20)

Lowell's play *Prometheus Bound* addresses the ancient myth of the eternal rebel and concerns itself with a philosophical concept that fascinated the Greeks—determinism.** Lowell's Prometheus is an intellectual who desires to see his ideas at work in the world, but hanging over him and the future is the will of Zeus. Forces in the universe he realizes are determined by the gods; however, this does not result in despair for Prometheus. As Meyers puts it,

> Prometheus recalls that with his help man was able to transform his life and transform the planet on which he lived. . . . Lowell has made Prometheus into an intellectual—for him to possess an idea is to have power, the power of understanding, and his body responds to such a possession of the mind. (Meyers, 157)

REFERENCES

Bloom, Harold, ed. *Robert Lowell.* New York: Chelsea, 1987.

Fein, Richard J. *Robert Lowell.* Boston: Twayne, 1979.

Manousos, Anthony. "Falling Asleep over the *Aeneid.*" *Comparative Literature Studies* 21, no. 1 (Spring 1984): 17–27.

Meyers, Jeffrey. *Manic Power: Robert Lowell and His Circle.* New York: Arbor House, 1987.

Ruddick, Nicholas. "A New Historiography of the Self: Robert Lowell's History as History." *WascanaR* 20, no. 2 (Fall 1985): 3–15.

Shin, Jeong-Hyun. "Stylistics of Survival in the Poetry of Robert Lowell." *DAI* 47, no. 2 (August 1986): 532A.

M

McCULLERS, CARSON. B. February 19, 1917, Columbus, Georgia. D. September 29, 1967, New York City, New York. American novelist, short-story writer, and playwright.

Carson McCullers studied writing at Columbia University in 1934, and in 1937 she married Reeves McCullers, a fellow southerner. Her first novel, *The Heart Is a Lonely Hunter* (1940), established her literary reputation. Much of a her life was tragic. During her twenties she suffered a series of crippling strokes; by the time her last novel, *Clock Without Hands* (1961) appeared, she was confined to a wheelchair, her left side completely paralyzed. Her other novels include *Reflections in a Golden Eye* (1941), *Ballad of the Sad Café* (1951), and a successful play, *The Member of the Wedding* (1950) which won the 1950 New York Drama Critics Circle Award.

Carson McCullers' major work, *The Member of the Wedding,* which methodically attempts to compensate for the split world during World War II, reveals a strong Jungian** influence. Critics have also recognized parallel theories of creativity between Carl Jung* and McCullers: that the creative process evolves from the subconscious.

In *The Member of the Wedding,* McCullers follows Jung's theories and uses archetypal images to create a myth for our time. Here the main archetype** is the so-called sacred wedding, which is one of wholeness. And so, throughout the story, we see the protagonist, Frankie, obsessed with this archetype and going through the process of arriving at wholeness and growth. Frankie is sick of her environment and is obsessed with the notion that she will join Jarvis and Janice in their wedding.

Frankie's experience is described precisely in Jung's words: "When a situation occurs which corresponds to a given archetype, that archetype becomes activated and a compulsiveness appears, which, like an instinctual drive, gains its way against all reason and will" (reported by Snider, 35).

Frankie's compulsion leads her through the process of individuation, which will make her a whole individual. In this process (as Jung has stated), she is guided by the unconscious as reflected by the occurrence of dreams and fantasies. What McCullers reenacts in the novel is a textbook blueprint of Jung's theories of inner growth and maturity.

There are other significant archetypes in *The Member of the Wedding*. For example, in the role of John Henry, we see the archetype of the child, called the "numinous character" by Jung, developing independence, Jung's archetype of the preconscious and postconscious essence of man.

The Jungian influence in this work of Carson McCullers is the dual archetype of the mother and the wise old woman, as personified by the middle-aged black cook, Berenice. As Snider says, "Berenice fits into the archetypal motif of the dual mother wherein the hero is raised by a foster mother (Oedipus and Moses are examples)" (Snider, 38).

From the above comments, it is evident that Jung influenced the writing of McCullers, and it is also obvious that a comparative study of Jung and McCullers' works will give the student of literature new insight into an understanding of *The Member of the Wedding*.

REFERENCES

Baldanza, Frank. "Plato in Dixie." *Georgia Review* 12 (1958): 151–67.
Durham, Frank. "God and No God in *The Heart Is a Lonely Hunter*." *South Atlantic Quarterly* 56 (1957): 494–99.
Natoli, Joseph P., ed. *Psychological Perspectives on Literature*. Hamden, Conn: Archon, 1984.
Petry, Alice Hall. "Baby Wilson Redux: McCullers' *The Heart Is a Lonely Hunter*." *SUST* 25, no. 2 (Summer 1986): 196–203.
Snider, Clifton. "Jungian Theory, Its Literary Application and a Discussion of *Member of the Wedding*." In *Psychological Perspectives on Literature*. Hamden, Conn.: Archon, 1984.

MALAMUD, BERNARD. B. April 26, 1914, New York City, New York. D. March 18, 1986, New York City, New York. American novelist.

Bernard Malamud received a national book award for *The Magic Barrel*

(1958) and a Pulitzer Prize for *The Fixer* (1966). His characteristic themes of moral involvement and the value of suffering are found in *The Assistant* (1957). In his novels, Malamud's characters search for a new direction, as in *A New Life* (1961) or *Dubin's Lives* (1979). He has been a leading figure in the liberal humanist (see humanism**) tradition, combating the nihilism** which threatens his culture.

Malamud, a versatile, clever, and learned writer, was familiar with the teaching of certain philosophers, whose thoughts he was inclined to weave into his novels, as he did most effectively in *The Fixer*. Here the character of Yakov Bok becomes a disciple of Baruch Spinoza* and attempts to follow the philosopher to a new life of freedom. "Spinoza's philosophy is an elaborate program for freedom, and Bok, naturally disinclined to politics, relieved of family responsibility by grace of his wife's desertion, goes outside the shtetl in search of enough economic security to follow his new master's example. As Bok understands him, Spinoza was out to make a free man of himself . . . by thinking things through and connecting everything up" (reported by Eigner, 101). Malamud was accustomed to putting his characters in the position where they either did not understand the philosophy they were studying or found it impossible to follow it. In the case of Bok, we see that he does not have the mind or the will to go through the process of strenuous thought that Spinoza went through in order to arrive at an understanding of his place in the universe. In other words, Malamud does not reject Spinoza's philosophy, but he does show that it is difficult to accept it as one's own.

There is probably no other modern American writer whose "Jewishness" is so obvious, so thorough, and so consistent. It is astonishing, therefore, that in *The Assistant* St. Francis becomes the hero and model for Frank Alpine because he says that the saint "took a fresh view of things, said poverty was a queen and he loved her like she was a beautiful woman" (Malamud, 31).

But Malamud returns always to Jewish themes, Jewish people, and Jewish suffering. As Alan Warkon Friedman states,

> For Malamud, man was nothing but the misery and intensity of his suffering. . . . But Malamud's characters not only define themselves by the force of existential [see existentialism**] anguish, they derive their special quality from the ancient Jewish teachings and spirit embodied in the Torah and the Talmud. Fundamental to the faith is the notion that God's ways are righteous and inscrutable, and that man must walk humbly and a little warily to survive from day to day. The vision is dual—simultaneously experiencing the harsh realities of limited morality and affirming an abiding

faith that God *is* in control of things and does indeed know what he is doing. (Friedman, 288, 291)

REFERENCES

Bloom, Harold, ed. *Bernard Malamud.* New York: Chelsea, 1986.

Eigner, Edwin M. "The Loathly Ladies." In *Bernard Malamud and the Critics,* edited by Leslie Field and Joyce W. Field. New York: New York University, 1970.

Field, Leslie, and Joyce W. Field, eds. *Bernard Malamud and the Critics.* New York: New York University, 1970.

Friedman, Alan Warkon. "The Hero as Schnook." In *Bernard Malamud and the Critics,* edited by Leslie Field and Joyce W. Field. New York: New York University Press, 1970.

Goldman, Mark. "Bernard Malamud's Comic Vision and the Theme of Identity." *Critique* 7, no. 1 (Winter 1964–65): 92–109.

Malamud, Bernard. *The Assistant.* New York: Dell, 1957.

Ratner, Mark. "Style and Humanity in Malamud's Fiction." *Massachusetts Review* 5 (1964): 663–83.

MALRAUX, ANDRÉ. B. November 3, 1901, Paris, France. D. November 23, 1976, Paris, France. French novelist, art critic, and politician.

After his publication of *La Condition Humaine* in 1933 (trans. S. Gilbert, *Man's Fate,* 1934) and his support of Charles de Gaulle in 1947, André Malraux was considered as a left-wing, committed writer. With the work *Le Temps du Mepris* (trans. H. M. Chevalier, *Days of Wrath,* 1936), he denounced Adolph Hitler and nazism.** During the Spanish civil war, Malraux fought on the Republican side, and this war experience resulted in a war novel *L'Espoir* (trans. S. Gilbert and A. McDonald, *Man's Hope,* 1938). In postwar France, Malraux was politically active but continued writing. During this period he published *The Voices of Silence* (1960) and *The Metamorphosis of the Gods* (1960).

It is interesting to note that, as a member of the editorial staff of Gallimaro Publishers, Malraux introduced the work of Albert Camus (q.v.). Both writers believed in the absurd (see absurdity**). In his essay on T. E. Lawrence, Malraux wrote: "[M]an is absurd. He is neither master of time, nor of anguish, nor of evil; the world is absurd because it implies the existence of evil, and evil is the sin of the world" (reported by Blend, 56).

There is a long history of Malraux's interest and affinities to Friedrich Nietzsche*: Both attacked the ability of science to resolve metaphysical** problems, and Malraux, in particular, declared again and again that science and reason have been completely unsuccessful in dealing with the elements of human destiny. Neither Nietzsche nor Malraux was so unen-lightened as to deny science a significant role in society, but both men lost faith in science and saw that it was the failure of science and reason that brought about the terrible inhumanity of the twentieth century. Fur-thermore, they both believed that it was science that had brought about the condition that Nietzsche made prerequisite for a rebirth of tragedy.

Malraux is no fatalist (in fact, he distrusts Marxism** because here fatality often gets the upper hand of the will), and, like Nietzsche, he believes in the power of the human will to move man from absurdity and angst** to a new and better world. In 1949, feeling that the element of fatality had triumphed, Malraux referred to Marxism as a ''Hegelian-ism[**] oriented toward an uncontrollable future—nothing could be fur-ther from the tragic effort of the human will that is the center of his own philosophy'' (Blend, 63).

André Malraux, whose education and knowledge were enriched by a wide range of experiences in politics, war, and art, was also well versed in Oriental art and philosophy, and he reveals in his writings a familiarity with many Western philosophers, ranging from Blaise Pascal,* Immanuel Kant,* and Nietzsche to the modern existentialists (see existentialism**), Camus and Jean-Paul Sartre*(q.v.). Finally, we close this entry on Mal-raux with a quote from Charles Blend concerning the possible influence of Nietzsche on Malraux and on his relationship to the Communist movement:

> The exact part played by Nietzschean philosophy in Malraux's movement toward and away from communism is difficult to ascertain exactly, but there is one conjecture that seems reasonable although the communists would deny the association. Nietzsche had written that anyone who wished to be a creator in either good or evil first had to destroy old values; the revolutionaries in the orient were doing just that. A growing awareness that this same group was actually betraying the new values they claimed to espouse brought about the consequent rupture. . . . In Malraux's case, it was hastened by orient-inspired doubts concerning the use of force. It was power and force which chained Prometheus to his rock. (Blend, 79)

REFERENCES

Bevan, David. *André Malraux: Towards the Expression of Transcendence.* Kingston, Ontario, Canada: McGill-Queens University Press, 1986.

Blend, Charles D. *André Malraux: Tragic Humanist.* Columbus: Ohio State University Press, 1963.

Cazenove, Michel. *Malraux.* Paris: Balland, 1985.

"The Human Condition." In *Men and Monuments,* edited by Janet Flanner. New York: Harper & Row, 1957.

MANN, THOMAS. B. June 6, 1875, Lübeck, Germany. Naturalized U.S. citizen, 1944. D. August 12, 1955, Kilchberg bei Zurich, Switzerland. German novelist.

Thomas Mann is one of Germany's most respected literary figures, and his works are considered classics of the very first rank. His first major novel, *Buddenbrooks* (1901), portrays three generations of a declining bourgeois family. *Death in Venice* (1912), a sombre story that helped establish Mann as an important writer of fiction, was followed by *The Magic Mountain* (1924) which, in a complex way, spanned German culture and the Romantic tradition of Richard Wagner and Friedrich Nietzsche.* In 1938 *The Joseph Trilogy* was published. Mann achieved the apex of his career with *Doctor Faustus* (1947), a massive work that explores the German culture in some depth. In 1952 Mann returned to Europe and settled in Switzerland. He won the Nobel Prize for Literature in 1929.

Philosophical influences are most obvious in Thomas Mann's later works where he reveals his admiration for Nietzsche, whom he called the epitome of the European spirit. Mann and Nietzsche were both deeply influenced by a feature that was also characteristic of T. S. Eliot (q.v.). Eliot had always said that modern writers had to tap into the stream of the past, and certainly Mann did this in his works, in *The Joseph Trilogy* as well as in *Doctor Faustus.* Mann in his novels is fascinated with characters who border on the fringe of society. Felix Krull, in the picaresque novel *Confessions of Felix Krull* (1954), despite his genius, is a crook, a rogue who steals from helpless old ladies. In several of Mann's stories men of integrity, like Aschenbach of *Death in Venice,* are driven by passion. In this novel, Mann believes, with Nietzsche, that all forms of human conduct are acceptable. Publicly, Aschenbach pretends to uphold morality, but his passion for Tadzio shows that, in truth, he acquiesces to passion.

It is significant that Thomas Mann describes Nietzsche as a mountain climber who has climbed too high among the glacial peaks. Such are the characters in Thomas Mann's literary works—people who push themselves to the point of no return. Aschenbach does this and destroys himself. In a sense even harmless characters like Tonio Kröger are truly Nietzschean. Tonio ventures into the world of art isolating himself from society and willingly accepting an awareness of art that results in pain. So when Mann says that Nietzsche "drove himself" into the pathless wastes and brought himself to a martyr's death on a cross, he is really describing the characters in his own literary works.

Mann's interest in Nietzsche began at the turn of the century while he was still a young writer. Mann's interest was based largely on *The Birth of Tragedy* (1872) which, according to John Foster, culminated in imaginative works like *Death in Venice, Fiorenze* (1905), and finally *Doctor Faustus*. In fact, in the early 1900s, Mann felt that the influence of Nietzsche was so strong that he feared losing his creative independence. In *Death in Venice,* Aschenbach fits Nietzsche's portrait of the decadent artist, and Mann's conception of *Doctor Faustus* is probably a fictional biography of Nietzsche. Foster claims that *Death in Venice* is an example of "[t]he appropriation of Nietzsche's literary legacy that also shows the special importance that *The Birth of Tragedy* (1872) could have for writers" (Foster, 147). Mann's reverence for Nietzsche's intellectuality provided him with a basis for confirmation of his own creative efforts.

Nietzsche's mental disease fascinated Mann, who was convinced that genius was linked to disease. To understand Mann's works, one must be aware of his fascination with disease as a sign of genius. In his penetrating analysis of Mann's *The Magic Mountain,* Frederick Hoffman stresses, Sigmund Freud's* influence on Mann's thinking and identifies Mann's debt to Arthur Schopenhauer* for the awareness of the artist's dependence upon disease and suffering for much of his inspiration.

> Thomas Mann has been called "The Ironic German" and under the influence of Nietzsche, irony became for him the chief means of rescuing art in a critical age. At various times of his life, Mann takes elements from Nietzsche's work that give him confirmation in his creative efforts. Accordingly his judgment also changes and waivers, but he always regards with reverence Nietzsche's intellectuality, which transcends itself and his tragic fate. (Berendsohn, 16)

REFERENCES

Berendsohn, Walter E. *Thomas Mann: Artist and Partisan in Troubled Times.* Tuscaloosa: University of Alabama Press, 1973.
Bloom, Harold, ed. *Thomas Mann.* New York: Chelsea, 1986.
Foster, John. *Heirs To Dionysius: A Nietzschean Current in Literary Modernism.* Princeton, N.J.: Princeton University Press, 1981.
Hoffman, Frederick John. *Freudianism and the Literary Mind.* 2nd ed. Baton Rouge: Louisiana State University Press, 1957.
Kolb, Jacelyne. "Thomas Mann's Translation of Wagner into *Buddenbrooks.*" *GR* 61, no. 4 (Fall 1986): 146–53. (Sources in Richard Wagner)
Roche, Mark W. "Laughter and Truth in *Doktor Faustus:* Nietzschean Structures

in Mann's Novel of Self-cancellation.'' *DVLG* 60, no. 2 (June 1986): 309–32. (Sources in Nietzsche)

MASTERS, EDGAR LEE. B. August 23, 1869, Garnett, Kansas. D. March 5, 1950, Philadelphia, Pennsylvania. American poet and novelist.

Edgar Lee Masters grew up on his grandfather's farm in New Salem, Illinois. He studied in his father's law office, then attended Knox College. In 1891, he was admitted to the bar and then pursued a successful law practice in Chicago. His first volume of verses appeared in 1898, followed by *Maximilian,* a drama in blank verse (1902). Other works that appeared in the early 1900s were *Blood of the Prophets* (1903) and *The Bread of Idleness* (1911). However, it was his *Spoon River Anthology* (1915) that finally earned him a distinguished place in American letters. Also notable is his autobiography, *Across Spoon River* (1936).

Although it is impossible to prove through direct statements that Edgar Lee Masters was directly influenced by the philosopher William James,* it is the opinion of several critics—specifically Howard Mumford Jones, Richard M. Ludwig, and Robert D. Narveson—that he was indeed. It has been documented that Masters read *Varieties of Religious Experience* by James while writing the anthology of poetry, and, as Narveson points out, the similarities of ideas between the two works are too great to be disregarded.

Varieties of Religious Experience is James's psychological study of religious experience, and the *Spoon River Anthology* is a collection of poetic epitaphs of people who are buried in a cemetery in the fictional town of Spoon River. James's work was the result of lectures delivered in Edinburgh in 1901–1902, and Masters's *Anthology* appeared in 1914 and 1915. Religious experiences are recorded in both books, and the similarities are so obvious that one must respect the evidence presented by Narveson in support of his view that Masters's work must have been influenced by James. Narveson points out the similarities of terms used both by James and Masters, for example, ''one birth minds'' (Masters) and ''once born'' by James. As Narveson points out, ''nearly all of the poems that follow are given over to similar discussions of philosophical issues and the experiences that inspired or accompanied them'' (Narveson, 90). A close reading of both works reveals interesting parallels of expressions.

REFERENCES

Burgess, Charles E. ''Spoon River: Politics and Poetry.'' *PLL* 23, no. 3 (Summer 1987): 347–63.

Narveson, Robert D. "The Kindred Spirits of William James and Edgar Lee Masters." *Mid-America* 10 (1983): 85–98.

Primeay, Ronald. *Spoon River: The Legacy of Edgar Lee Masters.* Austin: University of Texas Press, 1981.

Wrenn, John H., and Margaret M. Wrenn. *Edgar Lee Masters.* Boston: G. K. Hall, 1983.

MELVILLE, HERMAN. B. August 1, 1819, New York City, New York. D. September 28, 1891, New York City, New York. American novelist.

Herman Melville was raised in Albany, New York, and attended the Albany Classical School. Later, when the family was forced to move to Lansingburgh (New Troy), he studied surveying. In 1839, he became a cabin boy on the merchant ship *St. Larence* and in 1841 sailed on the whaler *Acushnet*. The adventure on this voyage provided him with material for his first novel *Typee* (1846). In 1841 he joined the crew of the Australian whaler *Lucy Ann* and took part in a mutiny which he recorded in *Omoo* (1847). Other works which describe his sailing experiences are *White-Jacket* (1850), *Mardi* (1849), and *Moby Dick* (1851), his masterpiece. In 1850, Melville settled in Massachusetts where he was a neighbor and friend of Nathaniel Hawthorne (q.v.).

Judging from the Platonic (see Platonism**) allusions in Melville's works, Melville was familiar with six of Plato's* dialogues: *The Apology, Phaedo, The Symposium, Timaeus, The Republic,* and *Phaedrus.*

> From *Mardi* (1849) until *Billy Budd* (1924) Melville's speculations on immortality are frequently expressed in Platonic language. Especially in *Mardi,* the arguments of the *Phaedo* on immortality and related subjects appear side by side with an equal number of passages contradicting the affirmations of Socrates[*] in the dialogue, for when writing *Mardi* (1849) Melville was just beginning to explore such philosophical problems. (Sealts, 64)

There was a time when Melville almost abandoned the philosophy of Plato. He disagreed with Plato on the dualism of good and evil. Melville felt not only that the problem of evil in the world had no solution but also that Plato evaded this issue.

> When Socrates offers Plato's objections to democracy or discusses the illusions of sense perception, Melville approves; when Socrates sketches Plato's plans for an ideal state or outlines his metaphysical[**] system, Melville replies that reason will never govern man, dispel illusion, or solve

the problem of evil. In short, Melville frequently accepted a Platonic analysis of a philosophic question but rejected its Platonic solution. (Sealts, 105)

Later in life, Melville regained his faith in Platonic thought and his faith in philosophy's role in helping struggling man.

The influence of Socrates and the Socratic tradition on Melville is apparent in the figure of Babbalanja, a character in *Mardi,* who emerges as a replica of Socrates through whom Melville's criticism of all that is false and morally corrupt in nineteenth-century civilization is expressed. Although one does not find numerous references to Socrates in Melville's works, in Babbalanja one finds an implicit expression of high regard for the Greek philosopher as a spiritual hero, a committed searcher for truth and wisdom.

In his examination of Melville's work, Merton Miller Sealts concludes that Melville's profound familiarity with philosophic literature is reflected in his characterizations and in his portrayal of various aspects of the human condition. Two thinkers in particular must be mentioned here: Seneca* and Marcus Aurelius Antoninus,* writers whose influence accounts for the strong strain of Stoicism** in Melville's works. The influence of Thomas Carlyle (q.v.) on Melville was far-reaching. He was inspired by Carlyle's writing, particularly *On Heroes, Hero-worship,* and *The Heroic in History* (collection, 1901), and he drew upon Carlyle's idea that paganism** expressed a valid awareness of the universe. This is revealed in Melville's rational and sympathetic treatment of Queequeg's paganism (Peach, 141). The sphinx, Carlyle's symbol for the mystery of the universe, appears in *Moby Dick.*

In conclusion, one must say that Melville's scholarship and learning in philosophy is probably one of the best kept secrets of American literary studies. His debt to philosophy, especially to the Platonic and Stoic systems of thought, was considerable.

REFERENCES

Bloom, Harold, ed. *Herman Melville.* New York: Chelsea, 1986.
Peach, Linden. *British Influence on the Birth of American Literature.* New York: St. Martin's Press, 1982.
Sealts, Merton M., Jr. "Herman Melville's Readings in Ancient Philosophy."*Dissertation Abstracts* 30: 1574A–75A (Yale).
Wenke, John. " 'Ontological Heroics': Melville's Philosophical Art." In *A Companion to Melville Studies,* edited by John Bryant. Westport, Conn.: Greenwood Press, 1986. (Treatment of philosophy)

Widmer, Kingsley. *The Ways of Nihilism: A Study of Herman Melville's Short Novels*. Los Angeles: California State Colleges, 1970.

MERTON, THOMAS. B. January 31, 1915, Prades, France. D. December 10, 1968, Bangkok, Thailand. American writer and mystic.

As a young man, Thomas Merton travelled throughout Europe with his artist parents and studied briefly at Cambridge, England. He returned to the United States and earned his master's degree (1939) from Columbia University. During these years, he turned from agnosticism to Roman Catholicism. In 1941 Merton decided to become a Trappist monk because of its discipline of silence and solitude. As a monk, he poured out massive amounts of poetry, meditations, and even works of social criticism. His writings, especially the very popular autobiography *The Seven Storey Mountain* (1948), brought him prominence in American letters.

An intellectual, schooled in Western and Oriental thought, Merton joined the Trappist monastery and developed into a celebrated theological writer whose mystical proclivity led him to Meister Eckehart* and Zen Buddhism.**

In addition to his interest in Zen Buddhism, Origen,* Seneca,* and Saint Thomas Aquinas* (Merton wrote a poem in honor of the great Catholic theologian), Merton was impressed with existentialism,** especially as represented in the work of Albert Camus (q.v.) whom he studied in depth and about whom he published four articles in 1960. Merton, however, was not an existentialist, but rather a mystical metaphysical** poet with philosophical inclinations. His poetry addresses the nature of "being" and the "inner experience," which undoubtedly results from years of monastic and contemplative living.

Although deeply learned in western as well as eastern thought, Merton always maintained the humble posture of the philosopher who spends his lifetime unraveling the mysteries of the universe; he ends with the words, "I don't really know." In the essay "The Study of Zen," Merton writes:

> But there eventually comes a time when like Moses we see that the Thornbush of cultural and religious forms is suddenly on fire and we are summoned to approach it without shoes—and probably without feet. Is the fire other than the bush? More than the bush? or is it more the bush than the bush itself? (Reported by Lentfoehr, 59)

REFERENCES

Lentfoehr, Sister Therese. *Words and Silence: On the Poetry of Thomas Merton*. New York: New Directions, 1979.

MILLER, ARTHUR. B. October 17, 1915, New York City, New York. American dramatist.

Arthur Miller lived through and was shaped by the Great Depression, when he experienced the financial ruin of his father, a small manufacturer. After graduation from high school, Miller worked in a warehouse and saved money for his college education. He attended the University of Michigan where he began to write plays. In 1956, Miller was called before the Un-American Activities Committee and was charged with contempt, but eventually he won an appeal for the contempt conviction. In the 1960s Miller married actress Marilyn Monroe, and his play, *The Misfits* (1961), is based on the life of the actress. His most celebrated play, *Death of a Salesman* (1949), depicted personal failure and self-deception, and it presented the dreams of the middle-class American. In *The Crucible* (1953), he turned to the theme of the Salem witchcraft trials, and here he satirized the McCarthy hearings. His other major plays include *A View from the Bridge* (1955), *After the Fall* (1964), and *The Price* (1968).

Ronald Hayman, an English critic, has called Arthur Miller a Sartrean playwright. This is undoubtedly true since Miller's plays fit the definition of Jean-Paul Sartre's* (q.v.) "theatre of situation." This affinity between Sartre and Miller is understandable when one considers the existential development (see existentialism**) of Miller's later plays. Beginning with *The Misfits,* Miller's works shift the tragic perspective from man's remediable alienation from society to man's hopeless alienation from the universe and from himself. The absurdist (see absurdity**) themes of personal solitude and moral ambivalence became central issues in *After the Fall, Incident at Vichy* (1964), and *The Price* (Lowenthal, 143).

It is clear that the later Miller does not entertain illusions about the perfectability of man; in his most recent works, man becomes a hopeless creature, groping for values out of the morass of human corruption. The theme of universal guilt (original sin) is despairingly affirmed, but Miller does not deny the possibility of personal redemption in the Godless world, insisting with Sartre on the free will and the potential for the recreation (transcendence) of self through choice.

Incident at Vichy, which illustrates man's power of resistance when faced with torture and death, clearly demonstrates Miller's existential concerns. The characters in *Vichy* are presented as free individuals who are placed in a crisis situation where they must make a choice. Yet, despite their limitations, they are always free to act according to their own morality. As Lowenthal says, "The Jew can resist or submit; the German can murder or rebel" (Lowenthal, 144). Although *Vichy* deals with the absurd, it nevertheless never loses its coherence or rationalistic structure. Evil in the play is expressed in Sartrean "dread" and the meaninglessness of the physical world. *Vichy* dramatizes, as well, the Sartrean notion of the man of "bad faith" who flees responsibility to a deterministic (see determinism**) situation. The Nazis represent, of course, the man of bad faith. *Incident at Vichy* is an explicit example of the influence of philosophy, particularly Sartre's existentialist philosophy, on Miller's work.

REFERENCES

Brashear, William R. "The Empty Bench: Morality, Tragedy, and Arthur Miller." *Michigan Quarterly Review* 5 (1966): 270–78.
Centola, Steven R. "Compromise as Bad Faith: Arthur Miller's *A View from the Bridge.*" *MQ* 28, no. 1 (Autumn 1986): 100–113. (Theories of Sartre and Freud)
Hayman, Ronald. "Arthur Miller: Between Sartre and Society." *Encounter* 37 (November 1971): 73–79.
Lowenthal, Lawrence D. "Arthur Miller's *Incident at Vichy:* A Sartrean Interpretation." In *Critical Essays on Arthur Miller,* edited by James J. Martine. Boston: C. K. Hall, 1979.
Martine, James J., ed. *Critical Essays on Arthur Miller.* Boston: C. K. Hall, 1979.

MILLER, HENRY. B. December 26, 1891, New York City, New York. D. June 7, 1980, Big Sur, California. American novelist.

Henry Miller was raised in Brooklyn. In 1924 he left his job with Western Union to devote himself to writing. In 1930 he settled in Paris, where he came under the influence of the surrealist movement (see surrealism**). In the 1950s and 1960s, Miller settled in the untamed area of Big Sur on the California coast, where he became the center of a colony of admirers including writers of the Beat generation. His first book, *Tropic of Cancer* (1934), was followed by other works, most of which dealt with his early life in New York. His books were banned as pornography until the 1960s. His later works include *Tropic of Capricorn* (1939) and *The Airconditioned Nightmare* (1945). Miller also wrote travel books and highly idiosyncratic literary criticism.

If one can get by the obscenity and what George Bernard Shaw (q.v.) calls "dirt for dirt's sake," one will find some solid Nietzschean philosophy in the novels of Henry Miller. "Of the many writers whose names he encountered during the days of young manhood, Friedrich Nietzsche[*] must have been the most important, for Miller wrote his first essay on the subject of Nietzsche's *Antichrist* while working in his father's tailor shop'' (Gordon, 36–37). Nietzsche called men to freedom and joy, but, if Gordon is correct that ''for both Miller and Nietzsche freedom is inward'' (Gordon, 38), then one wonders why Miller expresses this freedom in an obsession with the biological processes. One questions what this somewhat puritanical (see puritanism**) Nietzsche meant by ''Dionysiac freedom'' (see Dionysian**). Nevertheless Miller was true to the master in placing the individual at the center, and, throwing altruism aside, he made his own personal life the major purpose of life. Also like Nietzsche, Henry Miller set out to destroy existing cultural values, and he concerned himself with one thing—personal growth. He felt that development of the individual was the only way to survive.

> The influence of Nietzsche and his followers upon Miller goes deeper than a simple enhancement of individualism, a justification for self-assertion. In Nietzsche, as in Goldman and the anarchist movement, there is a strong acceptance of destruction . . . as one sees in studying Miller's individual works, aggression and destruction are important elements in his total feeling. (Gordon, 43, 44)

Furthermore,

> Nietzsche became for Miller, as for many others who dreamed of a better world, a prophet of the future direction of salvation for mankind. Salvation was to come through internal liberation. Restraints, institutions would fall, not by external attack, but from their own weight. Nietzsche and the anarchists [Miller] whom he influenced looked forward to a new man who would be the complete antithesis of western man as he had been up to then. (Gordon, 38)

Nietzsche had a tremendous influence on the thinking and values of Henry Miller. From Nietzsche he learned to face the problem of man in an evolving universe, to put the individual at the center and to remove God from the universe. But,

> According to his commentators, Nietzsche did not remain for long in a godless world. He turned around and defied the very Dionysiac force which he had at first balanced against the Apollonian.[**] Miller, too, accepted the Dionysian, but he went beyond Nietzsche in attributing to it a driving force. He accepted a cyclical view of history as did Nietzsche, but modified by a sense of destiny or purpose. Rejecting eternal recurrence, Miller, like Vico and [Oswald] Spengler,[*] accepted some kind of evolutionary progress as a future possibility if not as a historical fact. (Gordon, 47)

REFERENCES

Brown, J. D. *Henry Miller*. New York: Ungar, 1986.
Gordon, William A. *The Mind and Art of Henry Miller*. Baton Rouge: Louisiana
    State University Press, 1967.
Lewis, Leon. *Henry Miller: The Major Writings*. New York: Schocken, 1986.
Rahv, Phillip. "Henry Miller." In *Image and Idea*, edited by Rahv. New York:
    New Directions, 1957.

MILTON, JOHN. B. December 9, 1608, London, England. D. November 8, 1674, Chalfont St. Giles, Buckinghamshire, England. English poet.

John Milton received a classical education at Christ's College, Cambridge, and was writing poetry in Latin, Italian, and English at an early age. From 1632 to 1638 he lived as a recluse at his father's home and engaged himself in private study. At this time, he produced the masque *Comus* and the poem "Lycidas." Milton later became involved in the Puritan cause, and between 1641 and 1660 he wrote pamphlets for religious liberty. He also served as secretary for foreign languages in the Cromwell government. His great epic *Paradise Lost* was first published in 1667 and *Paradise Regained* and *Samson Agonistes* in 1671.

The one philosopher who had the greatest influence on Milton was Plato.* His undergraduate writings at Christ's College contain many allusions to Socrates* and Plato. *Comus* has been said to be the most Platonic of his works, yet here he did not set himself to express the doctrines of Plato, but, like poets from Homer to William Butler Yeats (q.v.), he simply used legend and myth to his own purposes (Samuel, 11). Since it is a fact that the works of Plato and Aristotle* were taught in European schools from the Renaissance** on and since it is well known that the Cambridge Platonists of the seventeenth century promulgated Plato's teaching in England, it is only natural that Milton would be familiar with Plato's teaching. The many references to the Greek philosopher in Milton's works provide convincing evidence of the direct impact of one great mind upon another.

The manifest relationship between Plato's dialogues and Milton's *Paradise Lost* and *Paradise Regained* leads one to agree with Irene Samuel that it is a mistake to read the works of Milton simply as Puritan poems. As Samuel states; "Everywhere in his [Milton's] work there are echoes of Plato, many that might have come from intermediate sources, some of them Christian, but many, too, that only a close reading of Plato by

Milton himself could produce'' (Samuel, vii). Samuel concludes in her comprehensive study of the Platonic elements in Milton's work, ''it became clear that the works of Plato had been not merely a source, but a stimulant, to Milton, and had acted as a catalytic agent on the heterogeneous materials of Pagan, Biblical, and Christian learning in his mind. Milton is, like Edmund Spenser [q.v.] and [Percy Bysshe] Shelley [q.v.], a Platonic poet'' (Samuel, viii).

In Milton's first political treatise, *Of Reformation*, he cites for his conception of the state the authority of Plato, Aristotle, and the Bible. In *Paradise Regained,* Milton has Jesus speak of Socrates as the ''next memorable'' to Job. Finally, Milton was familiar with Pythagorean** writings as evidenced from his reference to Pythagoras* in *Areopagitica.* Although critics (see Samuel) feel that Plato's teaching had the greatest influence on Milton, Aristotle was also a factor. For example, in *De Doctrina Christiana,* Milton makes an effort to disentangle the interwoven threads of Aristotelean and scholastic theology (see scholasticism**). Also, in his *Logic* Milton often cites Aristotle as evidence and authority.

REFERENCES

Curry, Walter Clyde. *Milton's Ontology, Cosmogony, and Physics*. Lexington: University of Kentucky Press, 1957.
Fallon, Stephen Michael. ''Degrees of Substance: Milton's Spirit World and 17th Century Philosophy.'' *DAI* 47, no. 2 (August 1986): 535A. (Treatment of monism** and influences of Cambridge Platonists)
Fletcher, Harris Francis. *The Intellectual Development of John Milton*. Urbana: University of Illinois Press, 1956.
Grace, William Joseph. *Ideas in Milton*. Notre Dame, Ind.: University of Notre Dame Press, 1966.
Hyman, Lawrence W. *The Quarrel Within: Art and Morality in Milton's Poetry*. Port Washington, N.Y.: Kennikat Press, 1972.
Rudat, Wolfgang E. H. ''Augustinian Theology and Milton's 'Manhood' in *Paradise Lost*.'' *JEP* 6, nos. 1, 2 (March 1985): 12–15. (Sources in Saint Augustine, *De Civitate Dei*)
Samuel, Irene. *Plato and Milton*. Ithaca, N.Y.: Cornell University Press, 1947.
Tillyard, Eustace Mandeville Wetenhall. *Milton*. New York: Collier, 1966.

MURDOCH, IRIS. B. July 15, 1919, Dublin, Ireland. British novelist.
Iris Murdoch, who, at one point in her career (1968), considered herself a Platonist (see Platonism**), is thought of as a moral philosopher as well as a novelist (as reported by Conradi, 15), but she was also familiar with many other philosophers, including Immanuel Kant* and Jean-Paul Sartre* (q.v.). She expressed a distrust for Sartrean existentialism** and

British philosophy: "In a radio talk in 1950 she criticized Sartre and [Albert] Camus [q.v.] for presenting worlds which were simultaneously too intelligible and transparent, and also too lacking in mystery" (Conradi, 12).

In her early novel *Under the Net* (1954), she implicitly criticized its existentialist hero and exhibits a romantic tendency and a Platonist view in the making, preferring "to be thought a reflective, religious or speculative novelist like [Feodor] Dostoevski,[*] than, like Sartre, directly a philosophical one" (Conradi, 31).

As early as 1950, Murdoch was writing philosophical essays as well as novels. Two of these, which appeared in 1950 and 1952, were entitled, respectively, "The Existentialist Hero" and "The Existentialist Political Myth." In 1977, she expressed her Platonist leanings in "The Fire and the Sun: Why Plato Banished the Artists," in which she discusses Plato's* objections to art and expresses sympathy and understanding of Plato, Kant, Leo Tolstoy (q.v.), and Sigmund Freud* and their opinions of art and morals. In this essay, as Conradi points out, Murdoch establishes a blending of Plato and Freud. She admired Freud as a thinker, but criticized him for concentrating on life in the cave and neglecting life in the sun.

Indeed, her works as well as her lectures (e.g., the 1982 Gifford Lectures) testify to her conviction that philosophical speculation plays a critical role in literature as well as in the more mundane aspects of human existence.

REFERENCES

Conradi, Peter J. *Iris Murdoch: The Saint and the Artist*. New York: St. Martin's Press, 1986.
Dipple, Elizabeth. *Iris Murdoch: Work for the Spirit*. Chicago: University of Chicago Press, 1982.

MUSIL, ROBERT. B. November 6, 1880, Klagenfurt, Austria-Hungary. D. April 15, 1942, Geneva, Switzerland. Austrian novelist.

Robert Musil began his career as an engineer, but he then went to the University of Berlin where he studied philosophy and psychology. The success of his first novel, *Young Torless* (1906), made him' decide to devote his life to literature. His most important work, *The Man without Qualities* (1930–1933), records Musil's own experiences and, although it was unfinished at his death, it is considered to be a brilliant synthesis of the main intellectual, social, political, and cultural elements within the Austrian and German civilizations.

Although Robert Musil's reputation lies in the area of fiction, it should be pointed out to students of literature that his formal university training was in philosophy and science. Musil came from a rich generation of writers, including Hugo von Hofmannsthal, Rainer Maria Rilke (q.v.), and Hermann Hesse (q.v.), and such important philosophers as Karl Jaspers* and Martin Heidegger.* Musil shared with these figures common problems: intellectual culture and political experience. As a young man, Musil "was attracted to symbolism[**] and [Friedrich] Nietzsche,[*] to the decadents, to [Immanuel] Kant[*] and [Arthur] Schopenhauer,[*] rather than to more historical or realistic [see realism**] philosophers" (Luft, 38). From Kant's *Critique of Judgement,* Musil learned the classical rationale of modern art: "Kant's emphasis on the incommensurability of the rational concept and the representation of the imagination allowed art to be something more than an inferior form of science. For Kant (and Musil), the aesthetic idea mediated between science and morality, between the phenomenal and the noumenal" (Luft, 39). Since Musil learned Kantianism** and aesthetics through Schopenhauer and Stéphane Mallarmé, he learned to emphasize subjective states and art for its own sake.

However, the overwhelming intellectual influence on Musil's development was Nietzsche, and this influence was not a temporary one, but one that increased as Musil grew older. From Nietzsche, Musil learned to identify science as a dead art and to regard psychology as the queen of philosophy. As Musil accepted Kant's criticism of eighteenth-century culture, he learned from Nietzsche to go beyond systematic philosophy without leaning toward pessimism.** "Nietzsche and the symbolists had not merely announced a new art and a new philosophy; they had condemned the psychic structure of the European burgher as a historical anachronism, cut off from its roots in Christian culture. This way of thinking appealed to Musil" (Luft, 41).

In 1903 and 1904, Musil matriculated in philosophy at the University of Berlin and studied philosophy and psychology under Karl Stumpf. At this time, he was completing his first novel *Young Torless,* a work which follows Schopenhauer's idea that a novel should stress inner events and concentrate on the inner monologue and psychological analysis. This novel was an excellent example of how philosophy spilled over into Musil's fiction just as later it strongly influenced his moral and political essays.

In conclusion, it must be emphasized that Robert Musil's philosophical training was far reaching—from Plotinus,* the Stoics (see Stoicism**) and Epicureans (see Epicureanism**) to Friedrich Schelling's* philosophy of nature, and the teachings of Baruch Spinoza,* Jean-Jacques Rousseau (q.v.), Thomas Carlyle (q.v.), Ralph Waldo Emerson (q.v.), and William James.*

REFERENCES

Erickson, Susan. "The Psychopoetics of Narrative in Robert Musil's 'die Portugiesin.' " *Monatshefte* 78, no. 2 (Summer 1986): 167–81.
Luft, David S. *Robert Musil and the Crisis of European Culture*. Berkeley: University of California Press, 1980.
Pike, Burton. *Robert Musil: An Introduction to His Work*. Ithaca, N.Y.: Cornell University Press, 1961.
Willemsen, Roger. "Dionysisches Sprechen: zur Theorie einer sprache der Erregung bei Musil und Nietzsche." *DBKG* 60, no. 1 (March 1986): 104–35.

O

O'CONNOR, FLANNERY. B. March 25, 1925, Savannah, Georgia. D. August 3, 1964, Milledgeville, Georgia. American novelist and short-story writer.

Flannery O'Connor graduated from Georgia State College for women and then went on to study creative writing at the University of Iowa. Her first published work appeared in 1946. Other works include two novels, *Wise Blood* (1952) and *The Violent Bear It Away* (1960). She published two collections of short stories, *A Good Man Is Hard to Find and Other Stories* (1955) and *Everything That Rises Must Converge* (1965). O'Connor's works are usually set in the rural south and, although they deal with human alienation, often concern themselves with the relationship between God and the individual.

At times it is difficult to ascertain whether a writer's words should be taken literally, as in the case of Flannery O'Connor's comments on her reading of the Greek philosophers: "I suppose I read Aristotle[*] in college but not to know I was doing it; the same with Plato[*]" (Letters, 93). In any case, there appears to be no evidence of influence by the Greek philosophers on her writing or thinking. However, it is quite a different case with Saint Thomas Aquinas* and Flannery O'Connor, who leaned toward religious thought and religious writing. The repeated references to the angelic doctor in her letters give evidence of serious reading of the *Summa*. For example, in September 1955, she quoted Thomas Aquinas who said that art did not require rectitude of the appetite. We mention this because it is one example of O'Connor's search in the *Summa* for theory that would enhance and clarify her own conception of art. This is not to say that the author always read theological and philosophical works with her literary work in mind. O'Connor believed that man was created in the image of God, and the reading of Saint Thomas Aquinas tended to strengthen her personal religious beliefs.

Flannery O'Connor had an inquiring mind and occupied herself with many varieties of philosophical writings. In September 1955, she read Etienne Gilson's *History of Christian Philosophy in the Middle Ages* and *The Unity of Philosophical Experiences*. A perusal of her reading list reveals her preference for philosophical writings. This is evident in her letters, where there are many references to diverse philosophers, including Martin Heidegger* and Søren Kierkegaard.* We must emphasize that she returns again and again to such religious thinkers as Saint Thomas Aquinas and the Frenchman Jacques Maritain,* whom she quotes freely. Her favorite work of Maritain's was *Art and Scholasticism* (1920).

Critics frequently remark that Flannery O'Connor should be characterized as a religious writer. If this is true, it should be no surprise that the thinkers who influenced her most were religious writers, namely, Saint Thomas Aquinas and Maritain. Indeed, there is evidence in her letters that she was a writer who concerned herself with universal philosophical problems, and she turned to philosophy for answers to the religious questions that concerned her.

REFERENCES

Currie, Sheldon. "Freaks & Folks: Comic Imagery in the Fiction of Flannery O'Connor." *AntigR* (Summer–Fall 1985): 62–63, 133–42.
Fitzgerald, Sally, ed. *The Habit of Being: Letters of Flannery O'Connor*. New York: Random House, 1979.
Friedman, Melvin J., and Lawson A. Lewis, eds. *The Added Dimension: The Art and Mind of Flannery O'Connor*. New York: Fordham University Press, 1966.
Kinney, Arthur F. "Flannery O'Connor and the Fiction of Grace." *MR* 27, no. 1 (Spring 1986): 71–96. (Treatment of grace and God)

O'NEILL, EUGENE GLADSTONE. B. October 16, 1888, New York City, New York. D. November 27, 1953, Boston, Massachusetts. American dramatist.

As the son of an actor, Eugene O'Neill experienced an insecure childhood. He studied at Princeton University for one year and spent the next six years as a roving seaman. He contracted tuberculosis and, while confined to a sanatorium, began to write plays. O'Neill began his career as a playwright in 1916 by participating in the productions of the Provincetown Players. His first New York production came in 1920 with *Beyond the Horizon*. In *The Emperor Jones* (1920) and *The Hairy Ape* (1922) he experimented with classical tragedy, and the result was *Mourning Becomes Electra* (1931). He experimented with masks in *The Great God Brown* (1926) and a chorus in *Lazarus Laughed* (1926). During his last years, he produced *The Iceman Cometh* (1946) and *Long Day's Journey into Night* (published posthumously, 1956).

In his excellent biography of Eugene O'Neill, Barrett Clark stated that the most powerful influences on the young O'Neill were Friedrich Nietzsche,* August Strindberg (q.v.), and Frank Wedekind. It is interesting that Strindberg is mentioned—he was highly regarded by O'Neill as a playwright—because Strindberg had genius and temperament very similar to those of Nietzsche. If both playwrights were strongly influenced by Nietzsche's Dionysian** view of life, O'Neill never went to Strindberg's extremes, and his characters are usually not as psychotic as Strindberg's.

Eugene O'Neill was introduced to Nietzsche by Benjamin R. Tucker, who owned The Unique Book Store on New York's Sixth Avenue. The work was *Thus Spake Zarathustra* (1883). Overwhelmed by Nietzsche's philosophy, O'Neill stated later,

> *Zarathustra* . . . has influenced me more than any book I've ever read. I ran into it through the bookshop of Benjamin Tucker . . . when I was eighteen and I've always possessed a copy since then and every year or so I reread it and am never disappointed, which is more than I can say of almost any other book. (Recorded by Gelb and Gelb, 121)

According to Gelb and Gelb, *Thus Spake Zarathustra* became O'Neill's catechism; the playwright even tried to emulate Nietzsche's poetic style (Gelb and Gelb, 122). O'Neill's intense attraction to Nietzsche led him in his early years to two other disciples of the philosopher: William Lawrence, a Latvian Jew whose total luggage when he arrived in America in 1909 was a copy of *Zarathustra*, and Terry Carlin, who considered himself a Nietzschean superman.** Critics agree that, in *The Great God Brown*, the Faustian self-torturing character of Dion was directly influenced by Nietzsche. *Lazarus Laughed* was also influenced by Nietzsche inasmuch as it deals with the rebirth of Dionysus, affirms life, and denies death in true Nietzschean fashion. As Edwin A. Engel emphatically states, "*Lazarus Laughed* proved more conclusively than ever that he [O'Neill] was a disciple of Nietzsche" (Engel, 177).

In following Nietzsche's ideas on tragedy, O'Neill faithfully reinstated the "drunken Dionysus" of mythology by proposing dreaming and drunkenness as man's way to peace. Indeed, Eugene O'Neill followed directly in the footsteps of Nietzsche and Richard Wagner because he saw that the drama of the future must be one of feeling, not of reason and understanding. From Nietzsche he learned, at once, of human suffering and the affirmation of life.

Even a cursory look at O'Neill must not ignore Roger Asselineau's "Eugene O'Neill's Transcendental Phase," which convincingly argues that O'Neill was more Nietzschean than transcendentalist (see transcendentalism**). The characters in *Desire Under the Elms* (1925), for example, seem to Asselineau to be in search of a Nietzschean rather than a Christian god. Asselineau also finds an interesting expression of John Calvin's* notion of predestination**—figures trapped in existence, controlled, predestined (see *The Web*). Man's key to transcendence over his animal nature is Nietzschean passion. Transcendentalism in O'Neill is to be seen only in his contention that the individual in society is supreme. This affirmation of the supremacy of the individual is indeed a form of transcendentalism, but of Nietzscheanism as well.

REFERENCES

Asselineau, Roger. *The Transcendentalist Constant in American Literature*. New York: New York University Press, 1981.

Clark, Barrett H. *Eugene O'Neill: The Man and His Plays*. New York: New York University Press, 1982.

Engel, Edwin A. *The Haunted Heroes of Eugene O'Neill*. Cambridge, Mass.: Harvard University Press, 1953.

Fambrough, Preston. "The Tragic Cosmology of O'Neill's *Desire Under the Elms*." *EON* 10, no. 2 (Summer–Fall 1986): 25–29. (Sources in ancient Greek tragedy)

Gelb, Arthur, and Barbara Gelb. *O'Neill*. New York: Harper & Row, 1960.

Long, Deborah Marie. "The Existential Quest: Family and Form in Selected American Plays." *DAI* 47, no. 4 (October 1986): 1119A. (Treatment of existentialism**)

P

PASTERNAK, BORIS. B. February 10, 1890, Moscow, Russia. D. May 30, 1960, Peredelkino, Moscow, USSR. Russian poet and novelist.

Boris Pasternak studied music, then philosophy in Moscow from 1909 to 1912 and in Marburg, Germany, in 1912. He began publishing volumes of verse: *Twin in Clouds* (1914) and *Above the Barriers* (1917). In 1925 his book of short stories appeared. He spent some years translating English, notably Shakespeare, and German and French poets. In 1957, his masterpiece *Doctor Zhivago* appeared in the west but was banned in the USSR. Two years later he was awarded the Nobel Prize but turned it down because of pressure from Soviet authorities.

As a student at the University of Moscow, and later at the University of Marburg, Pasternak was immersed in the study of philosophy and to a lesser extent in literature, especially from 1909 to 1912. Although Henri Bergson* (whom Pasternak studied) was very popular at the University of Moscow, Pasternak was probably more influenced by the works of Edmund Husserl* and the Gottingen School, which was supported by a young lecturer named Gustal Shpet. Pasternak moved closer (in ideology) to the Marburg School and the influence of the neo-Kantian Hermann Cohen.* Prior to this, Georg Wilhelm Hegel* had been a central figure in Pasternak's philosophical studies. The Marburg School attracted him because it looked to the very foundations of philosophical thought to primary sources in the history of knowledge. In April 1912, with the financial aid and encouragement of his mother and a friend named Dmitri Samarin, Pasternak decided to go to the University of Marburg.

In his first semester at Marburg, Pasternak enrolled in three courses: ethics, taught by Hermann Cohen; logic, taught by Paul Nattera; and modern philosophy, presented by Nocolai Hartmann. All three professors had good reputations as capable philosophers, but the most prominent, and the one who influenced Pasternak the most, was Hermann Cohen. Cohen was undisputably the leader of the Marburg neo-Kantian School, and he had written three books on logic, ethics, and aesthetics. The Marburg School maintained that life and thought were based on immutable laws, and it saw the world as a coherent, orderly system. For these philosophers, whose influence guided Pasternak's thinking, "intuition and irrationality did not exist; sensation was not known but was an object for study; religion was no more than a system of morality and God an ethical ideal to be imitated on earth" (de Mallac, 62). The Marburg School was most faithful to Immanuel Kant,* but it did venture to seek a blending of Kantianism** with Marxism.**

Although Cohen was strongly opposed to Bergson's philosophy, Pasternak became attached to Bergson's concept of the élan vital,** which challenged the teachings of Auguste Comte.* The influence of Bergson is seen in some sections of *Doctor Zhivago* in which Pasternak, in describing the elemental life force, used images close to those used by Bergson. "Pasternak sounds most Bergsonian when he proclaims that automation in all its forms entails a refusal to progress spiritually and is the very antithesis of the spirit of continuous creation" (de Mallac, 292).

REFERENCES

Cornwall, Neil. *Pasternak's Novel: Perspectives of Doctor Zhivago*. Keele, England: Keele University Press, 1986.
de Mallac, Guy. *Boris Pasternak: His Life and Art*. Norman: University of Oklahoma Press, 1981.
Dyck, J. W. "Doctor Zhivago: A Quest for Self-Realization." *The Slavic and East European Journal* 6, no. 2 (1962): 117–23.
Kun, Agnes, and Tunde Vajda. "Memories of Pasternak." *NHQ* 27, no. 104 (Winter 1986): 90–109.

PETRARCH (FRANCESCO PETRARCHA). B. July 20, 1304, Arezzo, Italy. D. July 18, 1374, Arqua, Italy. Italian poet and scholar.

Petrarch's inquisitive mind and love of classical authors led him to travel; he visited men of learning and searched monastic libraries for classical manuscripts. He was recognized as the greatest scholar of his age. As poet and humanist (see humanism**), he paved the way for the Renaissance.**

Although it is recognized by Petrarchan scholars that he had, albeit eclectically (see eclectic**), studied classical philosophy, the question of the extent to which he incorporated ancient thought into his own philosophy has not been resolved. Charles Trinkhaus finds that Petrarch saw himself as a moral philosopher as well as a poet and historian; he described himself as *poeta theologicus*. Accepting Aristotle's* claim that poetry is more philosophical than history, Petrarch attempted, with apparent success, to establish in his poetry the new mode of philosophical consciousness emerging in the later Middle Ages and the early Renaissance and reflected in the work of Dante Alighieri (q.v.).

Petrarch's work reveals an eclectic borrowing from the writings of several Greek thinkers. He was impressed with Pythagoras,* whom he regarded as a moral reformer; Heraclitus,* whom he came to know through Seneca;* Socrates* and Plato,* about whom he learned from his reading of Marcus Tullius Cicero's* *Tusculan Disputations;* and finally Aristotle, of whom he seems to have read at least *The Nicomachean Ethics,* the *Rhetoric,* and portions of the *Metaphysics.*

In spite of the inadequacies of his knowledge of classical philosophy, Petrarch came to the awareness that the classical Greek thought—Plato, Aristotle, and the Stoics (see Stoicism**)—could be drawn upon to serve and clarify the Christian goal of salvation. It is perhaps this awareness that constitutes Petrarch's contribution to philosophy and to theological speculations.

REFERENCES

Bouwsma, William J. "The Two Faces of Humanism: Stoicism and Augustinianism in Renaissance Thought." In *Itinerarium Italicum,* edited by H. A. Oberman and T. A. Brady, Jr. Leiden, Netherlands: Brill, 1975.
Lerner, Robert E. "Petrarch's Coolness toward Dante: A Conflict of Humanisms." In *Intellectuals and Writers in 14th Century Europe,* edited by Piero Britani and Awaa Torti. Tübingen, West Germany: Narr, 1986. (Treatment of Plato and Aristotle)
Stylianos, Andrew John. "Petrarch's Aesthetics of Poetry." *DAI* 47, no. 1 (July 1986): 197A.
Trinkhaus, Charles. *The Poet as Philosopher: Petrarch and the Formation of Renaissance Consciousness.* New Haven: Yale University Press, 1979.

PLATH, SYLVIA. B. October 27, 1932, Boston, Massachusetts. D. February 11, 1963, London, England. American poet.

Sylvia Plath attended Smith College where she received her bachelor's degree in 1955. The following year she received her master's degree from Newham College, and in 1956 she married the English poet Ted Hughes.

Her first collection of poems, *The Colossos,* was published in 1960, and in 1963 she wrote *The Bell Jar,* an autobiographical novel. Plath separated from Hughes in 1962 and took a flat in London where she devoted herself compulsively to poetry. On February 11, 1963, she committed suicide. Her posthumous volumes of poetry include *Ariel* (1965), *Crossing the Water* (1971), and *Winter Trees* (1972).

Sylvia Plath was a confessional poet whose work served as a not entirely successful catharsis of her profound sense of estrangement, of alienation, of the absurdity** of (her) human existence. Isolation, anxiety, and despair are recurring themes in her poetry and place her precisely in the existentialist (see existentialism**) camp. In "Ocean 1212-W" she expresses her intense awareness of her solitary existence and a deeply felt sense of loneliness; in "Mirror" she cries, "I am solitary as grass." Plath's assertions of her personal freedom are paradoxically juxtaposed with her consciousness of suffering and of death against which she must define herself. Tortured by the anguished sense of the absurdity of her universe, from which she struggles to free herself, Plath draws for us in her poetry, replete with "concrete images of annihilation," a path to sure obliteration (Kumar, 74).

REFERENCES

Chatterji, Ruby, ed. *Existentialism in American Literature.* New Delhi, India: Arnold-Heinemann, 1983.
Hardy, Barbara. "The Poetry of Sylvia Plath." In *Women Reading Women's Writing,* edited by Sue Roe. Brighton, England: Harvester, 1987.
Inoue, Fumiko. "A Myth Survived: A Reading of Sylvia Plath's Collected Poems." *CEMF* 26 (February 1983): 33–56.
Kumar, Sukrita Paul. "Sylvia Plath: A Self in 'Halflighted Castles'." In *Existentialism in American Literature,* edited by Ruby Chatterji. New Delhi, India: Arnold-Heinemann, 1983.
Plath, Sylvia. *The Collected Poems,* edited by Ted Hughes. New York: Harper & Row, 1960.
Walburg, Lori. "Plath's 'Brasilia.' " *Expl* 44, no. 3 (Spring 1986): 60–62.

POPE, ALEXANDER. B. May 21, 1688, London, England. D. May 30, 1744, Twickenham, England. English poet.

Alexander Pope, the son of a wealthy Roman Catholic linen merchant, received his education at home. In 1705 he wrote his "Pastorals," followed by *An Essay on Criticism* (1711) and *The Rape of the Lock* (1712–1714), a witty mock epic that established his reputation as a major writer

and poet. Between 1713 and 1726, Pope occupied himself with the translation of Homer. In 1728, *The Dunciad* appeared, an amusing attack on
literary pedantry. His most interesting poetry includes his major philosophical poem, *An Essay on Man* (1733–1734), and a presentation of the
classics in Augustan guise, an example being "Imitation of Horace."
Pope is regarded as a major poet and satirist of the English Augustan
Period.

As an educated man of the eighteenth century, Pope was well aware
of the progress of philosophy in that era. He was profoundly influenced
by Sir Isaac Newton and was cognizant of the rationalist systems of
Gottfried Leibniz* and René Descartes.*

Pope's major philosophical poem, *An Essay on Man,* was inspired by
and modelled on *De Rerum Natura,* the great philosophical, didactic
poem of the noted Roman poet Titus Lucretius Carus (98–54 B.C.) As
A. D. Nuttall says, "the interesting exposition of the philosophy of
Epicureanism[**] lay within his [Pope's] grasp. So, in 1730, he set to
work" (Nuttall, 43). "Pope addresses his poem to Lord Bolingbroke as
Lucretius addressed *De Rerum Natura* to Memmius. Pope was an unsystematic thinker; Bolingbroke was a philosopher of sorts; *An Essay on
Man* is a philosophic poem . . . Bolingbroke, it is said, must be 'the key'
to the philosophy of the essay" (Nuttall, 48). There is a story that can
be traced back to a letter from Lord Bathurst in 1763 to James Boswell
in which he stated that *"An Essay on Man* was originally composed by
Lord Bolingbroke in prose, and that Mr. Pope did no more than put it
into verse" (Nuttall, 49). When Boswell told this story to Dr. Samuel
Johnson, the celebrated doctor refused to believe it. Indeed, in modern
criticism, Maynard Mack has pointed out that Pope assimilates what
Bolingbroke excludes, and there is evidence that Bolingbroke's philosophy that has come down to us is different from Pope's philosophy.
Nuttall speaks further of Mack's opinion of the poem and mentions other
possible sources that Pope might have used: "For Mack, *An Essay on
Man* is a rich tapestry of Stoic [see Stoicism**] and Christian elements,
an utterly traditional fabric in which Pope is on excellent terms with his
peers across the intervening centuries, easily echoing the sentiments of
[Blaise] Pascal[*] and [John] Milton[q.v.]" (Nuttall, 51).

There are clear indications of multiple philosophical sources in Pope's
An Essay on Man. When the poet says, "But vindicate the ways of God
to Man," he is moving into theodicy and the tradition of Saint Augustine*
and Leibniz, both of whom argued that, if the world is imperfect, evil
originates with man and free will. There are also indications throughout

the work that Pope goes back to the original model, namely Lucretius's *De Rerum Natura,* and periodically inserts ideas of Lucretius's master in philosophy, Epicurus* himself.

An Essay on Man is perhaps one of the most complex philosophical poems in the English language, for which Pope tapped a multitude of classical (pagan) and Christian philosophical sources.

REFERENCES

Mack, Maynard, ed. *Essential Studies for the Study of Alexander Pope.* Hamden, Conn.: Arvhow, 1968.

Nuttall, A. D. *Pope's 'Essay on Man.'* London, England: Allen and Unwin, 1984.

Patey, Douglas Lane. "Art and Integrity: Concepts of Self in Alexander Pope and Edward Young." *MP* 83, no. 4 (May 1986): 364–78.

Sena, John F. "Melancholy as Despair: Pope's Eloisa to Abelard." *HTR* 76, no. 4 (October 1983): 443–54.

Tillotson, Geoffrey. *Pope and Human Nature.* Oxford, England: Clarendon Press, 1963.

POUND, EZRA. B. October 30, 1885, Hailey, Idaho. D. November 1, 1972, Venice Italy. American poet, critic, and translator.

Ezra Pound attended the University of Pennsylvania, transferred to Hamilton College, and returned to the University of Pennsylvania for graduate work, which he did not complete. His earliest poetry and his first book of prose consisted of imitations of troubadour poetic forms; *The Spirit of Romance* (1916) is a study of the Provencal and Italian troubadour models of classical satire. He founded the imagist movement, insisting on the use of colloquial language, the free phrase rather than forced metrics, and clarity of image and metaphor. Pound settled in Paris, but then moved on to Italy, where he engaged himself in all areas of modern art and, oddly enough, in economic theory, about which he published several polemical tracts and which led to his espousal of Fascism in the 1930s. After World War II, because of his broadcasts of a series of programs on Italian radio addressed to Allied troops, Pound was brought to Washington, D.C. and charged with treason; however, he was declared unfit to stand trial and was sent to a federal mental hospital. In 1958, as a result of a concerted appeal by American poets, led by Robert Frost (q.v.), the charges were withdrawn; Pound was released and he returned to Italy where he died in 1972. In 1948 he was awarded the Bollingen Prize for the *Pisan Cantos* (1948). His major works include "A Lume Spento" (1908), "Riposte" (1912), "Cantos" I–XVI (1925), "A Draft of XXX Cantos" (1930), "Eleven New Cantos" XXXI–XLI

(1934), "Fifth Decade of Cantos" (1937), "Cantos" LII–LXXI (1940), "Cantos" (1948), *Pisan Cantos* (1948), and *Collected Poems* (1950).

Even a cursory review of the poetic works of Ezra Pound reveals a profound knowledge of and insight into ancient Chinese literature and philosophy. In a 1953 review, after the publication of his translation of the 300 odes of ancient Chinese under the title *The Classic Anthology Defined by Confucius,** Pound was hailed as "The Confucian poet." This master work and other poems written under the Chinese influence was evidence that the thought of ancient China had made an impact on him, and his aim was to convey to English readers an understanding of what a good Chinese poem was.

One Confucian concept that permeates Pound's writing and thinking is the principle of good. Pound once said that the principle of good was promulgated neither by Christianity nor by Judaism, but he admitted that the early Quakers may have had some idea of the good principle.

Of all the modern poets, there are few who have been so well read in the classics of both the western and eastern traditions. He was well versed in them all from Sophocles and Homer (he wrote an essay on the early translators of Homer) to Plato* and Aristotle.*

> Perhaps Pound was more aware than T. S. Eliot [q.v.] of the gradual closing down of vistas, the erratic removal from our literary consciousness of sometimes quite important areas of creation and thought—a melancholy fact which is obvious to some students of Shakespeare and ought to be to all students of classical literature. But this awareness, which shows itself in some of his negative appraisals, say of Pindar, is perhaps compensated by Pound's optimism about the modern poet's ability to revivify by critical insights areas apparently abandoned to oblivion and about the possibility of grafting on to our tradition viable branches of oriental art and thought. (Sullivan, 216)

Pound was a critical reader and an independent thinker, and he did not always agree with the great tradition of Greek philosophy. He took all philosophy seriously, but he was critical of the Greek philosophy that dealt with mere abstractions and had no connection with the real world. For this reason, Pound approved of Epicurus* and Pythagoras*: they advocated a mode of living that was practical to the world of men.

REFERENCES

Dekker, George. *Sailing after Knowledge: The Cantos of Ezra Pound*. London: Routledge & Kegan Paul, 1963.

Emery, Clark. *Ideas into Action: A Study of Pound's Cantos*. Coral Gables, Fla.:
    University of Miami Press, 1958.
Gordon, David. "The Great Digest: A Pattern." *Paideuma*. 14, nos. 2–3 (Fall–
    Winter 1985): 253–57. (Sources in Confucius)
Hesse, Eva, ed. *New Approaches to Ezra Pound*. Berkeley: University of Cal-
    ifornia Press, 1969.
Sullivan, J. P. "Pound and the Classics." In *New Approaches to Ezra Pound*,
    edited by Eva Hesse. Berkeley: University of California Press, 1969.

R

RAND, AYN. b. February 2, 1905, St. Petersburg, Russia. Naturalized U.S. citizen, 1931. D. March 6, 1982, New York City, New York. Russian-American novelist.

In 1926, after graduating in history from the University of Leningrad, Rand emigrated to the United States where she became a citizen in 1931. Her first novel *We The Living* (1936) deals with the Russian Revolution. This was followed in 1943 by the novel *The Fountainhead*. Rand's other works include *Atlas Shrugged* (1957), the nonfictional *The Virtue of Selfishness* (1965), *Capitalism: The Unknown Ideal* (1966), and *The New Left: The Anti-Industrial Revolution* (1970).

Ayn Rand stated that, since the weltanschauung** that she desired as a novelist was lacking in her contemporary intellectual milieu, she had turned to philosophy. Thus the blending of literary artistry and philosophy established for her a foundation from which she could express her vision of human life.

Ayn Rand's philosophical posture is essentially that of Aristotle* (see Uyl and Rasmussen, 3). She insists on the existence of a world of beings where "existence is identity" (Rand, *Introduction to Objectivist Epistemology*, 55). Furthermore, her Aristotelianism is similar to that of William of Ockham as described by E. A. Moody: "Ockham's Aristotelianism is indicated by his complete adoption of the thesis that the reason of the fact is the being of the things of which the fact is true. It is in defense of this principle that Ockham opposes the traditional 'real distinction' between essence and existence within finite things'' (Moody, 311).

It is not unrealistic to draw the conclusion that Saint Thomas Aquinas's* thinking on relations influenced Rand's formation of concepts. Douglas Uyl and Douglas Rasmussen also believe ''that she seems to agree with [Jacques] Maritain[*] that a concept must signify more than just what we explicitly consider and more than a collection of individuals'' (Uyl and Rasmussen, 15). Finally, Rand's theory of concepts, though unorthodox, makes progress toward a better understanding of what concepts signify.

Modern philosophers who contributed essays to the volume *The Philosophic Thought of Ayn Rand* express mixed feelings about her philosophy. Robert Hollinger, for example, is highly critical of Rand's epistemology, and he points out that philosophers like Quine, Witgenstein, and Dewey, whom she attacks, are Aristotelians as well. Rand's ethical theory receives high grades: ''It is our view that Rand's ethical teaching has given renewed fuel to a light once thought to be flickering for the last time'' (Uyl and Rasmussen, 78).

REFERENCES

Branden, Barbara. *The Passion of Ayn Rand*. New York: Doubleday, 1986.
Greenberg, Sid. *Ayn Rand and Alienation*. Los Angeles: Brideberg, 1977.
Moody, E. A. *The Logic of William of Ockham*. New York: Sheed & Ward, 1935.
O'Neill, William F. *With Charity Toward None: An Analysis of Ayn Rand's Philosophy*. Lanham, Md.: Littlefield, 1977.
Rand, Ayn. *Introduction to Objectivist Epistemology*. New York: New American Library, 1979.
Uyl, Douglas J., and Douglas B. Rasmussen, eds. *The Philosophic Thought of Ayn Rand*. Chicago: University of Illinois Press, 1984.

RANSOM, JOHN CROWE. B. April 30, 1888, Pulaski, Tennessee. D. July 3, 1974, Gambier, Ohio. American poet and literary critic.

John Crowe Ransom taught at Vanderbilt University from 1914 to 1937, and in the 1920s he became a part of the Nashville Fugitive Group which included such writers as Robert Penn Warren (q.v.) and Allen Tate. After his retirement from Vanderbilt, he accepted the editorship of the *Kenyon Review*. His early poems consisted of two volumes called *Chills and Fever* (1924) and *Two Gentlemen in Bonds* (1927). His poetic reputation rests on these poems. Eventually Ransom, interested in social problems, defended the values of the old south in such essays as *I'll Take My Stand; The South and the Agrarian Tradition* (1930) and *God without*

Thunder (1930). He argued the superiority of art over science in *The World's Body* (1938).

One does not find it surprising that John Crowe Ransom draws substantially from major philosophers, including Plato,* Immanuel Kant,* and Georg Wilhelm Hegel,* among others. Ransom had studied classics and philosophy at Christ Church in Oxford, and he was a Rhodes Scholar under the tutelage of the famous neo-Kantian philosopher Francis Bradley.* Ransom once said publicly that Kant was his mentor, but F. P. Jarvis claims that it is really Bradley whose influence affected Ransom's critical theories and that the awareness of Bradley's influence on Ransom is essential to the understanding of Ransom's critical theory (Jarvis, 206). Bradley's metaphysical** system describes man as living in a phenomenal (see phenomenology**) world in which his experiences are appearances of an absolute. We make judgments about our environment, but our conclusions may differ from those of others. The impact of Bradley's metaphysics on Ransom's thought is most evident in Ransom's attempt at theologizing in *God Without Thunder,* in which he questions the claim that science offers comprehensive knowledge of the world and expresses the conviction that poetry does. Science, for Ransom, provides a limited, partial view of the world, poetry the whole truth.

Solidly grounded in the philosophical tradition, especially of Plato (whose transcendentalism** he rejects), Aristotle,* Kant, and Bradley, Ransom's critical thought is perceived as a synthesis of carefully selected concepts which emerge finally as a poetically expressed worldview.

REFERENCES

Grigson, Geoffrey. "John Crowe Ransom." *New Verse* 16 (August–September 1935): 12–17.

Jarvis, F. P. "F. H. Bradley's *Appearance and Reality* and the Critical Theory of John Crowe Ransom." In *John Crowe Ransom: Critical Essays and a Bibliography,* edited by Thomas Daniel Young. Baton Rouge: Louisiana State University Press, 1968.

Koch, Vivienne. "John Crowe Ransom's Poetry." *The Sewanee Review* 56, 3 (Summer 1948): 378–90.

Winters, Yvor. *In Defense of Reason.* Denver, Colo.: Alan Swallow, 1947.

Young, Thomas Daniel, ed. *John Crowe Ransom: Critical Essays and a Bibliography.* Baton Rouge: Louisiana State University Press, 1968.

RILKE, RAINER MARIA. B. December 4, 1875, Prague, Austria-Hungary. D. December 29, 1926, Valmont, Switzerland. Austrian poet.

In 1898, Rainer Maria Rilke visited Italy where he became acquainted with the Danish novelist Jen Peter Jacobsen, whose writing influenced his own work. In 1849 and 1920 he travelled with Lou Andreas-Salome in Russia, where he felt himself to belong spiritually to the Slavic race. A collection of poems entitled *Stundenbuch* (1905) was the result of his travels in Russia. From September 1905 to May 1906, Rilke served as Auguste Rodin's secretary. In 1908, when his *New Poems* appeared, the influence of his days spent as secretary to this great sculptor became evident. His greatest poetic project, which was spread over a ten-year period, was the *Duino Elegies* (1923). This work was the result of a two-year stay at the castle at Duino of Princess Marie von Thurn. Rilke completed these major poems on February 11, 1922. A few days later, he completed *Sonnets to Orpheus*. Rilke's work has been highly regarded in German literature and has had a lasting influence on English poetry.

Rilke's name appears in the memoirs of many distinguished Europeans. He is another of the nineteenth-century poets who had an academic background that was steeped not only in literature, but also in art, philosophy, psychology, and the classics. This background was enhanced by a life that brushed shoulders with the artist Paul Valéry, the philosopher Rudolf Kassner, and the poet Georg Brandes, who was the earliest champion of Friedrich Nietzsche.* Kassner, who leaned to Eastern mysticism** was a close friend of Rilke's, as was Lou Andreas-Salome, who introduced Rilke to the teachings of Sigmund Freud* whom Rilke had recognized as a revolutionary in the understanding of men.

In 1887, while a student at Berlin, Rilke attended lectures in philosophy given by the philosopher Kurt Breysig, "who has been called the German Toynbee because of his theories of historical development" (Bauer, 24). In 1904, while living in Rome, Rilke learned Danish and then proceeded to read the works of Søren Kierkegaard* in the original.

Rilke once said that, except for a few pages of Arthur Schopenhauer,* he was unread in philosophy, but this was a modest statement since he had read Plato* and Henri Bergson* and had associated with philosophers like George Simm from whose book, *Rembrandt,* Rilke had gleaned his friend's ideas on death, especially the idea that death is an extension of life. The readers of Rilke's poetry must recognize then that he was a mystical and philosophical writer who had always concerned himself with philosophy and who was influenced by the pantheism** of Meister Eckehart,* by Nietzsche, Freud, Kierkegaard, and others.

REFERENCES

Bauer, Arnold. *Rainer Maria Rilke.* New York: Ungar, 1972.
Hamburger, Kate. *Rainer Maria Rilke.* Stockholm, Sweden: Orlag, 1949.

Prater, Donald. *A Ringing Glass: The Life of Rainer Maria Rilke*. Oxford, England: Clarendon Press, 1986.

Shaw, Priscilla. *Rilke, Valery and Yeats: The Domain of Self*. New Brunswick, N. J.: Rutgers University Press, 1964

ROETHKE, THEODORE. B. May 25, 1908, Saginaw, Michigan. D. August 1, 1963, Puget Sound, Washington. American poet.

Throughout most of Theodore Roethke's adult life, he was associated with the University of Washington, first as a lecturer, from 1947 to 1948, then as a poet-in-residence, from 1948 to 1962. His first book of poems, *Open House* (1941), was well received by the reading public and, together with *The Lost Son and Other Poems* (1949), established Roethke as a romantic poet with a proclivity for nature mysticism** which probably evolved from Roethke's reading of Ralph Waldo Emerson (q.v.) and Henry David Thoreau (q.v.).

In Theodore Roethke's 1957 collection of poems, under the title *The Waking*, he was influenced by such existentialist (see existentialism**) thinkers as Søren Kierkegaard* and Martin Buber* (Malkoff, 13). In the following year, 1958, he was again reading these existentialist writers, and in *Words for the Wind*, published in that year, he records his reflections on the nature of the self and of its being-in-the-world, an expression of the important role which mysticism began to play in Roethke's life. He studied Paul Tillich's questions on the nature of reality and echoed the Kierkegaardian tradition in accepting despair as an aspect of faith. Malkoff sums up Roethke's existential concerns, especially angst**:

> He [Roethke] wrote about himself as universal man, not only in the sense that he contained within him the history of his race, but also that as a man of his age he was tormented by its characteristic anxieties, its existential anguish, its apparently unbridgeable gulf between the material and spiritual. (Malkoff, 224)

Roethke was constantly concerned with being and non-being. For example, in the poem "Words for the Wind," the poet is able to "see and suffer myself in another being." This is similar to Martin Buber's ideas of the I-Thou relationship in which the identity of an individual recognizes the self in another individual. Facing the possibility of non-being causes anxiety, a thought which is expressed in "Fearful Night." Here, Roethke calls upon Parmenides,* Jakob Böehme, and Plato,* but, as Malkoff states, "his list of philosophers was of no use that night" (Malkoff, 131).

Stanley Kunitz, a close friend of Roethke, and Roethke's wife, both testify that Roethke had read Carl Jung* and that he was familiar with

Maud Bodkin's *Archetypal Patterns in Poetry*. It is not surprising then that "Night Crow" expresses the collective unconscious, the racial memory held in common by all humanity.

REFERENCES

Arnett, Carroll. "Minimal to Maximal: Theodore Roethke's Dialectic." *College English* 17 (May 1957): 414–16.
Malkoff, Karl. *Theodore Roethke: An Introduction to the Poetry*. New York: Columbia University Press, 1966.
Stein, Arnold, ed. *Theodore Roethke: Essays on the Poetry*. Seattle: University of Washington Press, 1965.
Winters, Yvor. "The Poems of Theodore Roethke." *Kenyon Review* 3 (Autumn 1941): 514–16.

ROUSSEAU, JEAN-JACQUES. B. June 28, 1712, Geneva, Switzerland. D. July 2, 1778, Paris, France. French philosopher, essayist, and novelist.

Jean-Jacques Rousseau had little formal education. He was brought up by an aunt, and at an early age he was apprenticed to an engraver, who treated Rousseau badly. In 1728 Rousseau left Geneva to seek his fortune elsewhere. He came into the patronage and friendship of a Mme. de Warens who influenced his conversion to Catholicism. A brief experience as a private tutor in Lyons in 1740 created in him a lifelong interest in education. In 1743 Rousseau was appointed secretary to the French ambassador at Venice. His literary career began in 1750 with the publication of "Discourse on the Sciences and the Arts." His other works include "Discours sur l'Origine de inegalité" (1755), "Lettre à d'Alembert sur les Spectacles" (1758), *Julie, ou la Nouvelle Heloise* (1761), *Émile* (1762), and *Contrat Social* (1762).

Rousseau is listed in Dagobert Runes' *Dictionary of Philosophy* as a political thinker who for many decades had an enormous influence on other writers especially with his two works *Émile* and *Contrat Social*. Rousseau was influenced not only by the early thinkers, Aristotle* and Plato,* but also by such contemporaries as René Descartes,* Gottfried Leibniz,* and John Locke.* Although he never mastered Greek, he knew Aristotle's works, and it has been said that his political thought owes more to Plato than to any other single philosopher.

Among Rousseau's political and social theories, many of which were inspired by Plato, was his theory of a second revolution. He based this on the progress in agriculture and the increased usefulness of metals. As a result, he claimed that men would seek to acquire more than they need, and the outcome would be a state of war.

Rousseau's most significant contribution was his *Contrat Social,* but it is often said that the title of the book overemphasizes the significance of the social contract for Rousseau's standing as a political thinker; and this is certainly true inasmuch as many philosophers from Plato onwards have used the idea of a contract, or something like it. In this respect, his thought is unoriginal, and his claim to particular notice can only rest on the fact that in contrast to thinkers like [Thomas] Hobbes,[*] who manipulate the idea in such a way as to include a primary and secondary contract in order to justify absolute monarchy, Rousseau clings to a firmly democratic interpretation, using a single legitimate contract and reducing the government to a mere executive body authorized by a reuseable commission. (Broome, 62–63)

Although it is true that Rousseau was thought to be responsible for revolutionary changes in education, there were many precedents in French literature, especially in the educational criticism of Michel de Montaigne whose writings were familiar to Rousseau.

In modern times, Rousseau has become more reputable and comprehensible, and modern writers like Bertrand de Jouvennal give Rousseau the place he deserves: "Rousseau is the first great exponent of social evolution. His was the first attempt to depict systematically the historic progress of human society. Here he comes a full century before [Friedrich] Engels and all the others who were to make the evolution of human society a popular theme" (reported by Einaudi, 7–8).

REFERENCES

Broome, J. H. *Rousseau: A Study of His Thought*. New York: Barnes and Noble, 1963.
Einaudi, Mario. *The Early Rousseau*. New York: Cornell University Press, 1967.

S

SARTRE, JEAN-PAUL. B. June 21, 1905, Paris, France. D. April 15, 1980, Paris, France. French philosopher, novelist, dramatist, and critic.

Jean-Paul Sartre graduated from the École Normale Supérieure in 1929; between 1931 and 1945, he was a teacher at the Lycée. His first novel was *La Nausée* (Paris, 1938, trans. R. Baldick, *Nausea,* Harmondsworth, 1965). Between 1936 and 1940, he published three monographs on the imagination and the emotions in the phenomenological (see phenomenology**) style of Edmund Husserl.* With the publication of his chief philosophical work *L'être et Le Néant* (Paris, 1943, trans. E. Barnes, *Being and Nothingness,* New York, 1956), Sartre emerged as the leading existentialist thinker (see existentialism**). He continued to influence French philosophical and literary circles with such publications as *Critique de La Raison dialectique* (Paris, 1960, trans. A. M. Sheridan-Smith, *Critique of Dialectical Reason,* London, 1976). An important play that demonstrated his existential theories is *Les Mouches* (Paris, 1943, trans. S. Gilbert, *The Flies,* London, 1946). As a literary critic, his most important work is *Qu'est-ce que la Litterature?* (Paris, 1947, trans. B. Frechtman, *What Is Literature?,* London, 1950).

Jean-Paul Sartre was a rare combination of philosopher, literary critic, and fine weaver of fiction. Although he was in his own right an independent thinker, as is the case with most philosophers, there were seminal influences upon him by the great thinkers of the ages.

Between 1936 and 1940, Sartre wrote four phenomenological studies in which he made Husserl's phenomenological description his own. The phenomenological movement had been spearheaded by Husserl and furthered by Martin Heidegger,* but it was Sartre who developed it into a systematic body of work from his own perspective. In his work *The Transcendence of the Ego* (1936–1937), he dropped the last remnants of the idealistic philosophy that still clung to Husserl. According to Benjamin Suhl, "Sartre would not conceive of any content to consciousness, finding it transparent through and through, nothing but experience of the world" (Suhl, 11). Sartre read George Wilhelm Hegel* and held to Hegel's concept of a truth that becomes a totalization in a historical process. He read Karl Marx* and accepted the Marxist concept of history as a succession of class struggles.

Sartre's name has become synonymous with French existentialism, and, although it is difficult to earmark the significant factors of Sartrean existentialism in a few words, several salient points must be mentioned. First of all, for Sartre, existence (the consciousness of being in the world) precedes essence. Second, in the concept of nothingness, Sartre follows Baruch Spinoza* and Hegel and argues that "every negation is determination" (*Being and Nothingness,* 16).

In his critical study of Sartre, Suhl sums up some of Sartre's accomplishments: "Sartre is one of those philosophers—writers, who, like [Blaise] Pascal,[*] [Søren] Kierkegaard,[*] Heidegger and others before him, have returned to what Husserl called 'the being that can be seized as it is originally.' More than any other, Sartre has bridged the dichotomy civilization has cultivated between sensation and thought" (Suhl, 265).

REFEENCES

Aron, Raymond. "Sartre's Marxism." *Encounter* (London), June 1965, 34–39.
Barnes, Hazel E. "Sartre as Materialist." In *The Philosophy of Jean-Paul Sartre,* edited by Paul Arthur Schilpp. La Salle, Ill.: Open Court, 1981.
Knight, Everett W. *Literature Considered as Philosophy: The French Example.* New York: Macmillan, 1958.
Sartre, Jean-Paul. *Being and Nothingness.* New York: Philosophical Library, 1956.
Suhl, Benjamin. *Jean-Paul Sartre: The Philosopher As a Literary Critic.* New York: Columbia University Press, 1970.

SCHILLER, FRIEDRICH VON. B. November 10, 1759, Marbach, Germany. D. May 9, 1805, Weimar, Germany. German poet, dramatist, and literary theorist.

The son of an army officer, Friedrich von Schiller was educated at a military academy. He, however, disliked the military, and at an early age he began to write poetry and drama. His first play, *die Räuber* (The Robbers), an attack on tyranny, was published in 1782 at Mannheim. Shortly after, he became house dramatist to the Mannheim National Theatre. During this period he wrote and produced two plays: *Kabale und Liebe* (Intrigue and Love) (1784) and *Don Carlos* (1787).

In 1787, Schiller went to Weimar, where, in 1794, he met and began a close friendship with Johann Wolfgang von Goethe (q.v.). This friendship and residence in Weimar mark the turning point in Schiller's career. With Goethe's recommendation, Schiller obtained a professorship at the University of Jena. At this time, he produced his great historical drama, *Wallenstein* (1800). His last plays were also historical dramas: *Maria Stuart* (1801), *Die Jungfrau von Orleans* (The Maid of Orleans) (1801), *Die Braut von Messina* (The Bride from Messina) (1803), and finally, his most popular play, *Wilhelm Tell* (William Tell) (1804).

Students of world literature know Schiller primarily as a playwright who produced such masterpieces as *William Tell* and *Wallenstein,* and German students think of him primarily as a German poet, second in German literature only to his close friend, Goethe. Perhaps only scholars see him as a minor philosopher, an aesthetician (see aesthetics**), and an authority on Kantianism.**

Schiller was familiar with many philosophers, among them, John Locke,* David Hume,* and Gottfried Leibniz,* and he was a friend and associate of Johann Gottlieb Fichte* and Friedrich Schelling*; however, he was most profoundly influenced by Immanuel Kant.* He began to study works of the German philosopher seriously in 1791, when he read the *Kritik der Urtheilskraft* (Criticism of the Power of Judgement) and saw immediately that his experience as a poet helped him to understand the work on aesthetic problems more easily. At this time, he wrote to a close friend, "I am now working on Kantian philosophy with great fervor . . . I have made an irrevocable decision not to stop with it until I have grasped it fully, even if it should take me three years. I have already absorbed a great deal and made it my own" (reported by Regin, 102). Indeed, this absorption of Kant's philosophy was difficult for Schiller since he was inadequately trained in philosophy, especially in Greek, medieval, and Renaissance** philosophy. Nevertheless, Schiller's understanding of complex, abstract philosophical concepts is evident in his philosophical treatises.

Schiller accepted most of Kantian philosophy, but he "made an audacious attempt to correct Kant's view that there could not exist an objective principle of esthetic taste" (Regin, 104). He learned much about freedom and morality from Kant, but the result of his studies was his own aesthetics.** *Über das Pathetische* (Concerning the Pathetic) deals with the aesthetic judgment of suicide; in *Über Anmut and Würde* (Concerning Beauty and Dignity) the idea of dignity as an expression of ethical freedom (Regin, 112) is developed; finally, in *Über Naive und Sentimentalische Dichtung* (Concerning Naive and Sentimental Poetry), his most popular prose essay, he moves from philosophy to literary criticism.

The question naturally arises here that, although the philosophical essays were the fruit of his Kantian studies, how much did these philosophical studies influence his drama and his poetry? The answer is that, in German literature, Schiller has long had the reputation of being a philosophical poet. This issue cannaot be explored here, but let it suffice to say that, as early as 1909, Dr. Arthur Kutscher referred to Schiller's poetry as *Ideen-Dichtung* (poetry of ideas) (Kutscher, intro., p. 2). Students of literature and scholars who are interested and would pursue this further might investigate such poems as "Die Götter Griechenlands" (Gods of Greece) (1788); "Die Künstler" (The Artists) (1789); "Die Ideale" (The Ideal) (1795), an example of the poet's self-expression, "Das Ideal und Das Leben" (The Ideas and Life) (1795); and "Der Spaziergang" (The Walk) (1795), which deals with nature.

REFERENCES

Berns, Giselaln. *Greek Antiquity in Schiller's Wallenstein*. Chapel Hill: University of North Carolina Press, 1985.
Kutscher, Arthur. *Schillers Werke*. Vol. I. Berlin: Deutsches Verlagshaus Bong, 1969.
Lloyd, Tom. "High Air-Castles: Carlyle's Reactions to Schiller's Aesthetics." *VIJ* 12 (1984): 91–104.
Regin, Deric. *Freedom and Dignity: The Historical and Philosophical Thought of Schiller*. The Hague, Netherlands: Martinus Nijhoff, 1965.
Sharpe, Lesley. "Schiller and Goethe's *Iphigenie*." *PEGS*. 54 (1984): 101–22.

SHAW, GEORGE BERNARD. B. July 26, 1856, Dublin, Ireland. D. November 2, 1950, Ayot St. Lawrence, Hertfordshire, England. Irish dramatist and critic.

George Bernard Shaw's grandfather was the sheriff of county Milkenny, and his father was a civil servant who later became a wholesale merchant. In his early years Shaw was tutored in the classics, attended several different schools in Dublin, and under his mother's influence exhibited a voracious appetite for literature, art, and music. In 1876, he followed his mother to London where he worked as a journalist, and between 1879 and 1883, he completed five novels for which he could not find a publisher. Under the influence of Henry George, Shaw became a dedicated socialist, and he joined the Fabian Society in 1884. He began his career as a dramatist in 1885, although he continued to promote the Fabian cause and to write music and drama criticism. After an indifferent reception of his first play, *Widower's Houses* (1892), Shaw began to win popularity with *Arms and the Man* (1894), *The Devil's Disciple* (1897), and *Candida* (1894). Shaw's place in literature is assured notably by his prodigious output of plays as well as his extensive, controversial prefaces, published separately in 1934. His most well-known plays include *Man and Superman* (1903), *Major Barbara* (1905), *Androcles and the Lion* (1911–1912), and *Pygmalion* (1912).

Shaw was a learned man who, in his thirties, read Francis Bradley* and Arthur Schopenhauer* and was familiar with Georg Wilhelm Hegel.* The theories of love in *Man and Superman* are based on Schopenhauer's; Shaw's biographer, Maurice Valency, states that its composition was influenced by Schopenhauer's notion that the principle of life is an irrational energy and that reality is revealed to us in our sense of the will. "For Schopenhauer the evolution of the will to live ends in extinction; for Shaw [in *Back to Methuselah* (1923)] it ends in omnipotence" (Valency, 205). Shaw was familiar with Auguste Comte's* positivism,** John Stuart Mill's* empiricism,** and Henri Bergson's* theories as well as with Hegel's. Valency says that "Hegel's system had special validity for Shaw, as the basis for Marxism[**], and Bergson's notions seemed so congenial that Shaw claimed them for his own without even troubling to examine them" (Valency, 209).

To understand certain of Shaw's works, one must realize that Shaw was a creative evolutionist (see creative evolution**) who believed, with Pierre Teilhard de Chardin,* in the life force, or spiritual energy. Shaw believed that man could control the life force to speed up evolution and thereby struggle (as Bergson says) toward perfection. In *Back to Methuselah,* Shaw's characters use the life force to prolong their lives for three centuries. Shaw believed that, given a longer life span, man could solve his social problems.

In *Back to Methuselah,* Shaw presents his theory of long life through the Brothers Barnabas. We find them still alive in the year 2170, solving the world's problems through the motivating force of the human will. Except for the speed of the evolutionary process found in Shaw's works, the "Shavian version of evolution does not differ radically from orthodox Darwinism[**]" (Smith, 108).

In *As Far As Thought Can Reach,* which is set in A.D. 30,000, his characters are immortal, or nearly so. In the manner of science fiction,

Shaw presents his "Ancients" as people who have lost all interest in corporeal reality and have reached the state of pure thought. In the play, Shaw presents the idea that acquired characteristics, like habit and social conditions, can be inherited through an act of the will. In these plays Shaw demonstrates his skill as a dramatist and as a social and a political theorist.

REFERENCES

Amalric, Jean-Claude. "B. Shaw: Man and Superman." *CVE* 24 (October 1986): 153–60.

Carpenter, Charles. *Bernard Shaw and the Art of Destroying Ideals*. Madison: University of Wisconsin Press, 1969.

Smith, Warren S. *Bishop of Everywhere*. University Park: Pennsylvania State University Press, 1982.

Valency, Maurice. *The Cart and the Trumpet: The Plays of George Bernard Shaw*. New York: Oxford University Press, 1973.

Whitman, Robert F. *Shaw and the Play of Ideas*. Ithaca, N.Y.: Cornell University Press, 1977.

SHELLEY, PERCY BYSSHE. B. August 4, 1792, Field Place, Sussex, England. D. July 8, 1822, Leghorn, Italy. English poet.

Percy Bysshe Shelley was educated at Eton College and University College, Oxford. He was expelled from Oxford in 1811 for publishing a pamphlet that defended atheism,** and eventually he settled in the Lake District where he met Robert Southey and the anarchist William Godwin,* whose political ideas greatly influenced him. Shelley devoted himself to philosophy and poetry. In 1814 he eloped with Mary Godwin, and the two toured France, England, and Switzerland. In 1818 Shelley settled in Italy where he wrote *Prometheus Unbound* (1818), *The Cenci* (1819), and "Ode to the West Wind" (1819). While sailing with Edward Williams on July 8, 1822, Shelley was caught in a storm and drowned. His ashes were buried in a Protestant cemetery in Rome.

It has been said that Shelley was perhaps one of the most avid readers who ever lived. His favorite readings were the Greek tragedians and Plato.* Until 1816, he read John Locke;* George Berkeley* to 1817; David Hume* to 1818; and William Godwin (the nearest to Shelley) to 1820.

Some biographers have divided Shelley's life into periods of idealism** and periods of radicalism, and certain readings of great thinkers seem to match these periods. Plato (whom Shelley called "the Greek of Greeks") was his favorite, and his works accompanied Shelley throughout his career. He had been reading Plato's philosophy of love when he wrote *Prometheus Unbound*. A year later, while completing the fourth act of

Prometheus, he turned to *The Republic*. Shelley's "Discourse of the Manners of the Ancients Relative to the Subject of Love" and translation of *The Symposium* resulted in the preface to his translation of *The Symposium* where he states that "Plato is eminently the greatest among the Greek philosophers."

There is no doubt that Shelley was aware of contemporary philosophy. His wife testified to the fact that her husband was very familiar with the philosophy of George Berkeley, and as early as 1813, Shelley had studied the writings of David Hume and John Locke. In 1816, he wrote the poem "Mont Blanc," which has long been marked by various critics as showing the influence of Berkeley, Plato, and Baruch Spinoza* (Barrell, 127).

Although Shelley was cognizant of the theories of modern philosophy, his writings extol what Joseph Barrell calls "the Greek way" and he adds "that Shelley is Greek and western in the phrasing of his thoughts, in the logic of his style" (Barrell, 178). Indeed, there is evidence that Shelley's pursuit of philosophical speculation, far from hindering, positively promoted the growth of his poetical talent.

REFERENCES

Barrell, Joseph. *Shelley and the Thought of His Time: A Study in the History of Ideas*. Hamden, Conn.: Archon, 1967.
Bloom, Harold, ed. *Percy Bysshe Shelley*. New York: Chelsea, 1985.
Butter, Peter. *Shelley's Idols of the Cave*. Edinburgh, Scotland: Edinburgh University Press, 1954.
Pules, C. E. *The Deep Truth: A Study of Shelley's Skepticism*. Lincoln: University of Nebraska Press, 1954.

SIDNEY, SIR PHILIP. B. November 30, 1554, Penshurst, Kent, England. D. October 17, 1586, Arnhem, Netherlands. Renaissance critic and poet.

Philip Sidney attended Shrewsbury School, Christ Church, and Oxford. In 1572, he travelled to Europe where he studied Latin, French, and Italian. His first court appointment was in 1576 as cupbearer to Queen Elizabeth I. In 1583 he was knighted. From his literary output there were two major works, *Arcadia* (1580) and *The Defence of Poesie* (1595). Sidney was the ideal gentleman of his age, a master of social graces, a politician, a military leader, and a scholar learned in the arts and sciences. Sidney died of wounds received in the campaigns against the Spaniards.

The poetry of Sir Philip Sidney reveals a thinker who was responsive to the political and moral issues of his time, "a poet to the depths of his nature'' (Myrick, 314). Deeply versed in the classical tradition, Sidney studied Plato's* (see Platonism**) dialogues, especially *Ion, Phaedrus,* and *The Republic;* he knew Aristotle's* *Poetics,* as well as *Ethics, Rhetoric,* and *Politics,* which he described as being "most worth reading" in a letter to a friend.

An understanding of Sidney's work demands a knowledge of the Renaissance** tradition, Greek and Roman literature, and the forces that eventuated in Protestant Christianity in its formative stages at the time that Sidney was writing. In *Arcadia,* for example, Aristotle's *Politics* and Xenophon's *Cyropaedia* are obvious influences. His treatment of love, in Book II of *Arcadia,* owes much to Aristotle, who classified love as neither a virtue nor a vice but rather a passion, and to Plato.

A man of his time, Sidney exhibits the characters of the Renaissance man, deeply schooled in the tradition of western thought, concerned with the major philosophical and religious issues of his day, and sensitive to the aesthetic aspects of the world in which he lived.

REFERENCE

Myrick, Kenneth. *Sir Philip Sidney As a Literary Craftsman.* Lincoln: University of Nebraska Press, 1965.

SINGER, ISAAC BASHEVIS. B. July 14, 1904, Radzymin, Poland. American novelist.

Issac Singer, recognized as one of the greatest contemporary Yiddish authors, was born into a family of Hassidic rabbis. Although he received the traditional Jewish education at the Warsaw Rabbinical Seminary, he decided to become a writer instead of a rabbi. His first novel, *Satan in Goray,* appeared in 1935, the year Singer fled to the United States in expectation of a Nazi invasion of Poland. For some time he worked as a journalist for the Yiddish newspaper *Jewish Daily Forward.* English translations of Singer's works are widely known in the English-speaking countries. Among his major novels are *The Family Moskat* (1945), *The Magician of Lublin* (1960), *The Slave* (1962), *The Manor* (1967), *The Estate* (1969), and *Enemies, A Love Story* (1972).

In the introduction to *Conversations with Isaac Bashevis Singer,* Richard Burgin describes Singer as "a remarkably honest man." The *Conversations* reveal as well that he is a scholar of considerable depth, not only in literature and theology, but also in the tradition of Western philosophy from the classical Greeks to the nineteenth- and twentieth-century philosophers. His work reveals a writer and thinker whose interests range from the ethical principles raised in the Talmud to mysticism,** materialism,** and contemporary social and moral issues.

Samuel Mintz tells us, "He [Singer] acclaimed as one of the greatest contemporary Yiddish writers, is an avid student of [Baruch] Spinoza[*] and has attempted in *The Spinoza of Market Street* (der Spinozist) an analysis of Spinoza's character." The work has been the subject of considerable critical attention.

> He [Singer] has evidently read the philosopher with care and with an accurate understanding. Spinoza is not an easy philosopher to read; ... but Singer has perceived very clearly the essential shape of Spinoza's mind. He understands that Spinoza's system embraces the whole universe and man's place in it and that it is a powerful vision of moral order, an order into which man can rise when he comprehends the universe under the aspect of eternity. (Mintz, 77)

Dr. Fichelson, the protagonist in the story, attempts to mold his mind and character after his master, Spinoza. Reason becomes for him the guiding principle; yet, as Mintz points out, Dr. Fichelson discovers during his life that the old cliche "the flesh is weak" is only too true. He discovers that the world is not rational as Spinoza would like it to be. "In it lurk evil presences" (Mintz, 77).

Singer's sometimes cynical perception of the romantic (see romanticism**) view of the human condition was wishful thinking. His admiration for Arthur Schopenhauer* is based, at least in part, on "his [Schopenhauer's] courage to be a pessimist [see pessimism**]" (Singer and Burgin, 83). He goes on to say, "Most philosophers tried one way or another to paint a beautiful universe and to give people hopes which were nothing more than wishful thinking. Schopenhauer had the courage to say that we are living in a world of evil" (Singer and Burgin, 83).

REFERENCES

Isenberg, Charles. "*Satan in Goray* and Ironic Restitution." *R & L* 18, no. 3 (Fall 1986): 53–69.

Kresh, Paul. *Isaac Bashevis Singer: The Story of a Storyteller*. New York: Dutton, 1984.

Maltz, Herman. "Point of View in Isaac Bashevis Singer's 'The Penitent.' " *ESA* 29, no. 2 (1986): 131–39.

Mintz, Samuel. "Spinoza and Spinozism in Singer's Shorter Fiction." *Studies in American Jewish Literature* 1 (1981): 75–82.

Singer, Isaac Bashevis, and Richard Burgin. *Conversations with Isaac Bashevis Singer*. New York: Doubleday, 1985.

Zeitlin, Aaron. "Aaron Zeitlin on Singer." Translated by Joseph C. Landis. *Yiddish* 6, nos. 2–3 (Summer-Fall 1985): 81–85.

SMOLLETT, TOBIAS. B. March 19, 1721, Cardross, Scotland. D. September 17, 1771, Leghorn, Italy. Scottish novelist.

In 1740, Tobias Smollett entered the navy as surgeon's mate and sailed to Jamaica where he met and probably married Anne Lassells. In 1748, after returning to England, he wrote a wonderful picaresque novel *The Adventures of Roderick Random,* which drew largely on Smollett's naval experiences. This success was followed by *The Adventures of Peregrine Pickle* (1751), another picaresque novel. In 1756, Smollett became editor of a Tory paper, *The Critical Review,* but a libelous article led to a short imprisonment, which became the subject of *The Adventures of Sir Launcelot Greaves* (1762). As a satirist and portrayer of comic characters, Smollett is unrivalled by his contemporaries in the early English novel.

In his *History of England* (1757), Smollett wrote: "Many ingenious treaties on metaphysics and morality appeared during the course of this reign [Geroge II], and a philosophic spirit of inquiry diffused itself" (reported by Bruce, 30). Thus Smollett exhibited a first-hand knowledge of philosophical thought because he was never far removed from the circle of philosophers who dominated the thinking of his era. He was the first to edit Voltaire's* work in English, and he was a close friend of David Hume,* the most influential philosopher of Smollett's time.

Smollett sided with John Locke* against the Cambridge Platonists (see Platonism**) who had followed Plotinus* in adopting the doctines of Plato's* *The Symposium* and *Phaedrus.* In his *Essay on the Human Understanding,* Locke denied the existence of innate ideas, maintaining that our direct contact with the world is limited to that of our sensations and that all understanding is derived from sense experience. The main aspect of Locke's philosophy that Smollett accepted was related to determinism.** There is a possibility that, in this area of philosophical thought, Smollett was influenced by his friend Hume.

Smollett was an ardent admirer of Hume and Voltaire, and he approved of Voltaire's exposition of Locke's doctrine on sensory perception. Conversely, Smollett had nothing but contempt for Gottfried Leibniz* and his optimism, and in *Peregrine Pickle* he satirizes the Neoplatonists (see Neoplatonism**) and their theory of innate ideas.

It is unlikely that Smollett ever adopted a formal system of philosophy; however, his incorporation of various aspects of the philosophies of Locke, Hume, and David Hartley* in his novels reveals a profound awareness and an understanding of philosophical tradition.

REFERENCE

Bruce, Donald. *Radical Doctor Smollett*. Boston: Houghton Mifflin, 1965.

SPENSER, EDMUND. B. 1552/1553, London, England. D. January 13, 1599, London, England. English poet.

Edmund Spenser was born in London and began his education at the Merchant Tailors School from which he went to Pembroke Hall at Cambridge. After completing his B.A. and M.A. degrees, he served as courier and secretary to several influential figures at court, including Sir Henry Sidney and the Earl of Leicester. His first major poem "Shepherd's Calendar," a series of twelve pastoral ecologues, was published anonymously in 1579. His satirical *Mother Hubbard's Tale* offended several influential figures and resulted in a political appointment in Ireland where he spent the remainder of his life. Of the projected twelve books of *The Faerie Queene,* a long, allegorical poem glorifying Elizabeth and England, only six books and a fragment of the seventh were completed. Spenser returned to London with his family in 1598 and died there in January 1599. He was buried in Westminster Abbey near Geoffrey Chaucer (q.v.).

Edmund Spenser, with a sensitive mind trained in the classics, is an excellent representative of the English Renaissance** thinker and author. He derived his Platonism** almost wholly through Italian channels and throughout his life maintained a veneration for Plato* and the ancient poets. One of the most important features of his masterpiece *The Fairie Queene* (1590) is allegory; Spenser had learned early from the Platonists that myth and allegory have infinite possibilities as themes for poetry. He compounded his scheme of allegorical devices on Aristotle's* ten virtues, enumerated in the *Ethics;* but, as B. E. C. Davis points out,

> his debt to Neoplatonic [see Neoplatonism**] sources was far more effective. The scheme of personified abstractions reacting upon each other is comparable with Plato's dramatic presentation of differing types of mind brought into relation or conflict and ultimately compelled to submit to the verdict of a superior intelligence. The whole conception of faeryland, the vision of a perfect world swayed by images of virtue that exist only in heaven, beyond the bounds of time and space, is the philosophy of ideas in romantic dress. . . . It may be safely asserted that, without Plato and the Platonists, *The Fairie Queene* would never have reached its present form. (Davis, 109–10)

The influence of Lucretius,* Boethius,* and Renaissance Platonists is also to be found in Spenser's work. Spenser's references to the one deity worshipped by all, the Venus Cenetrix, he borrowed most likely from Lucretius's verses in *De Rerum Natura;* but the major concepts extracted from Lucretius deal with the ideal of self-control and an indifference to death and calamity.

Spenser was influenced by his contemporaries as well as by the ancients. Giordano Bruno* was in England between 1583 and 1585, and, according to Spenser's biographer Davis, Spenser

> was the first English writer, by nearly half a century, to show any traces of his [Bruno's] influence in the domain of natural philosophy . . . the similarity both in thought and phrasing is sufficiently distinct to suggest that Spenser was acquainted with the two Italian dialogues, *La Cend de le Ceneri* and *Della Causa, Principio et uno,* in which Bruno developed his philosophy of nature. (Davis, 235, 236)

Spenser tapped many classical sources, and his studied eclecticism (see eclectic**) produced a critical view of life reflective of the intellectual climate of his time.

REFERENCE

Davis, B. E. C. *Edmund Spenser, A Critical Study.* New York: Russell and Russell, 1962.

STEVENS, WALLACE. B. October 2, 1879, Reading, Pennsylvania. D. August 2, 1955, Hartford, Connecticut. American poet.

On leaving Harvard University in 1900, Wallace Stevens began to contribute poems to the *Monthly* and *Advocate.* For a while, he tried his hand at journalism in New York and finally became a lawyer in 1904. His first book of poems, *Harmonium* (1923), was not well received. He wrote little for several years but became more prolific and popular in the 1930s with *Ideas of Order* (1935.) His *Collected Poems* appeared in 1954. His poetry is speculative and meditative and often betrays a dissatisfaction with American life.

Wallace Stevens's biographers constantly make references to his interest in philosophy, and in the last decade the question had been raised as to whether he was a philosophical poet. In any case, he was well read in philosophy, and in his prose work *The Necessary Angel* (1951), a collection of essays dealing primarily with poetry, he does make such specific references to philosophers that his knowledge of their teaching is obvious.

In the first essay of *The Necessary Angel,* Stevens acknowledges the

influence of two widely accepted philosophers in modern aesthetics**:
I. A. Richards and Benedetto Croce. The essay, however, develops from
a discussion of Plato's* figure of the charioteer traversing the heavens,
a figure expressing the nobility of the soul. Stevens accepts Henri Bergson's* notion of reality as a perceptual flux: "Bergson conceived of the
world as a single organism, continually evolving, and containing within
it innumerable small organisms, each sharing in the life principle of the
whole" (Peterson, 67). Bergson offers an organic world in which the
artist is supreme. "For the most part, Stevens's most obvious reliance
upon Bergson is in his stress upon change and upon the poet's ability to
express the novelty of the moment" (Peterson, 71).

There are two other Harvard philosophers to whom Stevens alludes
with respect: William James* and George Santayana.* It should be mentioned here that Stevens's poem "To an Old Philosopher in Rome" was
about Santayana. One may be tempted to read the poem in a Christian
context, but the biographical facts are that it is a tribute by an atheist
poet to an atheist (see atheism**) philosopher. Finally, an example of
William James's influence occurs in Stevens's first volume of poems,
Harmonium. The major themes of *Harmonium* are the loss of Christian
faith and traditional values and the philosophical position of idealism**
and materialism.**

The attentive reader of Wallace Stevens's essays and poetry cannot
help but see philosophy as a central component of his poetry. "At the
very least, Stevens's poetry has exposed something of the philosophical
heritage of modern aesthetics" (Peterson, 161).

REFERENCES

Beehler, Michael T. "Kant and Stevens: The Dynamics of the Sublime and the
    Dynamics of Poetry." In *The American Sublime,* edited by Mary Ar-
    ensberg. Albany: State University of New York Press, 1986.
Doggett, Frank. *Stevens: Poetry of Thought.* Baltimore, Md.: Johns Hopkins
    University Press, 1968.
Imber, Jonathan B. "The Vocation of Reason: Wallace Stevens and Edmund
    Husserl." *Humans* 9, no. 1 (1986): 3–19. (Relationship to phenom-
    enology**)
LaGuardia, David M. *Advance on Chaos: The Sanctifying Imagination of Wal-
    lace Stevens.* Biddeford, Me.: University Press of New England, 1983.
Peterson, Margaret. *Wallace Stevens and the Idealist Tradition.* Ann Arbor:
    University of Michigan Research Press, 1983.
Stevens, Wallace. *The Necessary Angel: Essays on Reality and the Imagination.*
    New York: Knopf, 1951.

STRINDBERG, AUGUST. B. January 22, 1849, Stockholm, Sweden. D. May 14, 1912, Stockholm, Sweden. Swedish dramatist, novelist, and critic.

After surviving a difficult and insecure childhood, August Strindberg entered the University of Uppsala but left without taking a degree to become a free-lance writer. His three unhappy marriages increased his misogyny which is demonstrated in several of his plays. In the realm of drama, Strindberg excelled in historical plays, tragedy, dream plays, and fairy tales. Early in his career he wrote the successful *Master Olaf* (1882). From 1875 to 1877 he produced many short stories and dramas, which were in keeping with naturalistic doctrines (see naturalism**). Some of his most important works are *Dance of Death* (1901), *To Damascus* (1898), *A Dream Play* (1902), and *The Ghost Sonata* (1907), in which he experimented with expressionism** and surrealism.**

August Strindberg's work reflects a profound acceptance of the naturalist view that one's life is the product of heredity and environment, a view established and promulgated by nineteenth-century writers in response to the work of thinkers from Arthur Schopenhauer* to John Lyle and Charles Darwin.* Between 1887 and 1901, the influence of Darwin and Schopenhauer helped Strindberg to produce four major naturalist plays: *The Father* (1887), *Miss Julie* (1888), and *Dance of Death,* which deal with Emile Zola's "slice of life" and characterize the lower classes as victims of their environment.

From Schopenhauer, Strindberg derived his pessimism** and from Nietzsche the glorification of the superman** and "the will to power." In *The Father,* Strindberg created a Nietzschean character, a superior, "civilized" human being. The captain is a strong man who believes that women, including his wife, Laura, are inferior and must be looked after. Ironically, Laura is also a superior person who wants to control everything and everyone in her environment.

For a time, Strindberg corresponded with Nietzsche, and Strindberg's biographer, Elizabeth Sprigge, mentions that Strindberg had sent a copy of *The Father* to Nietzsche: "It amazed Nietzsche to find his own conception of love-hatred so powerfully expressed" (Sprigge, 120).

> At first, critics regarded *By the Open Sea* (1913) as the most conspicuous expression of Strindberg's "Nietzscheanism." But subsequent scholarship makes it clear that the ideology represented by Inspector Borg in *By the Open Sea* (1913) is essentially different from the philosophy of the mature Nietzsche. Even though the atmosphere occasionally recalls Nietzsche, it really derives from a positivistic and pessimistic outlook that is more likely to suggest Max Nordau and Schopenhauer. (Brandell, 57)

In fact, Schopenhauer had as much influence on Strindberg as did Nietzsche: "in Schopenhauer and [Edward von] Hartmann, his philosophical masters when he was young, he had become acquainted with ideas that stemmed from the prescientific traditions of natural philosophy. Through them he found the road back to Aristotle[*] and to Ionion natural philosophy" (Brandell, 183).

In the realm of religion, Strindberg was a pessimist to whom salvation was never a certainty. This pessimism, probably derived from Schopenhauer, was expressed in three essays composed in 1864. In these he depicted a life of pain, salvation as illusory, and happiness beyond the reach of man. "Christianity, as Strindberg understood it, is not very far from philosophical pessimism, which he was later to embrace. In fact, in his old age, he readily spoke of Schopenhauer as a disciple of Christ" (Brandell, 13).

REFERENCES

Bellquist John Eric. "Strindberg's Father Symbolism, Nihilism, Myth." *MD* 29, no. 4 (December 1986): 532–43.

Brandell, Gunnar. *Strindberg in Inferno*. Cambridge, Mass.: Harvard University Press, 1974.

Greenway, John L. "Strindberg and Suggestion in *Miss Julie*." *SoAR* 51, no. 2 (May 1986): 21–34. (Relationship to science)

Mitchell, Stephen A. "The Path from *Inferno* to the Chamber Plays: *Easter* and Swedenborg." *MD* 29, no. 2 (June 1986): 157–68.

Sprigge, Elizabeth. *The Strange Life of August Strindberg*. New York: Macmillan, 1949.

STYRON, WILLIAM. B. June 11, 1925, Newport News, Virginia. American novelist.

After serving three years in the U.S. Marines, William Styron attended Duke University and graduated in 1947. While living in New York, he wrote his first novel, *Lie Down in Darkness* (1951), which won for Styron the Prix de Rome. He was recalled into military service during the Korean War, and *The Long March* (1953) was the literary result of this experience. Styron's third novel, *Set This House on Fire* (1960), deals with an American expatriate in Italy. In 1979, Styron wrote *Sophie's Choice*, a powerful and popular novel that explores the nature of evil through the story of a young writer and his relationship to two doomed lovers. Styron's major work, *The Confessions of Nat Turner* (1967), which won him the Pulitzer Prize in 1968, is a controversial fictionalized version of the 1831 revolt of Nat Turner and a small band of fellow slaves in Virginia.

The existentialist content (see existentialism**) in William Styron's novels has been addressed by several critics, including Lewis Lawson, Robert Gorham Davis, David L. Stevenson, and John Howard. Lawson argues that *Set This House on Fire* is a direct product of Søren Kierkegaard's* *The Sickness unto Death:* "only when Cass Kinsolving, the protagonist, is viewed as a Kierkegaardian man of despair does his life take on enough significance to justify its full presentation. For although he seems unaware of it, Kinsolving's descriptions of his thoughts and actions during his exile in Europe are couched in Kierkegaardian terms" (Lawson, 98). The influence of Kierkegaard is readily apparent in Styron's work, not only in his use of Kierkegaardian theories, but also in his borrowings of such expressions as "self-loathing" and "sick unto death."

In fact, Styron takes his character Kinsolving through Kierkegaard's stages of despair and leads him painfully to faith, which is Kierkegaard's only solution to despair. In *The Sickness unto Death,* the Danish philosopher explains that there are two types of despair: despair where the person is not conscious of the state and "despair viewed under the aspect of consciousness" (Kierkegaard, 8). Kinsolving, at various times, suffers from both types of despair, and his state is described in Kierkegaardian images.

In the novel, Styron applies Kierkegaard's theory of "the immediate man," placing the character in a state of immediacy, in which he experiences false happiness, a Kierkegaardian state of despair. Styron's use of Kierkegaard's terminology and concepts contribute significantly to the success of the novel.

REFERENCES

Casciato, Arthur D., and James L. W. West. *Critical Essays on William Styron.* Boston: C. R. Hall, 1982.
Kierkegaard, Søren. *The Sickness unto Death.* Translated by Hanny Alistair. New York: Penguin, 1989.
Lawson, Lewis. "Cass Kinsolving: Kierkegaardian Man of Despair." In *Critical Essays on William Styron,* edited by Arthur D. Casciato and James L. W. West. Boston: C. R. Hall, 1982.
West, James L. W. III., ed., and William Styron, Foreword. *Conversations with William Styron.* Jackson: University of Mississippi Press, 1985.

SWIFT, JONATHAN. B. November 30, 1667, Dublin, Ireland. D. October 19, 1745, Dublin, Ireland. Irish poet and satirist.

Born of Anglo-Irish parents, Jonathan Swift was educated in Ireland at Trinity College. For some time he was a literary assistant to Sir William

Temple. By 1704, Swift had published two of his first important satires: *A Tale of a Tub* and *The Battle of the Books*. By 1713 he had become disenchanted with Whig policies and had allied himself with the Tory party, whose leading writer he became. The famous essay "A Modest Proposal" appeared in 1729, and in 1726 his masterpiece *Gulliver's Travels* was published. To this day, he is considered the greatest satirist in the English language.

Jonathan Swift's satire not surprisingly exhibits a substantial knowledge of philosophical literature. His training in the classics enabled him to use classical models for his own purposes, and he found these purposes in his critical perceptions of several aspects of the social, political, ecclesiastical, and philosophical milieu of his time, as well as in classical literature. *The Battle of the Books,* in which Aristotle* shoots an arrow, which misses its mark, at Francis Bacon,* and *Redarqutic Philosophiarum* (Refutation of Philosophers) are cases in point.

His regard for Bacon is quite clear; he respected and praised Bacon as "the learned and incomparable author," "the Patriarch of Experimental Philosophy," a monument of human learning (Vickers, 92). But even Bacon was not free from the jibes of the satirist for, as we see in *A Tale of a Tub,* Swift associated Bacon with the absurdities of the modern author and satirized Bacon's use of the Renaissance** division of the intellectual faculties. "[I]n *A Tale of a Tub* Bacon and his followers take quite a beating" (Vickers, 99).

Swift's critical posture found an ally in Thomas Hobbes* to whom he owed more than he may have realized. Hobbes's pessimistic (see pessimism**) view of human nature was expressed in his description of the life of man as one of "continual fear, and danger of violent death, solitary, poor, nasty, brutish and short" (*Leviathan,* 82). Swift's biting satire, however, rarely went to such extremes. In fact, Swift probably had more in common with John Locke* than he did with Hobbes. That Swift approved of Locke's metaphysical** speculations is clear in his use of Lockean concepts in his works.

REFERENCES

Harth, Philip. *Swift and Anglican Rationalism: The Religious Background of "A Tale of a Tub."* Chicago: University of Chicago Press, 1961.
Hobbes, Thomas. *Leviathan,* edited by M. Oakeshott. New York: Penguin, 1982.
Hunting, Robert. *Jonathan Swift.* Boston: Twayne, 1967.
McKenzie, Gordon. "Swift, Reason and Some of its Consequences." In *Five Studies in Literature,* edited by Bertrand H. Bronson. New York: Roth, 1978.

Quintana, Ricardo. *The Mind and Art of Jonathan Swift.* Gloucester, Mass.: Peter Smith, 1965.

Vickers, Brian, ed., *The World of Jonathan Swift.* Cambridge, Mass.: Harvard University Press, 1968.

T

THOREAU, HENRY DAVID. B. July 12, 1817, Concord, Massachusetts. D. May 6, 1862, Concord, Massachusetts. American essayist.

Henry David Thoreau was educated at Harvard University and after
he graduated he began an unsuccessful career in teaching. Thoreau was
a friend of Ralph Waldo Emerson (q.v.) and other famous New England
transcendentalists (see transcendentalism**). In 1845 Thoreau moved into
a cabin at Walden Pond where he lived a solitary life until 1847. His
experiences at Walden Pond he recorded in *Walden: Life in the Woods*
(1854). One of his most famous essays is "Civil Disobedience" (1849).
A confirmed abolitionist, Thoreau lectured against slavery. He is sometimes regarded as a practical philosopher, one who lived and recorded
the doctrines of transcendentalism.

During his college years at Harvard, Thoreau, although his major
interest was literature, read German transcendentalism, immersed himself
in the writings of Thomas Carlyle (q.v.), and accepted the doctrine that
one must search for that work which fits him best and dedicate himself
to it.

Although Thoreau read the works of Confucius* as early as 1839, his
critics agree that he was no Confucian. However, through his reading of
the Chinese philosopher, he came into contact with Taoist teaching. John
Emerson argues that there is evidence for the affinities between Thoreau
and the Taoist philosophers, namely, the devotion to nature, hostility to
social convention, and a suspicion of philanthropists and reformers.

Through Emerson Samuel Taylor Coleridge (q.v.), Thoreau came to a knowledge of Emanuel Swedenborg* and Neoplatonism.** It is also mentioned in several biographies (see LeBeaux, Emerson) that Thoreau was familiar with Hinduism.** Although Thoreau was neither Confucian nor Hindu, the Oriental influences on his thinking must not be minimized. The philosophical influences on Thoreau are quite varied and range from Emersonian transcendentalism to Hinduism. The result of it all, according to John Emerson, is that "Thoreau, while not a completely perfected sage, is recognizably a traveller on the mystic path" (Emerson, 9).

As a young man, Thoreau found the quest for identity an agonizing one. A dedicated disciple of Emerson, with whom he lived and worked for a period of time, he sought individual growth through an adherence to Emerson's transcendentalism. The acceptance of transcendental idealism** was natural for Thoreau, who rejected material success and who reveals himself in works like *Walden* as one of the most conscientious and independent of men. In conforming to the ideology of the transcendentalist, Thoreau glorified nonconformity and self-reliance. Under Emerson's tutelage, Thoreau developed as a writer and transcendentalist, and he identified himself with Johann Wolfgang von Goethe (q.v.) Carlyle, Michel dé Montaigne, and Lord Byron.

REFERENCES

Canby, Henry Seidel. *Thoreau*. Boston: Houghton Mifflin, 1939.

Dombrowski, Daniel A. *Thoreau the Platonist*. New York: Peter Lang, 1986. (Sources in Plato)

Emerson, John. *Thoreau's Construction of Taoism.'' Thoreau Quarterly Journal* (1980): 5–12.

LeBeaux, Richard. *Young Man Thoreau*. Amherst: University of Massachusetts, 1977.

Porte, Joel. *Emerson and Thoreau: Transcendentalists in Conflict*. Middletown, Conn.: Wesleyan University Press, 1965.

Richardson, Robert D. *Henry Thoreau: A Life of the Mind*. Berkeley: University of California Press, 1986.

Spiller, Robert, ed. *Literary History of the United States*. New York: Macmillan, 1953.

TOLSTOY, LEO. B. September 9, 1828, Yasnaya Polyana, Russia. D. November 20, 1910, Astapovo, Russia. Russian writer.

Leo Tolstoy intended for his writings to bring about social reform. An opponent of all social institutions, he believed change had to begin with the individual. His major novels were *Anna Karenina* (1876), *The Kreutzer Sonata* (1890), and *War and Peace* (1868). Tolstoy has long been regarded as one of the greatest internationally recognized world authors.

There is an excellent quote by Ernest J. Simmons that sums up Tolstoy's attitude toward philosophy: "Philosophy was an intellectual brew that Tolstoy always stirred the wrong way. He was hostile to systems of thought or to systems of any sort" (Simmons, vol. I, 328). During his university years, Tolstoy read Voltaire,* but his skepticism** had no effect on the Russian writer. He also read Georg Wilhelm Hegel,* but he firmly rejected Hegel's assumption of civilization's progress. "He was already developing a philosophy hostile to the pragmatic ideal that progress could be achieved only by social education of the people through the medium of democracy" (Simmons, vol. I, 220).

> Hegel's words struck him as an "empty collection of phrases," but in August 1869 he wrote to his friend, "Do you know what this summer has been for me? An endless ecstasy over [Arthur] Schopenhauer,[*] and a series of mental pleasures such as I've never experienced before. I have bought all his works and have read and am reading them (as well as [Immanuel] Kant's[*]) . . . I do not know whether I shall ever change my opinion, but at present I'm confident that Schopenhauer is the greatest genius among men." And he concluded with an offer to collaborate with Fet on a translation of Schopenhauer. (Simmons, vol. I, 328)

The author who influenced Tolstoy during his university years and had a permanent influence on his thought was Jean-Jacques Rousseau (q.v.). He read Rousseau's complete works and found Rousseau's thoughts to be so similar to his own that it seemed as though he had been the author of many of Tolstoy's pages. Tolstoy admitted that Rousseau's *Confessions* (1778) had a "very great" influence on him and that *Julie, ou la Nouvelle Heloise* (1761) and *Émile* (1762) had an "enormous" influence. He could be critical of Rousseau, however. The fundamental difference between them was that Rousseau repudiated all civilization, whereas Tolstoy rejected only what he referred to as pseudo-Christianity. He wrote: " . . . will devote the rest of my life to drawing up a plan for an aristocratic, selective union with a monarchical administration on the basis of existing elections. Here I have an aim for a virtuous life. I thank thee, O Lord. Grant me strength" (reported by Simmons, vol. I, 104). In 1856, Tolstoy wrote a moralistic (Rousseauean) tract called "Lucerne," in which he developed his notions of the beauty of primitive art and the opposition of nature to government and civilization.

The scope of Tolstoy's study of philosophy is revealed in a statement which he made to an admirer in 1905:

Having read not only Marcus Aurelius [Antoninus],[*] Epictetus,[*] Xenophon, Socrates,[*] and Brahmin, Chinese, and Buddhist wisdom, Seneca,[*] Plutarch, [Marcus Tullius] Cicero,[*] but also the later ones:
Montaigne, Rousseau, Voltaire, Lessing, Kant, Lichtenberg, Schopenhauer, [Ralph Waldo] Emerson [q.v.], Channing, Parker, Ruskin, Amiel
and others, I've become more and more surprised and horrified at the
ignorance, at the "cultured" barbarism in which our society is steeped.
(Reported by Simmons, vol. II, 370)

REFERENCES

Edel, Leon. "Dialectic of the Mind: Tolstoy." In *The Modern Psychological
    Novel,* edited by Edel. Gloucester, Mass.: Smith, 1972.
Jamosky, Edward. "Moral and Philosophical Problems of Military Life in the
    Early Writings of Leo Tolstoy." *PKFLG* 4, no. 1 (1986):44–52. (Treat-
    ment of philosophy)
Sherman, David J. "Philosophical Dialogue and Tolstoy's *War and Peace.*"
    Slavic and East European Journal 24 (1980):14–24.
Simmons, Ernest J. *Leo Tolstoy.* Vol. I (1823–1879). New York: Vintage, 1960.
———. *Leo Tolstoy.* Vol. II (1880–1910). New York: Vintage. 1960.

TROLLOPE, ANTHONY. B. April 24, 1815, London, England. D.
December 6, 1882, London, England. English novelist.

Anthony Trollope wrote a series of books with the imaginary setting
of the county of "Barsetshire." He also wrote novels of political life,
which were convincing and successful. He was educated at the public
schools of Winchester and Harrow. From 1834 to 1841 he was a junior
clerk at the General Post Office but luckily was transferred as a postal
surveyor to Ireland, where he began to enjoy a social life. *The Warden*
(1855), his first novel, is a penetrating study of a warden of an old people's
home. His most famous novel, *Barchester Towers,* appeared in 1857
followed by *Doctor Thorne* (1858) and *Framly Parsonage* (1861). *Barchester Towers* excels in memorable characters and depicts well the landed
aristocracy.

Between 1877 and 1880, Trollope, displaying mature thought and great
artistic power, wrote a two-volume study of Marcus Tullius Cicero.* It
is a deliberate piece of scholarship of the man whom Dagobert Runes
describes as "[f]amous for his eclectic exposition of general scientific
knowledge and philosophy, by which he aimed to arouse an appreciation
of Greek culture in the minds of his countrymen, the Romans" (Runes,
56).

While conducting the necessary research for his biography of Cicero,
Trollope made himself completely familiar with Cicero's works; and

Trollope's biographer, Ruth Aproberts, emphasizes how much Trollope incorporated the ideas from Cicero's works into his own novels.

Cicero's philosophy, which is probably the most important aspect of Trollope's study, reflects Trollope's own philosophical interest and his intellectual attitude. Apparently, some critics have made slurs about Trollope as a nonthinker, but Aproberts jumps to his defense on this issue:

> Some of the comments on Trollope as non-thinker seem to imply that we expect a systematic philosophy from any artist worth his salt. Professional philosophers do not, as far as I can see, expect so much from philosophy. I think it can be shown that Trollope's own position consists in "anti-systematism," and that it is a deliberate, considered position, and that it is in itself basic to an extraordinarily humane artistic product. (Aproberts, 65)

If it is difficult to assess Trollope's involvement in philosophy, so is it equally difficult to assess his mentor Cicero's position as philosopher. We have already quoted Runes who categorized Cicero's works as eclectic in nature, and this can be explained. One of Cicero's aims was to make the ideas of the prolific Greek thinkers available to his countrymen. Therefore, Cicero often wrote summaries of Greek philosophy and added his own comments. It might not be commonly known that Cicero became the source of much late Greek philosophy for western civilization, and, "because Cicero has given us the greater part of our philosophical terms, as he translated or imported Greek words into Latin, he has controlled our thinking immeasurably" (Aproberts, 66). The important point in question here is the transmission of knowledge through the centuries. Cicero was the Roman philosopher and writer who transmitted the learning of the Greeks to western Europe. Trollope, in turn, through his scholarly study of Cicero, did western civilization a double favor: He became the agent who promoted an understanding of both Greek and Roman culture and philosophy.

REFERENCES

Aproberts, Ruth. *The Moral Trollope*. Athens: Ohio University Press, 1971.
Booth, Bradford A. *Anthony Trollope: Aspects of His Life and Art*. Bloomington, Ind.: Indiana University Press, 1958.
Gragg, Wilson B. "Trollope and Carlyle." *NCF* 13 (1958–1959): 266–70.
Runes, Dagobert David, ed. *Dictionary of Philosophy*. New York: Philosophical Library, 1983.

Smith, Shelia M. "Anthony Trollope: The Novelist as Moralist." In *Renaissance and Modern Essays Presented to Vivian de Sola Pinto in Celebration of His Seventieth Birthday,* edited by G. R. Hibbard. New York: Barnes & Noble, 1966.

U

UNAMUNO, MIGUEL DE. B. September 29, 1864, Bilbao, Vizcaya, Spain. D. December 31, 1936, Salamanca, Spain. Spanish thinker, novelist, and poet.

Miguel de Unamuno was a professor of Greek and later the rector of the University of Salamanca. He was a great linguist who read sixteen modern languages as well as Latin and Greek. In practically all of his works, there is an obsessive longing for assurance of a personal afterlife. His first major work was *The Tragic Sense of Life in Men and Women* (1912). *The Agony of Christianity* appeared in 1928, and *The Life of Don Quixote and Sancho* in 1927. The latter work is one of the most interesting commentaries ever written on Don Quixote. This book, and the essays on Spain that followed, reveal much about the personality and mind of the author. Unamuno's greatest achievement as a poet was *El Cristo de Velázquez* (1920, trans. E. L. Tornbull, *The Christ of Velázquez*, 1951).

Although considered primarily an imaginative writer, Unamuno's commitment to philosophy is amply demonstrated in the extensive reference which one finds in his work to such thinkers as Saint Augustine,* René Descartes,* Baruch Spinoza,* Blaise Pascal,* Immanuel Kant,* Georg Wilhelm Hegel,* Henri Bergson,* Søren Kierkegaard,* and William James,* to name a few. Not a systematic philosopher in the Hegelian or Kantian sense, he did produce a number of philosophical papers which addressed the problem of being, the theory of knowledge, and the ultimate meaning of life and death. Philosophy was to Unamuno a vital aspect of human existence, a discrete enterprise, separate from science and the enemy of religion. His equating of philosophical knowledge with poetry reminds one of Aristotle's* claim that the "friend of myth" is in a sense a philosopher.

Unamuno's profound interest in epistemology led him to Kant's *Critique of Practical Reason* (1788), in which Kant defines the philosophic enterprise. His insistence that man relive his past, his refusal to accept the notion that man is lost in the nothingness of time, brought him into precise concurrence with Friedrich Nietzsche's* *Ewige wiederkunft* (the eternal return of all things), which posits the notion that each discrete phenomenon repeats its fleeting existence and does not escape into time. His doctrine of eternal return, or recurrence, is not simply a matter of repetition. It speaks to the eternality of that which was.

Like Samuel Beckett (q.v.) and E. M. Forster (q.v.), Unamuno addressed the classical philosophical questions in his fiction and in his thought-provoking essays. An independent thinker himself, he drew selectively from among the great classical thinkers and thereby enriched his own thought and the lives of those who read him.

REFERENCES

Fasel, Oscar A. "Observations on Unamuno and Kierkegaard." *Hispania* 37 (1955): 443–50.
Huertas-Hourda, José. *The Existentialism of Miguel de Unamuno*. Gainesville: University of Florida Press, 1963.
Hyslop, T. "Miguel de Unamuno as a Religious Philosopher." *Modern Churchman* 27 (1937–1938): 646–52.
Marias, Julian. *Miguel de Unamuno*. Cambridge, Mass.: Harvard University Press, 1966.

UPDIKE, JOHN. B. March 18, 1932, Shillington, Pennsylvania. American novelist.

John Updike studied at Harvard and began to produce novels in 1959 with *The Poorhouse Fair,* a work that has death as its central theme. His other major works include *Rabbit, Run* (1960), *Couples* (1968), *Rabbitt Redux* (1971), *Marry Me* (1978), and *Rabbit Is Rich* (1981). Updike, in a clever blending of the erotic and the spiritual, examines the trials of the bourgeois in a modern universe. In the 1980s, Updike has published *Facing Nature* (1985), a collection of poems, and *Roger's Version* (1986), a novel.

There are recurring allusions to Søren Kierkegaard* in the writings of John Updike, and he has written two lengthy essays on Kierkegaard that demonstrate his thorough knowledge of the teachings of the Danish philosopher. Updike appended lengthy comments on Kierkegaard's ideas in the afterward to the play *Buchanan Dying* (1974). The comments are not passing ones but treat the philosophical ideas in depth and with understanding. Also in his work *A Month of Sundays* (1975), Updike has the narrator, Rev. Thomas Marsh Field, make constant allusions to Kierkegaard and other Christian theologians. The references to the philosopher are so constant and so important to the flow of the novel that it is evident that Updike not only has knowledge of Kierkegaard's teaching, but does not hesitate to incorporate the ideas into his own writing; an influence of the philosopher is thus established.

Updike exhibits an interest and expertise on the theology of Karl Barth, a fact that has been well documented (see Hunt, 15–16). Although Kierkegaard and Barth lived a century apart, both reacted strongly against the tendency to make Christianity a lofty rationalistic and humanistic (see humanism**) philosophy. Both men strove to remind Christians that Christianity was founded on revelation and that Christians should not attempt to bypass this divine element. The autobiographical poem of Updike entitled "Midpoint" echoes the fears of Kierkegaard and Barth over this humanism that was threatening to undermine traditional Christian beliefs. The first line states the problem explicitly: "An easy humanism plagues the land."

In the 1950s Updike read the major works of Kierkegaard and then proceeded to write short stories that would reflect "Kierkegaardian sensations." His biographer, George Hunt, lists ten stories that were influenced by this philosophy and adds: "All betray to a greater or lesser degree an appropriation of or a grappling with a theme proper to Kierkegaard" (Hunt, 21). In the story that shows the most influence by Kierkegaard, "The Astronomer," Updike touches upon the heart of the philosopher's teaching—fear and angst.** Undoubtedly other philosophers have influenced Updike; however, his fascination with Kierkegaard is well established.

REFERENCES

Detweiler, Robert. *John Updike*. New York: Twayne, 1972.
Galloway, David D. *The Absurd Hero in American Fiction*. Austin: University of Texas Press, 1970.
Hunt, George W. *John Updike and the Three Great Secret Things: Sex, Religion and Art*. Grand Rapids, Mich.: Eerdmans, 1980.
Neary, John M. "The Centaur: John Updike and the Face of the Other." *Renascence* 38, no. 4 (Summer 1986):228–44. (Theories of Emmanuel Levinas)

W

WARREN, ROBERT PENN. B. April 24, 1905, Guthrie, Kentucky.
D. September 15, 1989, Stratton, Vermont. American poet, novelist, and
critic.

Robert Penn Warren entered Vanderbilt University in 1921 and graduated in 1925 and then did graduate work at the University of California,
Yale University, and Oxford University as a Rhodes Scholar. At Vanderbilt he joined a group of poets who called themselves The Fugitives,
under the leadership of John Crowe Ransom (q.v.). This group published
an influential literary magazine called *The Fugitive*. From 1930 to 1957,
he was on the faculty of several colleges including Vanderbilt and the
University of Minnesota, and, with Cleanth Brooks, he edited *The Southern Review* (1935–1942). From 1951 to 1956 he taught playwriting at
Yale. In 1957 his volume of poetry *Promises* won both the National Book
Award and the Pulitzer Prize. His career as a novelist reached a high
point with *All The King's Men* (1946), a work which won a Pulitzer Prize
in 1947. Warren is a major figure in literary criticism; *Understanding
Poetry* (1938) and *Understanding Fiction* (1943), which were written in
collaboration with Cleanth Brooks, are established classics of the New
Criticism.

Although most readers of Robert Penn Warren might not mark him as
a religious writer, it must be remembered that the most important scene
in his greatest work, *All the King's Men*, is the conversion of Jack Burden,
a scene that is faithfully modeled on William James's* work *The Varieties*

plains it, is a psychological condition in which the "sick soul" experiences an identity change. James's "sick souls" must be reborn to be happy, and that is what happens to Jack Burden. He experienced his second birth when he awoke to his mother's scream at his father's suicide. James says that this conversion is the only way to overcome "anger, worry, fear, and despair" (Straudberg, 28). Warren's concern with the religious experience is apparent in "The Ballad of Billie Potts" and "Small Soldiers" and in "Winners and Losers, Pickers and Choosers," in which he describes the universe as dangerous and ends with James's religious pragmatism.**

Warren makes some reference to Freudian** psychology in *Brother to Dragons* (1953), but he is unable to accept Sigmund Freud's* predisposition to atheism.** He turned to another explorer of the subliminal consciousness, Carl Jung,* seeing in Jung's "collective unconsciousness" redemptive qualities and the unconscious as the only accessible source of religious experience (reported by Straudberg, 137).

Warren explores a variety of penetrating and often mysterious themes, especially the secret religious experiences that venture on the mystical (see mysticism**). His *New and Selected Essays* (1989) reveal a vast knowledge of literary figures ranging from Joseph Conrad (q.v.) to William Faulkner (q.v.), as well as a solid grasp of philosophical thought from Ralph Waldo Emerson (q.v.) and Arthur Schopenhauer* to George Santayana* and Jean-Paul Sartre* (q.v.). It must be said, however, that, if "the cure of selves" is Warren's main concern, then William James is his primary source and the greatest philosophical influence in his writings. Through the stimulus of philosophy, Warren has contributed to our awareness of what Martin Buber* calls "the injured wholeness of man." As a philosophical poet, Warren expresses versatility and excellence, and he is marked as one of the finest talents of his age.

REFERENCES

Byrne, Clifford M. "The Philosophical Development in Four of Robert Penn Warren's Novels." *McNesse Review* 9 (Winter 1957): 56–58.
Gross, Seymour L. "The Achievement of Robert Penn Warren." *College English* 19 (May 1958): 361–65.
Straudberg, Victor. *The Poetic Vision of Robert Penn Warren.* Lexington: University of Kentucky Press, 1977.
Welker, Robert. "The Underlying Philosophy of Robert Penn Warren: A Study in the Poetic Attitude." Master's thesis, Vanderbilt University, 1952.

WEST, NATHANAEL. B. October 17, 1903, New York City, New York. D. December 22, 1940, near El Centro, California. American novelist.

Born in New York City, Nathanael West attended high school there and then enrolled at Brown University and graduated in 1924. During a fifteen-month stay in Paris, he completed his first novel, *The Dream Life of Balso Snell*. This work was influenced by the surrealist emphasis on dream and fantasy (see surrealism**). After his return to New York, West supported himself as a hotel manager but continued writing, and in 1933 he produced his second and most popular novel, *Miss Lonelyhearts*. In 1934, he published the novel *A Cool Million,* which successfully satirized the American dream. In his last years, he worked as a Hollywood screenwriter and wrote *The Day of The Locust* (1939), considered by some critics to be the best novel ever written about Hollywood. West was killed in an automobile accident in 1940. Although never widely read in his lifetime, his works attracted attention after World War II, especially in France.

The influence of William James* on West's fiction—that he borrowed heavily from *The Varieties of Religious Experience* (1902) as well as from an earlier study by I. D. Starbuck that James integrated into his own work—is expressed by West in published notes about *Miss Lonelyhearts:* "*Miss Lonelyhearts* became the priest of our time who had a religious experience. His case is classical and is built on all the cases in James' *Varieties of Religious Experience* and Starbuck's *Psychology of Religion*" (reported by Schoenewolf, 80).

Miss Lonelyhearts, especially the final chapter, addresses the phenomenon of religious conversion, and West makes such extensive use of *The Varieties* that one is tempted to see the novel as a fictional expression of James's work. Manifest instances occur throughout the novel: the concept of a "disordered world" in which disorder in the universe is responsible for the dual nature of evil. Additionally, West's notion that Christ is the answer to disorder is Jamesean. The authority of James is also apparent in the protagonist's recognition "that man must struggle against nature to achieve both internal and external order" (Schoenewolf, 83) and in the efficacy of religious conversion as a corrective for the physical and mental deterioration which James calls the "sick soul."

It must be noted that, although West made extensive use of James in his fiction, he did not accept religious conversion as a meaningful or efficacious experience. He suggests, in *Miss Lonelyhearts,* finally, that to submit to the ecstasy of conversion is to succumb to evil.

REFERENCES

Bloom, Harold. *Nathanael West*. New York: Chelsea, 1986.
Bloom, Harold, ed. *Nathanael West's Miss Lonelyhearts*. New York: Chelsea, 1987.

Schoenewolf, Carroll. "James in Psychology and Nathanael West's *Miss Lonelyhearts.*" (November 1981): 80–86.
Young, Gloriea. "*The Day of the Locust:* An Apocalyptic Vision." *SAJL* 5 (1986): 103–10.

WHARTON, EDITH. B. January 24, 1862, New York City, New York. D. August 11, 1937, St. Brice-Sous-Forêt, France. American novelist.

Edith Wharton was educated privately at home and in Europe. In 1885, she married Edward Wharton, a Boston banker, and several years later she embarked upon her literary career. Deeply influenced by Henry James (q.v.), her stories and novels reveal a concern with ethical issues in the lives of the members of the American upper class into which she was born. *The Valley of Decision* was published in 1902, but the work that established her as a leading writer was *The House of Mirth* (1905). In the next two decades, she wrote such novels as *The Reef* (1912), *The Custom of the Country* (1913), *Summer* (1917), and *The Age of Innocence* (1920), for which she won the 1921 Pulitzer Prize. Her best known work, however, was *Ethan Frome* (1911), a long tale that portrays the grim realities of New England farm life. From 1907 to her death, Mrs. Wharton lived in France and visited the United States only on rare occasions.

In her autobiography *Backward Glance* (1934), Edith Wharton tells of her excitement on first reading such evolutionist writers as Charles Darwin,* Aldous Huxley (q.v.), Herbert Spencer,* and Ernst Heinrich Haeckel* (see evolution**). The influence of evolutionist thought on her work is revealed in the character Lily in *House of Mirth*, whose struggle is with her environment. *House of Mirth* is a classical naturalistic (see naturalism**) novel, à la Theodore Dreiser (q.v.), in which Lily is portrayed as the product of her heredity and environment. Wharton abandons her characters to the spirit of pessimism, and the attentive reader anticipates the tragic ending where the forces of heredity and environment prevail. Edith Wharton's biographer Blake Nevius emphasizes her penchant for fatalistic novels: "The rare imaginative force with which she was able to project the inner drama is inseparable from the controlling vision of her characters' destiny. As in the *House of Mirth* and *Ethan Frome,* the influence of nineteenth century determinism[**] is more than simply implied" (Nevius, 171–72).

REFERENCES

Bloom, Harold. *Edith Wharton.* New York: Chelsea House, 1986.
Lewis, R. W. *Edith Wharton: A Biography.* New York: Fromm Intl., 1985.

Nevius, Blake. *Edith Wharton: A Study of Her Fiction.* Berkeley: University of
California Press, 1961.
Singley, Carol J. "The Depth of the Soul: Faith, Desire, and Despair in Edith
Wharton's Fiction." *DAI* 47, no. 5 (November 1986): 1730A.
Wharton, Edith. *The Collected Letters of Edith Wharton.* New York: Scribners,
1988.

WHITMAN, WALT[ER]. B. May 31, 1819, Long Island, New York.
D. March 26, 1892, Camden, New Jersey. American poet.

Walt Whitman educated himself in classic literature, reading the works
of William Shakespeare, Homer, and Dante Alighieri (q.v.), among others. In 1839, he taught in a Long Island school and was engaged in
journalism in his spare time. By 1841 he had become a full-time journalist
in New York City. In 1846 he became editor of the *Brooklyn Eagle,*
printed *The Literature of Leading American Writers,* and wrote articles
supporting slavery; he felt that slavery would gradually be abolished with
the growth of the democratic spirit. In 1847 he had began work on twelve
poems which resulted in the publication of his greatest work, *Leaves of
Grass* (1855). In 1863, he moved to Washington, D.C. where he worked
as a voluntary nurse in an army hospital during the Civil War. In 1873,
suffering from partial paralysis, he took up his residence in Camden,
New Jersey, where he lived out his life except for visits to Colorado
(1879) and to Canada (1880). Whitman's most well-known poems include
"Crossing Brooklyn Ferry," "Out of the Cradle Endlessly Rocking,"
and "When Lilacs Last in the Dooryard Bloom'd."

Whitman's works reflect the influence of several philosophical thinkers;
among these was Thomas Carlyle (q.v.) who became Whitman's spiritual
guide and social critic. Whitman's biographer, Justin Kaplan, states that
"Carlyle's heroic affirmations had a long induction period in Whitman's
intellectual system" (Kaplan, 172). Kaplan continues: "Carlyle's essays
introduced him [Whitman] to [Johann Wolfgang von] Goethe [q.v.],
[Friedrich von] Schiller [q.v.], and the *Niebelungenlied*" (Kaplan, 172).

However, the greatest influence on Walt Whitman was undoubtedly
Ralph Waldo Emerson,* whom Whitman called "friend and master."
Critics have often said of *Leaves of Grass* that it was Emersonian in
content, unmeasured poetry in praise of America. Of course, it must be
pointed out that, although the work exhibits Emerson's thoughts, Whitman's language is reckless, sometimes coarse and defiant, and not in the
Emerson manner. Nevertheless, Emerson praised the work. Whitman
learned from Emerson that the American spirit walks on its own feet,

works with its own hands, and speaks its own mind (Emerson paraphrased).

Roger Asselineau, in *The Transcendentalist Constant in American Literature,* calls Whitman "The Transcendentalist Poet Incarnate" and claims that Emerson lauded *Leaves of Grass* because he saw in the work a definite exposition of transcendentalist thought (see transcendentalism**). Whitman stresses idealism, individualism, and mysticism,** all traits of the transcendentalist movement. Whitman praises the current of life that engulfs the entire cosmos and sees God as the force that pulsates through the universe. William James* identifies passages of "Song of Myself" as examples of the true mystical state in his book *The Varieties of Religious Experience* (1902). Asselineau sums up Whitman's transcendentalism: "Even in those early days, he was, by instinct as it were, a transcendentalist to whom material surfaces were only appearances and the terminus of some mysterious, intangible, but absolutely real spiritual presence" (Asselineau, 36).

Other influences on Whitman include the Stoic (see Stoicism**) and Epicurean philosophers (see Epicureanism**). For example, from Epictetus,* Whitman learned that "the basis of happiness was in behaving comfortably to nature. These philosophers had helped to release him from the terror of death and offered him a way of controlling life" (Kaplan, 154).

Whitman's reading of the works of Georg Wilhelm Hegel,* perhaps as early as 1857, is apparent in "As I Ebb'd with the Ocean of Life," in which Whitman attempts a reconciliation of the individual "I" with the democratic "we." He accepts Hegel's concept of art as a function of mind and poetry as the universal art of mind, concepts that are discussed in Hegel's essay "The Philosophy of Fine Art."

REFERENCES

Asselineau, Roger. *The Transcendentalist Constant in American Literature.* New York: New York University Press, 1981.

Bell, Ian F. A. "Lockean Sensationalism and American Literary Language." *JAmS* 20, no. 2 (August 1986): 291–93.

Crowley, Malcolm. "Walt Whitman—The Philosopher." *New Republic* 117 (September 29, 1947): 29–31.

Daiches, David. "Walt Whitman's Philosophy." In *Literary Essays.* New York: Philosophical Library, 1957.

Kaplan, Justin. *Walt Whitman, A Life.* New York: Simon & Schuster, 1980.

Kemnitz, Charles. "A Construction of Hegelian Spirit in Whitman's 'As I Ebb'd with the Ocean of Life.' " *Walt Whitman Review,* 59–63.

WILDER, THORNTON. B. April 17, 1897, Madison, Wisconsin. D. December 7, 1975, Hamden, Connecticut. American novelist and playwright.

Thornton Wilder graduated from Yale University in 1920 and taught dramatic literature from 1930 to 1937 at the University of Chicago. His most successful novel, *The Bridge of San Luis Rey* (1927), won for him the Pulitzer Prize. *The Ides of March* (1948), which deals with the last days of Julius Caesar, was not as successful. Wilder was extremely influential as a playwright with popular hits like *Our Town* (1938); *The Matchmaker* (1954), which was later adapted into the musical *Hello, Dolly;* and finally *The Skin of Our Teeth,* which also won the Pulitzer Prize in 1943. In his novels and plays, Wilder addresses what he perceived as the universal truths in human nature, and he expresses his bias against realistic naturalism, an active literary movement in the 1920s.

Thornton Wilder's philosophical knowledge was not extensive and, realizing his limitations in philosophy, Wilder, in 1935, commissioned one of his students, Robert Davie, to tutor him in classical philosophy. Wilder also studied Sigmund Freud* in his early years and met Freud in Vienna in the fall of 1935 where the two discussed the incorporation of psychoanalysis into fiction. Freud had read all of Wilder's novels and regarded him as a *Dichter* (poet) and not a mere *Romanschriftsteller* (story teller). Finally, one of Wilder's plays entitled *Childhood* (1931) brings Freudian psychology to a light one-acter.

Wilder's tendency to follow the Puritan ethic was rooted in nineteenth-century New England traditions and awareness. During his teaching years at Harvard University, he had closely applied himself to the life and work of Henry David Thoreau (q.v.). It is no wonder then that ''[t]he protagonist of *The Eighth Day* (1967) shares with Thoreau modes of behavior that we associated with American individualism: inventiveness, ingenuity, and manual dexterity; indifference to religious dogma and organized Christianity, but belief in the intuitive self as the true source of moral law'' (Goldstone, 252). Wilder's brother Amos's book on Thornton provides additional information on the influence of Søren Kierkegaard*: ''The hero of *The Eighth Day* can rightly be viewed as a Kierkegaardian knight of faith, but Kierkegaard's point about this kind of hero is that he is unrecognizable as such and does not even know his own merit'' (Wilder, 44).

In 1952, in an interview in Edinburgh, Scotland, Thornton Wilder explained that his play, *The Alcestiad* (1958), was ''existentialist in its philosophy'' (see existentialism**); and he spoke at length about ''the leap of faith,'' an expression used by Kierkegaard in *The Courage to Be.*

In his later years, Wilder was to regard himself as an existentialist (Goldstone, 79). We do not know how extensive his readings of the existentialist philosophers actually was, but we do know that he incorporated their philosophy into *The Ides of March*. In this controversial novel (it was never accepted by the best critics), Julius Caesar acquires his existential freedom once he acquires power. Goldstone notes that Wilder was the first American novelist to create an existentialist hero based on the models of Kierkegaard and Jean-Paul Sartre* (q.v.). and poses the question as to whether the book's failure to receive a serious evaluation was a reflection upon the work or upon the critical establishment (Goldstone, 221).

There is evidence that Wilder had been exposed to other philosophical influences. For example, he had studied Baruch Spinoza,* Immanuel Kant,* Georg Wilhelm Hegel,* Friedrich Nietzsche,* and Sartre.

REFERENCES

Castronovo, David. *Thornton Wilder*. New York: Ungar, 1986.
Corrigan, Robert W. "Thornton Wilder and the Tragic Sense of Life." In *The Theatre in Search of a Fix,* edited by Corrigan. New York: Delacorte, 1973.
Goldstone, Richard H. *Thornton Wilder: An Intimate Portrait*. Upper Montclair, N.J.: Saturday Review Press, 1975.
Lifton, Paul Samuel. "Thornton Wilder and the 'World Theatre.' " *DAI* 46, no. 9 (March 1986): 2486A.
Wilder, Amos. *Thornton Wilder and His Public*. Philadelphia: Fortress Press, 1980.

WILLIAMS, THOMAS LANIER (TENNESSEE) B. March 26, 1911, Columbus, Mississippi. D. April 25, 1983, New York City, New York. American dramatist.

Tennessee Williams became interested in playwriting while he was a student at the University of Missouri and at Washington University in St. Louis. The depression interrupted his studies, and he worked in a St. Louis shoe factory, experience which he worked into the *Glass Menagerie* (1945), a play which presented the American family in a state of failure. With *A Streetcar Named Desire* (1947), which won the Pulitzer Prize, and *Cat on a Hot Tin Roof* (1955), Williams acquired a reputation for exploring sexual themes, but he continued to deal with the pain and loneliness of modern civilization in works like *Camino Real* (1953) and *The Rose Tatoo* (1951). Although Williams's recent works have not had an impact on either the public or the critics, his earlier plays have already been added to the classics of the modern American theater.

There were many philosophical and theological influences in the career of Tennessee Williams. His Puritan background (see puritanism**) gave him a strong sense of guilt; he wrote in the foreword to *Sweet Bird of Youth* (1959), "Guilt is universal. I mean a strong sense of guilt" (reported by Asselineau, 154). Williams expresses his conviction that man is determined by heredity, environment, and social forces which he cannot resist. In *Glass Menagerie,* Amanda, Laura, and Tom are all victims of social forces.

A Streetcar Named Desire reveals the influence of Blaise Pascal* and his doctrine of man's dual nature: the angelic nature of his soul and the beastly nature of his body. This concept is illustrated in the character of Blanche who rejects the beastly side of her nature and is punished by an unending yielding to the demands of her body. Stella, on the other hand, accepts her dual nature and consequently finds peace and contentment.

Williams, like the theistic existentialist (see existentialism**), is obsessed with man's mortality and the necessity for belief in the immortality of the soul, the denial of which posits the meaninglessness and absurdity of human existence.

In his *Memoirs* (p. 101), Williams uses Henri Bergson's* phrase "élan vital,"** and it is obvious in his works that in choosing between the material and the spiritual, or God and the devil, the most important thing is the impulse or urge. "His characters, like himself, feel lonely and walled in their ego. They try desperately to communicate, through the flesh if necessary, with the spiritual presence which they feel outside themselves. God present in others. But they succeed only intermittently" (Asselineau, 158).

And so the influences on Tennessee Williams seem to be a mixture of Pascal, Bergson, and Christianity, especially puritanism. Though it cannot be documented, Sigmund Freud* seems to be looking over Williams's shoulder in most of his works; Williams certainly defines sexuality as the "primal life urge" (Asselineau, 157). William idealizes sexual desire, but it is always tempered by tenderness and love. In fact, in an interview, Williams once said, "I don't think there can be truly satisfactory sex without love" (*Playboy,* April 1972, p. 74). One must see through the sex and violence of Williams's plays to see an author who called himself "a lover of God and a believer" (*Partisan Review,* 1978, vol. 45, no. 2, p. 296).

REFERENCES

Asselineau, Roger. *The Transcendent Constant in American Literature.* New York: New York University Press, 1980.

Jackson, Esther Merle. *The Broken World of Tennessee Williams*. Madison: University of Wisconsin Press, 1986.

Minyard, John Douglas. "Classical Motivations in Tennessee Williams." *CML* 6, no. 4 (Summer 1986): 287–303.

Nelson, Benjamin. *Tennessee Williams: The Man and His Work*. New York: Ivan Obolensky, 1961.

Williams, Tennessee. *Memoirs*. 1st ed. Garden City, N.Y.: Doubleday, 1975.

WOLFE, THOMAS. B. October 3, 1900, Asheville, North Carolina. D. September 15, 1938, Baltimore, Maryland. American novelist.

In 1916 Thomas Wolfe entered the University of North Carolina, and in 1920 he enrolled in George Pierce Baker's 47 workshop at Harvard University. He aspired to be a playwright, but his plays, although produced on stage, never brought him fame. In 1923 Wolfe left Harvard for New York City. While aspiring to be a playwright, he taught at the Washington Square College of New York University. In 1929 he published his first novel, *Look Homeward, Angel,* then gave up teaching to write full time. His next novel was *Of Time and the River* (1935), which was followed by *The Web and the Rock* (1939) and his masterpiece *You Can't Go Home Again* (1940).

Thomas Wolfe's first introduction to the world of philosophy and philosophers came in his junior year at Chapel Hill when he enrolled in a course entitled 'A Story of the Forces That Shape Life.' The course was offered by Horace Williams, a philosophy professor who, as one of Wolfe's biographers, says, "was a mixture of kindliness and charlatanism, and this particular course mixed George Berkeley,* David Hume,* Immanuel Kant,* Georg Wilhelm Hegel,* and Herbert Spencer* into Williams's own special brew" (Kennedy, 50–51). In Wolfe's last year, he took Williams's course in logic, "which was not a study of logic in the usual sense; it was a rehash of Hegel's *Science of Logic* and certain parts of the *Phenomenology of Mind,* in which Williams illustrated that thought and absolute idea was totality" (Kennedy, 50). "Although Wolfe was only a somewhat better than average scholar at Chapel Hill, he had a great delight in primary questions, and to his untrained mind, which delighted in undergraduate discussions of being and essence, the one and the many, truth and goodness, time and immortality, Williams's intellectual nurturing seemed to supply final answers" (Kennedy, 51).

Wolfe went to Harvard under the influence of Williams's ideas, but a first draft of a letter to his friend Greenlaw in March or April 1922, shows that by the close of the second year at Harvard Wolfe was doubtful of the Hegelian monism[**] that Williams had preached to his college classes:

"If I'm ever to be a dramatist I must believe in struggle. I've got to believe in dualism, in a definite spirit of evil, and in a satan who is tired from walking up and down upon the earth. These are things I can visualize, when we erase the struggle, our power of visualization seems to fade. I have the utmost difficulty in bringing into my mind the picture of Professor Williams absorbing a negation. Life as he was now living it and writing as he wished to practice it made him feel that the doctrine of the *Begriff* was only classroom theory that he could forget with no great loss: "I'm beginning to know the kind of thing I want to do now. And it calls for a grasp on the facts of life. When I attended philosophy lectures I was told that there was no reality in a wheelbarrow, that reality rested in the concept or plan of that wheelbarrow. But the wheelbarrow is the thing you show on the stage." (Kennedy, 52)

Professor Williams's influence on the young Thomas Wolfe was lasting. Williams's doctrine of individualism, which was Hegel's concept of life as a progress, led to Wolfe's acceptance of the doctrine of vitalism.**

Wolfe is revealed by his biographer Richard Kennedy as being more the intellectual than earlier critics recognized. One thing that he always had was a yearning and absolute interpretation of the meaning of life, a demand of the philosophers that probably was never realized. Early in 1922 he wrote in a letter to Williams: "Time after time it has seemed as if mankind was about to come upon the absolute; to plunge into and discover the ultimate impenetrable mystery; and then they quit; or turn to something else, to baffle and foil themselves anew" (Kennedy, 65).

REFERENCES

Beebe, Maurice, ed. Thomas Wolfe Special Number. *Modern Fiction Studies* 11, no. 3 (Autumn 1965).

Kennedy, Richard S. *The Window of Memory*. Chapel Hill: University of North Carolina Press, 1962.

McElderry, Bruce R. *Thomas Wolfe*. New Haven, Conn.: College and University Press, 1964.

"The Wolfe Pack: Bibliography." *TWN* 10, no. 2 (Fall 1986): 72–74.

WOOLF, VIRGINIA. B. January 25, 1882, London, England. D. March 28, 1941, Rodmell, Sussex, England. British novelist and critic.

The daughter of Sir Leslie Stephen, a scholar and editor of *The Dictionary of National Biography*, Virginia Woolf was acquainted with several major writers and scholars during her early years. She was educated at home, and at the age of thirty she married Leonard Woolf, an historian and a political essayist. In 1917 they founded the Hogarth Press which published her books. Very early, she wrote critical essays, published in *The Common Reader,* two volumes (1925–1932), and *The Death of the Moth* (1942). *Mrs. Dalloway,* a successful novel which appeared in 1925, was followed by *To the Lighthouse* (1927) and *The Waves* (1931). Her short fiction appears in *Monday or Tuesday* (1921) and in *A Haunted House* (1947).

Together with such writers as D. H. Lawrence (q.v.) and James Joyce (q.v.), Virginia Woolf rejected the positivistic (see positivism**) realism that characterized many writers of the preceding generation and sought, in her early years, a new direction, a new vision, a search which led finally to the works of Henri Bergson,* one of the more prominent and influential thinkers at the turn of the century.

Bergson's influence on Virginia Woolf's thought is explicitly apparent in her novels as well as in her shorter fiction. In "Kew-Gardens," for example, borrowing the Bergsonian élan vital,** she sees life as a pure spiritual force, a timeless human consciousness beyond, free from time and space. In *Jacob's Room* (1923), Woolf illustrates the Bergsonian notion that the vital force is not always successful in its battle with the physical, but what matters is that one tries, repeatedly, and the trying is all. Granting the influence of Marcel Proust and Joyce, among others, in her work, the knowledgeable reader cannot but recognize Bergson as a major factor in the thought as well as the form of Virginia Woolf's fiction.

Virginia Woolf's biographer, James Hafley, discusses the elements of Bergsonian thought that he sees in the novel *Jacob's Room.* In one scene, Jacob as a child catches a large sand crab and puts it in his sand bucket. Later a powerful rainstorm hits, and the bucket fills with water. The author goes into considerable detail to describe the crab's valiant attempts to climb up the side of the bucket, only to fall back again and again. Hafley says of this scene, "This too is perfectly consistent with Bergson and Bergsonistic thinking, the vital impetus does not, in each particular manifestation, win its battle with matter; what is important is that it tries, acts, fights the fight" (Hafley, 54).

Virginia Woolf was influenced to such an extent by the philosophy of Henri Bergson that in some cases she used the same symbols that Bergson used. The symbol of water to suggest life is one example: "The use of water in this novel [*The Voyage Out* (1920)] is another indication that Virginia Woolf was ready to receive with open arms certain concepts— notably the Bergsonian—soon to become part of the contemporary intellectual climate" (Hafley, 23).

In short, when one takes an overview of the art of Virginia Woolf and studies her works, one arrives at the conclusion that several literary figures, namely Proust and Joyce, and Bergson influenced her work.

REFERENCES

Hafley, James. *The Class Reef: Virginia Woolf as Novelist*. New York: Russell and Russell, 1963.
Harvard-Williams, P. M. ''Perceptive Contemplation in the Work of Virginia Woolf.'' *English Studies* 35 (1954): 96–116.
Moody, A. D. *Virginia Woolf*. Edinburgh, Scotland: Oliver and Boyd, 1963.
Schaefer, Josephine O'Brien. *The Three-fold Nature of Reality in the Novels of Virginia Woolf*. The Hague, Netherlands: Mouton, 1965.

WORDSWORTH, WILLIAM. B. April 7, 1770, Cockermouth, Cumberland, England. D. April 23, 1850, Grasmere, Cumberland, England. English poet.

William Wordsworth was educated at Cambridge University. In 1795 he settled with his devoted sister, Dorothy, in Dorsett, where he met Samuel Taylor Coleridge (q.v.). Their friendship resulted in a collaboration on the *Lyrical Ballads* (1798), which is regarded as the beginning of the English Romantic movement (see romanticism**). By 1805 Wordsworth had completed his autobiographical masterpiece *The Prelude*. He was appointed poet laureate in 1843.

The influence of David Hartley's* implicit empiricism** is evident in Wordsworth's poetic theory, which argues that the poetic response arises out of ''reminiscences of things past,'' out of ideas that survive from sensations of daily life. His search for the elemental source of poetic expression led Wordsworth to the view that the rustic life was the preferred subject matter of poetry. Closer to nature than the urban and the sophisticated, the rustic condition provides a context free from repression and given to free associations. The poems contained in *Lyrical Ballads* reflect this theory of poetry (see naturalism**).

Wordsworth's biographer, Newton P. Stallknecht, generally agrees that his philosophical poetry was also significantly influenced by William Godwin.* One recalls the advice of the poet to a young student: ''Burn your books on Chemistry and read Godwin on necessity.'' The reference here is that the attainment of the good and human progress are the consequence of necessity, of unqualified determinism.** In 1791 Wordsworth, disillusioned with the French Revolution which had degenerated into the Reign of Terror, worked on *Guilt and Sorrow* (1842), which tells of a soldier's destitute widow and of a discharged soldier who is driven to crime by the miseries of war. The poem is hardly an optimistic affirmation of human progress but is, on the contrary, a Godwinian indictment of society. It must be added that Godwin, like the ancient Stoics (see Stoicism**), emphasized reason and not passion. To follow reason is an essential of Godwinism, but in Wordsworth's *The Borderers* (1796–1797) the poet strays from Godwin's influence inasmuch as neither the hero nor the villain follows reason.

Godwinian Stoicism finds expression in Wordsworth's *The Convict* (1798) and *Guilt and Sorrow* (1842), in which Wordsworth expresses his admiration for the stoical fortitude of the sufferers; however, it is important to note that Wordsworth does finally repudiate Godwin's philosophy and turns for consolation to the healing influences of nature.

> Wordsworth's interests led him to demand more of philosophy than do most reflective men; besides seeking a criterion of the good and probing into the problem of human freedom, he looked for an explanation of his own strange communion with nature. Thus his philosophical life, proving as it did the source of some of the finest metaphysical[**] and religious poetry in literature, was a deep and rich one. It led him to absorb the teachings of many thinkers and to incorporate their doctrines in his poems. (Stallknecht, 1)

REFERENCES

Havens, Raymond Dexter. *The Mind of a Poet: A Story of Wordsworth's Thought with Particular Reference to the Prelude*. Baltimore: Johns Hopkins University Press, 1941.
Stallknecht, Newton P. *Wordsworth and Philosophy*. New York: [N.P.], 1929.
————. *Strange Seas of Thought: Studies in William Wordsworth's Philosophy of Man and Nature*. Durham, N.C.: Duke University Press, 1945.
Stoddard, Eve Walsh. "Flashes of the Invisible World: Reading *The Prelude* in the Context of the Kantian Sublime." *WC* 16, no. 1 (Winter 1985): 32–37.

WRIGHT, RICHARD. B. September 4, 1908, Natchez, Mississippi. D. November 28, 1960, Paris, France. American writer.

Born in Natchez, Mississippi, of a very poor family, Richard Wright began writing early in life and published a short story, "The Voodoo of Hell's Half Acre," in a Jackson, Mississippi, newspaper. His first major work was a volume of four novels, entitled *Uncle Tom's Children* (1938), which was followed by *Black Boy* (1945) and *The Outsider* (1953), a work that attacks both communism and fascism. Wright's works provide a realistic picture of the sordid living conditions of blacks in the south as well as in northern inner-city ghettos.

When Richard Wright emigrated to France in the 1940s, he came to know men like Jean-Paul Sartre* (q.v.) and was consequently exposed to existentialism.** This exposure and his existentialist studies resulted in his commitment to "the existentialist ideal of the committed intellectual, the man who was always willing and able to testify to and fight against injustice" (Fabre, 316). In the 1950s, his second maturative period, he studied philosophy, was involved in political action, and arrived at the conviction that the salvation of humanity would come from the Third World.

Wright's study of Søren Kierkegaard,* Edmund Husserl,* and Martin Heidegger,* rather than Sartre and Albert Camus (q.v.), led to the awareness that his isolation, which he blamed on his color, was actually the fate of all men. He also learned from these existentialist thinkers that the individual is responsible for the creation of his own values. The novel that came out of this period, *The Outsider,* prophesized the demise of industrial civilization and the coming of a "dehumanized society that would give birth to a moral monster" (Fabre, 374). During this era he also turned to humanism** as a universal solution to the world's problems, a worldwide humanism that would go beyond the barriers of race and beyond those of nation and religion.

Wright developed his own brand of existentialism based on a freedom which society must guarantee to man: the freedom and dignity that were the rights of American negroes which America must guarantee to them.

For some time, Wright had been aligned with and dependent on Sartre, but when the French existentialist moved closer to the Communists in 1953 (Sartre had agreed to attend the Vienna Peace Conference along with Communist representatives), he divorced himself from Sartre. He realized at this time that he was too much of a "world intellectual" and that Sartre was too exclusively European.

Wright's biographer, Michel Fabre, maintains not only that he was susceptible to existentialism but also that he had an "exaggerated reverence for books and too much faith in ideas" (Fabre, 531). This would account for the fact that Wright lived through several intellectual stages and periods. At times he was an existentialist, and in other periods he was a Marxist (see Marxism**). Nevertheless, it is fairly obvious that entertainment was not his aim, just as it is obvious that his mind was easily influenced by the works of yet greater minds.

[U]ncertainly at times, but more often quite consciously, he was grappling with a definition of man. Although his solitary quest ended prematurely and did not allow him to find one, his achievement as a writer and a humanist makes him, in the Emersonian sense, a truly "representative man" of our time. (Fabre, 531)

REFERENCES

Bone, Richard. "Richard Wright and the Chicago Renaissance." *Callaloo* 9, no. 3 (Summer 1986): 446–68. (Relationship to Marxism)

Cappetti, Carla. "Sociology of an Existence: Richard Wright and the Chicago School." *MELUS* 12, no. 2 (Summer 1985): 25–43. (Relationship to sociology)

Fabre, Michel. *The Unfinished Quest of Richard Wright.* New York: William Morrow, 1973.

Margolies, Edward. *The Art of Richard Wright.* Carbondale: Southern Illinois University Press, 1969.

Y

YEATS, WILLIAM BUTLER. B. June 13, 1865, Dublin, Ireland. D. January 28, 1939, Roguebrune, Alpes-Maritimes, France. Irish poet.

Born into a Protestant Irish family, William Butler Yeats grew up in Dublin and London. He returned to Ireland in his late adolescence because of his fascination with its myths and legends. He began his literary career in London but returned to Dublin in 1896, where he became active in the creation of the Irish Literary Theatre. His first major publication, *The Crew Helmet and Other Poems* (1910), was followed by *Responsibilities* (1914). At this time, Yeats became interested and involved in politics and civic matters, but his major pursuit was poetry, and he seized upon myth in his search for an understanding of man's nature. His other major works include *A Vision* (1925), *The Tower* (1928), and *The Winding Stair* (1929). Yeats received the Nobel Prize for Literature in 1923.

The influence of Carl Jung* on Yeats has been well documented, and the influence of philosophy on his thinking is apparent in his work. Yeats and Jung both drew on the Platonic tradition (see Platonism**); two examples are "archetypes" (see archetype**) and "anima mundi" (see anima**). T. R. Henn has pointed out Platonic elements in Yeats. Furthermore, F. A. C. Wilson's two books "are the standard by which Yeats' debt to Neoplatonism[**] must be measured" (Olney, 15).

Yeats seized eagerly on the mysteries of Pythagoras.* As Olney states: "Yeats and Jung were Pythagoreans through and through, it would be fair to say, in tendency and temperament, if not in learning and ability"

(Olney, 55). Indeed, Yeats accepted all the Pythagorean** doctrines, with only a few qualifications on the subject of reincarnation.

The influence of Heraclitus* is revealed in the poem "Easter" (1916), which expresses the Heraclitean doctrine that all things human and natural are in a state of flux and transformation (see Heraclitean flux**). Many of the poems of Yeats's maturity—"Sailing to Byzantium," "The Tower," "All Soul's Night," and others—demonstrate Yeats's acceptance of Heraclitus's doctrine of opposition and paradox projected into a dictum of psychological theory holding that everything psychic is paradoxical and contradictory.

Yeats also studied Parmenides.* "Yeats and Jung had reason to be grateful to Parmenides, for there is much of his thought in the writings of both men" (Olney, 133). In his copy of Burnet's *Early Greek Philosophy,* Yeats wrote in the margin on the section of Parmenides, "Time is illusion," and then went on to write "A Meditation in Time of War," a poem that expresses the Parmenidean denial of the reality of time.

One of Yeats's major preoccupations was with supernaturalism and occultism**. He believed in magic. He "attended spiritualist seances, became for a while a disciple of Madame Blavatsky, studied Rosicrucianism,[**] and joined the secret order for the study and practice of magic" (Stock, 81).

Yeats's proclivity for mysticism** led to a profound interest in Hinduism.** While still a student at the Dublin Art School, he attended the lectures of a young Brahmin, Mohini Chatterjie, which convinced him that the world of the imagination was just as real as the world of matter, a fact which affected his art and poetry and possibly led him to an art for art's sake position.

Yeats's critics rank him as a philosophical poet, one who assimilated western thinkers like Heraclitus, Parmenides, and Plato,* but who expanded his studies to Eastern philosophy and incorporated much of Western and Eastern thought into his poetry.

REFERENCES

Barker, Vara Sue Tammings. "W. B. Yeats: Poetry as Meditation." *DAI* 47, no. 6 (December 1986): 2165A.

Griffin, Jon. "Profane Perfection: 'The Statues.' " *CollL* 13, no. 1 (Winter 1986): 21–28. (Sources in ancient Greek philosophy)

Henn, T. R. *The Lonely Tower.* Portsmouth, N.H.: Methurn, 1965.

More, Henry. *Philosophical Poems,* edited by Geoffrey Bullough. Manchester, England: Manchester University Press, 1937.

Olney, James. *The Rhizome and the Flower: The Perennial Philosophy—Yeats and Jung*. Berkeley: University of California Press, 1980.

Stock, A. C. *W. B. Yeats: His Poetry and Thought*. Cambridge, England: Cambridge University Press, 1964.

PROFILES OF PHILOSOPHERS

ANTONINUS, MARCUS AURELIUS. B. April 26, 121, Rome, Italy. D. March 17, 180, Vienna, Austria. Roman emperor and Stoic philosopher.

In 138, Marcus Aurelius was adopted by the emperor Antoninus Pius, and a few years later he married his daughter Annia Galeria Faustina. On the death of Antoninus, he succeeded to the throne. Marcus Aurelius had been educated by the best tutors in Rome and Athens, and throughout his life he was devoted to learning, especially the philosophy of Stoicism.** The book that he bequeathed to posterity is titled *Meditations*. This work presents his mature reflections on Stoicism.** In spite of his philosophical view of life, he was consistently hostile to Christianity, which he perceived as a threat to the established order.

AQUINAS, SAINT THOMAS. B. 1224, Roccasecca, Italy. D. 1274, Fossanova, Italy. Italian theologian and scholastic philosopher.

At the age of five, Thomas Aquinas was placed in the Benedictine monastery of Monte Cassino. Later he studied liberal arts at the University of Naples. In 1244, against the violent opposition of his family, Aquinas joined the Dominican order and completed his novitiate and theological training in Paris and Cologne. At this time he studied under the renowned Albertus Magnus. From 1252 to 1259, Thomas taught theology at the Dominican house of studies in Paris; from 1259 to 1269 he was an attaché at the Papal court in Rome. During his years as a teacher (1252–1273) Aquinas produced an extensive literature, including several theological

treatises, commentaries on the Bible, disputations on theological and philosophical issues, and numerous miscellaneous sermons, letters, and notes. In 1274, while traveling to the Council of Lyon, he fell ill and died. His greatest work, the *Summa Theologica,* occupied him from 1267 to 1273. Saint Thomas's greatest achievement was the synthesis of faith and reason in Catholic theology.

ARENDT, HANNAH. B. October 14, 1906, Königsberg, E. Prussia. D. December 4, 1975, New York City, New York. German/American philosopher.

Hannah Arendt's father died when she was seven years old, and she was raised by her mother, Martha Arendt. At a young age she exhibited high intelligence, which was enhanced by her avid reading. In 1924 she matriculated at the University of Marburg, Germany, and at this time began an intellectual and romantic relationship with the renowned philosopher, Martin Heidegger.* Arendt studied under three of the greatest philosophers of the twentieth century: Heidegger, Edmund Husserl,* and Karl Jaspers.* Under Jaspers's tutelage, Arendt wrote her dissertation on Saint Augustine.*

In 1929 she married Gunther Stern, and the two took up residence in Berlin. In 1933, after experiencing some harassment by the Gestapo, she left for Paris. By 1936 her marriage had dissolved, and she married Heinrich Blutcher. The Blutchers lived in Paris until 1939, but the German occupation presented danger, and in 1940 they sailed to New York. Arendt worked at several jobs in America, including the position of senior editor for Schocken Books (from 1940 to 1948). In 1951 she published her book, *The Origins of Totalitarianism.* In 1952 she received a Guggenheim Foundation grant to sudy the Marxist elements of totalitarianism. During the 1960s Arendt lectured widely and published some essays entitled *Men in Dark Times.* In 1967 she accepted a professorship at the New School for Social Research. Her other works include *The Human Condition* (1958), *The Life of the Mind* (1977), *Crises of the Republic* (1973), and *Politics in the Modern Age* (1978).

ARISTOTLE. B. 384 B.C., Stagira, Greece. D. 322 B.C., Chalcis, Greece. Greek philosopher.

In his eighteenth year, Aristotle became a pupil of Plato* and remained for twenty years a member of Plato's Academy. For several years after the death of Plato, he acted as tutor to the young Alexander of Macedon. In 335, he returned to Athens where he established and headed a school of philosophy commonly known as the Peripatetic School. An enthusiastic defender of Platonism** in his early years, Aristotle came to reject the essential features of Plato's metaphysics (see metaphysical**). Reality for Aristotle involves both matter and form, and it unfolds in phenomena. The two are inseparable, with the exception that the First Cause is transcendent pure form. In his theory of knowledge, Aristotle deviates significantly from Plato in that he argues that the object of knowledge is that which enables the rational faculty to explain what is perceived, not the Platonic world of ideas. Scientific knowledge, demonstrated knowledge of the causes of things, is arrived at through deduction. The highest good is achieved in philosophical inquiry and in contemplation of truth, which is the activity of that most important element of human nature: *nous* or intuitive reason. In his aesthetic theory, Aristotle observes that man is the most imitative creature in the world, but he contends that art is more than pure *mimesis,* that great art evokes pity and fear and effects *catharsis* or purgation of those emotions. Through his vicarious participation in art, man is cleansed of the unpleasant emotions and experiences and thereby gains a sense of elation. His major philosophical works are the *Organum, De Anima, Metaphysics,* and the *Nicomachean Ethics.*

AUGUSTINE, SAINT. B. 354, Tagaste, North Africa. D. 430, Hippo, North Africa. Roman philosopher and theologian.

As a young man, Augustine followed a career as teacher of rhetoric, first in Rome and then in Milan, Italy. Although he was at first attracted to the Manichaen religion, he converted to Christianity in 386. While in Milan, he came under the influence of Bishop Ambrose and the Christian Neoplatonists (see Neoplatonism**). In 400, Augustine wrote his *Confessions* in which he states that the teaching of the Platonists (see Platonism**) had prepared his way to Christianity. In 395, he became Bishop of Hippo and from the 390s onward, Augustine was devoted to the service of his church. Although he led a semimonastic life, he continued to fulfill his administrative responsibilities and to write. The center of Augustine's thought is morality. He argues that philosophy is a search for wisdom with the aim of achieving happiness. But happiness depends on right living as much as true thinking. Although his theories on human conduct were guided primarily by the New Testament, the influence of Plato* is readily apparent in his work. In addition to the *Confessions,* his major works include *De Doctina Christiana* and *City of God,* both of which are found in the Loeb classical library.

BACON, FRANCIS. B. January 22, 1561, London, England. D. April 9, 1626, London, England. English statesman, essayist, and philosopher.

Francis Bacon attended Cambridge University for two years and then spent three years in France. In 1579 he began to study law at Gray's Inn. He became a member of Parliament in 1584. In about 1592 he became a political adviser to the Earl of Essex, but when the earl attempted to lead a rebellion against the Crown, Bacon was instrumental in convicting the earl of treason. Bacon's chief literary contribution is the *Essays,* which was a product of twenty years of work. His main interests, however, were philosophy and science, and his philosophical teaching was organized in his work *Novum Organum* (1620). Bacon divided knowledge into reason, memory, and imagination. Memory and imagination govern events and facts; reason, on the other hand, is concerned with general laws and ideas. Bacon is most famous for his so-called scientific method. His other works include *The Advancement of Learning* (1605) and *New Atlantis* (1627).

BERGSON, HENRI. B. October 18, 1859, Paris, France. D. January 4, 1941, Paris, France. French philosopher.

The son of a prosperous Polish Jewish musician and an English mother, he studied at the École Normale Supérieure from 1877 to 1881, and for the next sixteen years he was a philosophy teacher in several Lycées. In 1900 he was made professor at the Collège de France where he lectured until 1914. He was awarded the Nobel Prize for Literature in 1928. For Bergson, the real world is the Heraclitean flux.** Thus, the world for him is one of continuous becoming or process. Bergson's most original thinking is to be found in his doctrine of the élan vital,** or vital impetus, which he considered to be a "current of consciousness" that penetrates matter, gives rise to living bodies, and determines the course of their evolution. In the years preceding World War I, Bergson was the object of a fashionable cult, and his lectures were attended by large crowds. Most important of his philosophical writings are *An Introduction to Metaphysics* (1912) and *The Two Sources of Morality and Religion* (1935).

BERKELEY, GEORGE. B. March 12, 1685, County Kilkenny, Ireland. D. January 14, 1753, Oxford, England. Irish philosopher.

In 1700, at the age of fifteen, Berkeley entered Trinity College, Dublin where he studied mathematics, logic, languages, and philosophy. He became a fellow in 1707, and two years later he published his first significant book, *The Essay Towards a New Theory of Vision.* The following year, he published *A Treatise Concerning the Principles of Human Knowledge,* in which he established his posture as an immaterialist, a position which he continued to defend throughout his life. He argued that the mind reasons only about particular sense experiences, that abstract ideas have no equivalents in reality, that *esse est percipi* (to be is to be perceived), and that the existence of sensible objects unperceived is inconceivable. However, he argued that sensible objects depend, finally, on their perception not by the human mind but by God. In addition to those mentioned above, his works include *Three Dialogues between Hylas and Philoman* (1713), *De Motu* (1721) (a criticism of Sir Isaac Newton's theory of nature), and *The Analyst* (1734), an attack on Newton's doctrine of fluxions.

BOETHIUS, ANICIUS MANLIUS SEVERINUS. B. ca. 480, Rome, Italy. D. 524, Pavia, Italy. Late Roman statesman and philosopher.

Boethius was born into the ancient Anician family in Rome. A precocious young student, he was educated in the liberal arts and philosophy. He entered public life at an early age, and at fifty-one he became consul under King Theodoric the Ostrogoth. It has never been thoroughly explained, but Boethius was arrested for treason, imprisoned for a year at Pavia, and executed in 524. Boethius's influence on the scholars of the early scholastic period (1000–1150) was so great that it has been called the Boethian Age. Using both Stoic (see Stoicism**) and Neoplatonic (see Neoplatonism**) arguments, Boethius, in the *Consolation,* maintained that the just man who suffers arrives at the conviction that happiness may be found in adversity. His most influential work is *On the Consolation of Philosophy* (edited and translated in 1925), but he also wrote other works, such as *The Commentaries on Porphry* (ed. 1906) and *Theological Tractates,* which were translated and edited by H. F. Stewart and E. R. Rand in 1918.

BONAVENTURE, SAINT. B. ca. 1217, Bagnorea, Italy. D. 1274, Lyons, France. Italian scholastic philosopher.

After obtaining a Master of Arts degree at Paris, Bonaventure joined the Franciscan Friars and began his theological studies under Alexander of Hales and John of LaRochelle. In 1248, as a bachelor of scripture, he began lecturing on the books of scripture. In 1253 he was licensed by the chancellor of the University of Paris and was regent master of theology there until 1257. A major work that came out of this period was *De Mysterio Trinitatis* (On the Mystery of the Trinity), which contains the best exposition of his proofs for the existence of God. In February 1257, he was elected minister general of the Franciscan order and resigned his chair at the university. Bonaventure's fame rests primarily on his reputation as a theologian rather than as a philosopher. According to Bonaventure, the philosopher who does not accept revelation cannot understand the full significance of man's existential situation. His most important publication in theology is *Itinerarium Mentis in Deum* (The Journey of the Mind to God) (1259).

BRADLEY, F[RANCIS] H[ERBERT]. B. January 30, 1846, Clapham, England. D. September 18, 1924, Oxford, England. English idealist philosopher.

Francis Bradley was educated at Oxford University, and in 1870 he was elected to a fellowship at Merton College, Oxford, and was able to devote himself to philosophical writing. He read and admired Georg Wilhelm Hegel,* but much of Bradley's writings attacked the utilitarianism** and empiricism** of John Stuart Mill* and his followers. Later in his career, he became involved in philosophical disputes with William James* and Bertrand Russell.* In ethics, Bradley was Hegelian (see Hegelianism**) and was critical of both Mill and Immanuel Kant.* His philosophical works include *The Presuppositions of Critical History* (1834), *Ethical Studies* (1876), *Principles of Logic* (1883), *Appearance and Reality* (1893), *Essays on Truth and Reality* (1914), and *Collected Essays* (1938).

BRUNO, GIORDANO. B. 1548, Nola, Italy. D. February 17, 1600, Rome, Italy. Italian philosopher.

At an early age, Giordano Bruno joined the Dominican order, but in 1576, when he was accused of heresy, he fled and abandoned the order. He reached Paris in 1581, where he gave public lectures and published two books on the art of memory. Early in 1583 Bruno went to England where he delivered lectures, repetitions of Ficino's work on astral magic. Late in 1525 Bruno returned to Paris where he lectured on his philosophy, but it was received with strong opposition. He fled to Germany in 1586 and was favorably received at the University of Wittenberg. In August 1591, Bruno returned to Italy and was arrested in Venice for heresy. He was sentenced by the Inquisition as a heretic and was burned at the stake in 1600. Bruno considered his most important work to be in the art of memory. Here he continued a Renaissance** tradition of the Hermetic revival, which he contended was grounded in the reflection of the universe within one's own mind and memory. His published works include *Dialoghi Italiani* (ed. 1957), *Opera Latine* (ed. 1879–1891), and *The Heroic Enthusiasts* (tr. 1887).

BUBER, MARTIN. B. February 8, 1878, Vienna, Austria. D. June 13, 1965, Jerusalem, Israel. Israeli religious philosopher.

Martin Buber, a Jew, contributed some of the richest religious experiences available to Judeo-Christian theology. He studied philosophy at the universities of Vienna and Berlin and received his Ph.D in 1904. In 1898 he had joined the Zionist movement and became editor of the Zionist journal *Die Welt*. In 1902 he helped found the Judischer Verlag, a German Jewish publishing house. In 1938 he left Germany for Palestine, where he became professor of social philosophy at the Hebrew University in Jerusalem. Buber's most well-known theory is what he called the ''I-Thou'' relationship, which he claims to be genuine since this relationship is between me and the thou that addresses me. The I-Thou concept demonstrates the difference between the way people relate to inanimate objects on the one hand and to human beings on the other. Buber's published works include the very influential *I and Thou* (1937) and *The Prophetic Faith* (1960). His views have been widely studied and embraced, and he has especially influenced such European Catholic writers as Jacques Maritain* and Gabriel Marcel.

CALVIN, JOHN. B. July 10, 1509, Noyon, France. D. May 27, 1564, Geneva, Switzerland. French theologian.

From 1521 to 1526, Calvin studied in Paris where he was introduced to humanistic studies. He began to study law at his father's bidding, but when his father died in 1531, he turned to the study of the classics and theology. About 1526, he experienced a Protestant conversion. Because of his religious beliefs and teaching, he was forced to flee to Basel, Switzerland, in 1535. By 1536, he published his *Institutes of the Christian Religion,* a work that clearly declared the Bible as the final authority. In the *Institutes,* Calvin concerns himself with two types of knowledge: knowledge of God and knowledge of ourselves. He further argues that knowledge of God can be achieved if one nourishes one's subjective awareness of the Deity. Calvin's social and political theory, especially that of man's fellowship in society, has proved most influential. Man, he says, is a creature of fellowship who has natural tendencies for groupings of which the church is an instance. Calvin's religious reforms were first established in Geneva, Switzerland, where he spent fourteen years establishing the ''Genevan Reform.'' Calvin's influence spread quickly throughout the western world but was felt especially in Scotland through the work of John Knox.

CICERO, MARCUS TULLIUS. B. 106 B.C., Arpino, Italy, D. December 7, 43 B.C. Caieta, Italy. Roman philosopher, orator, and statesman.

Cicero had a lifelong interest in philosophy and wrote a number of philosophical works. Among his friends were the Epicureans (see Epicureanism**), Phraedrus, Zeno, and the Stoic Posidonius (see Stoicism**). One of Cicero's major contributions to philosophy was the reconstruction of lost Greek originals. The most conspicuous feature of Cicero's thought is the union of philosophy and rhetoric which led him to a humanistic ideal. This blending of the philosopher-rhetorician (statesman) was for him the highest human achievement. Philosophy supplies the knowledge, and rhetoric disseminates it among his fellow men. His philosophical works consist of *Academica* (45 B.C.), *De Natura Deorum* (45 B.C.), *De Divinatione* (44 B.C.), and *De Fato* (44 B.C.). His major ethical writings are *De Finibus Bonorum et Malorum* (45 B.C.), *De Officiis* (44 B.C.), and ethics based on Stoic principles.

COHEN, HERMANN. B. 1842, Coswig, Germany. D. 1918, Berlin, Germany. German philosopher.

Hermann Cohen attended the gymnasium at Dessau, Germany, and later pursued philosophical studies at the University of Breslau and the University of Berlin, where he was awarded the doctorate of philosophy in 1865. His first philosophical book, *Kants Theorie der Erfahrung* (1871) (Theory of Experience), was followed by *Begrundung der Ethik* (Foundation of Ethics) in 1877. His teaching and his published works reinforced his reputation as an authority on Immanuel Kant,* and he became a renowned neo-Kantian philosopher. After retirement from the chair of philosophy at the University of Marburg, Cohen returned to Berlin, gave lectures, and turned in his writings to theology. The book that came out of this period was *Die Religion aus den Quellen des Judentums* (Religion from the Sources of Judaism) (Leipzig, 1919). "In spite of the stock of questions left unanswered by Cohen's principles, he continued to live in the memory of philosophers as a Kantian who dominated to a great extent the philosophical discussion of his time" (*Encyclopedia of Philosophy*, edited by Paul Edwards. New York: Macmillan, 1972, vol. 2, 128.)

COMTE, AUGUSTE. B. January 19, 1798, Montpellier, France. D. September 5, 1857, Paris, France. French philosopher.

Auguste Comte was educated at the École Polytechnique, and for some years he served as secretary to the socialist Claude-Henri de Rouvroy, Comte de Saint-Simon. Auguste Comte is called the founder of positivism.

> Positivism is best defined as a general attitude of mind, a spirit of inquiry, an approach to the facts of human existence. Its central feature is first of all negative in that it rejects the assumption that nature has some ultimate

purpose or end. Secondly, positivism gives up any attempt to discover either the "essence" or the internal or secret causes of things. On the positive side, its spirit is expressed in the attempt to study facts by observing the constant relation between things and formulating the laws of science simply as the laws of constant relations between various phenomena. (Stumpf, 347, 348)

His two major works are *Système de Politique Positive* (1824) and *Cours de Philosophie Positive* (1830–1842).

CONFUCIUS. B. ca. 551 B.C., Shantung Province, China. D. ca. 479 B.C. Chinese philosopher.

Confucius was the son of a magistrate at a city in the dukedom of Lu and a peasant woman. His father died when Confucius was three years old, and the boy grew up in poverty. For a while, he was a government official, but he resigned in 517 and began to teach and attracted many disciples. At age fifty, Confucius was invited to take public office and after one year as a magistrate, he was Minister of Justice, the highest position in the state open to a commoner. As a philosopher, he supported his teaching by the authority of the ancient sages. In ethics, he stressed two virtues: *Li,* the rules of proper conduct, and *ren,* benevolent love. China's first professional teacher, Confucius devoted himself to the teaching of literature and the principles of conduct, and he felt that education should be available to all.

DARWIN, CHARLES. B. February 12, 1809, Shrewsbury, England. D. April 19, 1882, Down in Kent, England. British naturalist.

Charles Darwin attended the universities of Edinburgh and Cambridge, and his friendship with J. T. Henshow, professor of botany at Cambridge, eventually led Darwin into a career as a biologist. An important event in his intellectual development and in the assimilation of material for his work *The Origin of Species* was a trip to the Southern Hemisphere on the *H. M. S. Beagle.* In 1842, Darwin took up residence at Down in Kent where he settled for the next forty years, did his research, and completed *The Origin of Species* (1859). Darwin's theory argues that there are three mechanisms that affect the process of evolution: natural selection, sexual selection, and the inheritance of characteristics acquired during the lifetime of the organism. The theory created reverberations in scientific, social, theological, and philosophical thoughts beginning with its presentation to the Linnaean Society in 1858. The term Darwinism** refers to Darwin's theory of evolution as well as to its impact on other disciplines.

DEMOCRITUS. B. ca. 460 B.C., Abderz, Thrace. D. ca. 370 B.C. Greek philosopher.

Although most sources recognize the fact that knowledge of Democritus' life is limited to untrustworthy tradition, it is generally accepted that he is important in the development of the atomic theory of the universe.

Tradition has it that Democritus was a wealthy citizen of Abdera, in Thrace, and that he travelled widely in the East. Only a few hundred fragments of his works have survived and these deal mostly with ethics.

Democritus explained the origin of the universe through the manifestation of the nature of atoms, which he claimed are uncaused and eternal.

In theology, Democritus was one of the first philosophers to attribute belief in the gods as a desire to explain extraordinary phenomena in nature such as thunder, lightning, and earthquakes.

DESCARTES, RENÉ. B. March 31, 1596, Touraine, France. D. February 1, 1650, Stockholm, Sweden. French philosopher.

René Descartes was educated at the Jesuit College of La Fleche where he specialized in mathematics, logic, and philosophy. Disturbed by the doubts and disputes in the tradition of philosophy, he addressed the problem of intellectual certainty, and he established a set of rules to harness the powers of the mind, turning to mathematics for examples of clear and precise thinking. The Cartesian** method, known as the method of doubt, calls into question all propositions no matter how true they may seem in order to arrive at one that cannot be doubted. Since, as he says, "I could not feign that I was not," he was led to the necessary conclusion that "I think; therefore I am." From an epistemological point of view, it is the clarity and distinction of ideas that make them undoubtable. Such ideas for Descartes are innate and await recognition. Descartes's principal works are *Discourse on Method* (1637), *Meditations on First Philosophy* (1641), *Principles of Philosophy* (1644), and *The Passions of the Soul* (1649).

DEWEY, JOHN. B. October 20, 1859, Burlington, Vermont. D. June 2, 1952, New York City, New York. American philosopher.

John Dewey was born in Burlington, Vermont, and entered the University of Vermont in 1875 where he expressed an interest in philosophy during his last two years. After graduating, he taught high school in Oil

City, Pennsylvania, from 1879 to 1881, then he returned to Vermont and continued to teach. He was subsequently accepted into the graduate school at Johns Hopkins University to begin his study of philosophy. Dewey's early interest in Georg Wilhelm Hegel* and the idealists (see idealism**) gradually gave way to a profound interest in the application of philosophy to practical issues, resulting in several publications in theoretical and applied psychology. In 1894, Dewey was appointed chairman of the department of philosophy, psychology, and education at the University of Chicago, where he was instrumental in creating what came to be known as the Dewey School, which served as a forum for testing his hypotheses. In 1904 he left Chicago for Columbia University where his educational philosophy gained international prominence.

The core of Dewey's thought is to be found in his eventual focus on a naturalistic analysis of experience, and he considered himself a participant in the development of a new empiricism,** an empiricism that attempted a synthesis of the naturalism** of classic Greek thinkers with the methods of contemporary science. His most well-known publications include *Human Nature and Conduct* (1922), *The Quest for Certainty* (1929), *Experience and Education* (1935), and *Logic, the Theory of Inquiry* (1938).

DUNS SCOTUS, JOHN. B. ca. 1266, Duns, Scotland. D. 1308, Cologne, Germany. Scottish theologian.

John Duns Scotus, called *Doctor Subtilis* (subtle doctor), was born in the village of Duns, Scotland. After joining the Franciscan order, he studied and taught at Oxford and Paris. His major work, the *Opus Oxoniensis* (Oxford Work), came out of this period. The *Reportata Parisiensia* (Paris Reports) are students' reports of his lectures at Paris. Primarily a metaphysician, Duns Scotus's major concern focused on what philosophy had to say about God, a necessary a priori condition for any contingent truth to be possible and which must be a part of God's nature. Duns Scotus's profound criticism of his predecessors, Saint Thomas Aquinas* in particular, is based on his contention that their philosophical arguments were inconclusive since it is impossible for philosophy (reason) to solve many of the theological problems which Thomas claims lay in the province of philosophy.

ECKEHART, MEISTER. B. 1260, Hochheim, Germany. D. 1327, Cologne, Germany. German mystic.

At an early age, Eckehart entered the Dominican order and pursued higher studies at Cologne and Paris. In 1312 he became superior-general of the Dominican order for all of Germany. His teaching resulted in charges of heresy in the last part of his life. Eckehart's account of God and the universe was based not just on theology and metaphysics (see metaphysical**) but also on mystical experience (see mysticism**). He evolved a complex psychology in which he posited the notion of the spark within the soul, which led contemporaries to believe that he taught that the soul was uncreated. His surviving works, including treatises, sermons, and fragments, may be found in *Meister Eckehart,* by F. Pfeiffer, ed., 4th ed., Gottingen, Germany, 1924. A more thorough and more readable treatment, including an extensive bibliography, was prepared by R. B. Blakney in 1957: *Meister Eckehart, a Modern Translation.*

EMPEDOCLES. B. ca. 484 B.C., Acragas, Sicily. D. 424 B.C. Greek physician, poet, and philosopher.

What is known of Empedocles's life and thought has been garnered from commentaries, such as that of Theophrastus, and from remnants of two poems: *On the Nature of Things* and *Purifications.* He is said to have played a significant role in politics, was later exiled from Acragas, and spent the remainder of his life wandering in southern Italy. During his travels he acquired a significant reputation as a healer, and in one of his poems he refers to himself as ''a deathless god'' He is best known for the doctrine that the universe consists of four elements: earth, air, fire, and water—a doctrine that dominated Western metaphysics (see metaphysical**) and is reflected in the literature of the Middle Ages. The apparent contradiction in his predilection for the scientific and the mystical (see mysticism**) has posed irreconcilable problems for scholars. Fragments of his poems and other sources of information regarding his life and thought are to be found in *Die Fragmente der Vorsokratiker* (Fragments of the Presocratics), edited by H. Diels and W. Krang, vol. 1, 6th ed. Berlin: N.P., 1951, p. 51.

EPICTETUS. B. 50, Asia Minor. D. 130, Nicopolis, Greece. Greek philosopher.

As a young man, Epictetus attended the lectures of the Stoic Musonius Rufus (see Stoicism**). In 90, he and certain other philosophers were expelled from Rome because of Stoic resistance to tyranny. Epictetus wrote nothing, but his lectures were preserved by his pupil Arrian under the titles *Discourse* and *Enchiridion.* Concerned primarily with ethics, Epictetus claimed that morality is to be sought in the disposition of the will and not in external actions. Epictetus taught submissiveness to the inevitable and saw all events as gifts of God. Though not a religious activist, Epictetus furthered moral activism, which insisted on rigorous moral instruction, and he recommended daily self-examination, which enables one to judge one's actions correctly. Like the modern existentialists (see existentialism**), he insisted that man has the faculty of choice and refusal, and he is, therefore, totally responsible for his actions.

EPICURUS. B. 341 B.C., Samos, Greece. D. 270 B.C., Athens, Greece. Greek philosopher.

Born of Athenian parents on the island of Samos, Epicurus began his philosophical studies at an early age on the Aegean islands and the coast of Asia Minor where he met followers of Plato* and Democritus.* About 311 B.C. he began to teach at Mytilene, but then he moved to Lampascus where he gained a group of followers which included the future leaders of the Epicurean School (see Epicureanism**). In 307 B.C. he returned to Athens and established an Epicurean community. Here he remained for the rest of his life. Epicurus taught that the pleasure and pain, which accompany sense experiences, are the ultimate good and evil and that knowledge comes from sense experience. He rejected much of traditional education, especially geometry and rhetoric, which he considered an abuse of language. Three of Epicurus's letters which contain summaries of his doctrine have been preserved in Diogenes Laertius's *Life of Epicurus*. Most of his writings have been lost, but *On Nature* was recovered from the Epicurean library at Herculaneum. In modern philosophy modified Epicureanism finds expression in Jeremy Bentham and John Stuart Mills's* utilitarianism.**

FEUERBACH, LUDWIG. B. July 28, 1804, Landshut, Bavaria. D. September 13, 1872, Rechenberg, Bavaria. German philosopher, theologian, and moralist.

In 1825, under the influence of Georg Wilhelm Hegel,* Ludwig Feuerbach transferred to the faculty of philosophy at Berlin. He received his doctorate at Erlangen where he stayed to teach as Dozent until 1832. In 1830 he published *Gedanken uber den Tod und Unsterblichkeit* (Thoughts on Death and Immortality), which created a minor scandal since it characterized Christianity as an inhumane religion and resulted in his dismissal from the faculty. In 1836 he retired to Brockberg where he lived on a pension and on income from his writings and money provided by his wife's interest in a pottery factory. Feuerbach's reputation lies in his materialistic (see materialism**) adaptation of Hegelian philosophy (see Hegelianism**), which he saw as the culmination of rationalism.** He pointed out that a certain religious element led Hegel to a downgrading of the material world and the senses. Feuerbach, on the other hand, taught that the body was man's ego and his existence in itself. This materialistic stance, which did not deify consciousness, broke new ground in philosophy and provided a point of departure for Karl Marx* and Friedrich Engels. Feuerbach's works include *The Essence of Christianity* (1841) and *Foundations of the Philosophy of the Future* (1846). His collected works of ten volumes were edited and published in 1903 to 1910.

FICHTE, JOHANN GOTTLIEB. B. May 19, 1762, Rammenau, Germany. D. January 27, 1814, Berlin, Germany. German philosopher.

Johann Gottlieb Fichte was the son of a ribbon maker and the eldest of a large family. As a result of his procosity, he was adopted by Baron von Miltite, who educated the boy. In 1780 he attended the University of Jena and from there he went to the universities of Wittenberg and Leipzig. When the baron died, he left no financial provision for Fichte, and for several years Fichte suffered serious economic privations. Profoundly influenced by Immanuel Kant,* as well as by Gotthold Ephraim Lessing (q.v.), Fichte's opportunity came when Kant reacted favorably to his manuscript, *Critique of all Revelation* (1792), and this in addition to an interest by Johann Wolfgang von Goethe (q.v.) led to a professorship at Jena. At the university, he became friends with Friedrich von Schiller (q.v.). Fichte's adamant adherence to the principles of ethical idealism** and his unorthodox views resulted in a charge of heresy and the loss of his position at Jena. His moral and religious proclivities led to and were largely formed by his studies of Lessing, from whom he acquired a commitment to intellectual freedom and a social culture of tolerance; Baruch Spinoza,* whose pantheism** influenced his philosophical development; and Kant, whose moral philosophy was most influential in Fichte's formulation of his ethical position, which is most specifically addressed in *Das System der Sittenlehre nach den Principien der Wissenschaftslehre* (1798; trans. A. E. Kroeger, *The Science of Ethics as Based on the Science of Knowledge,* London, 1907). His collected works appeared under the title *Sammtliche Werke,* 8 vols., in 1845–1846.

FOURIER, CHARLES. B. April 7, 1772, Besançon, France. D. October 10, 1837, Paris, France. French social philosopher.

Except for his secondary education in a Jesuit school, Charles Fourier was entirely self taught. Apparently influenced by Jean-Jacques Rousseau (q.v.), his work reflects concepts drawn from the Enlightenment** and early nineteenth-century thought. In 1808 he published *Theory of the Four Movements and of General Destinies,* and he developed his ideal system of the social organization in *Treatise on Domestic Agricultural Association* (1822) and *The New World of Industry and Partnership* (1829). Fourier, claiming that man lived in misery because he did not carry out the divine plan of a benevolent deity, established a new social system which would bring happiness and harmony to men. Specifically, he recommended communal living. Organized in phalanxes of about 1800 men, women, and children, participants could give full expression through work and useful activities to all their tastes and capacities. His communities were actually extremely complicated and interdependent socialist societies, in which men own property, work, and live in common. Fourier's system eventually influenced many groups throughout the world; in New England, the Brook Farm experiment was Fourierist in nature.

FREUD, SIGMUND. B. May 6, 1856, Freiberg, Moravia. D. September 23, 1939, London, England. The founder of psychoanalysis.

Sigmund Freud's early years were spent in Vienna, Austria, and in 1873 he entered the university there to study medicine. He specialized in neurology and published research on the subject in 1885 and 1886. Eventually Freud turned to the psychological aspects of neurology. He was the first to recognize neurotic systems as the expression of essentially childish fears and anxieties. He began psychoanalysis as therapy, enabling the patient to become aware of the unconscious through free association. The aim was to enable the patient to recover lost memories in which the unconscious motives are rooted. Freud's major works are the *Interpretation of Dreams* (1899), *Introductory Lectures in Psycho-Analysis* (1916), *Beyond the Pleasure Principle, The Ego and the Id,* and *Group Psychology and Analysis of the Ego.* These last three works are included in *The Standard Edition of the Complete Psychological Works of Sigmund Freud,* edited by James Strachey, London, 1953–1964.

GEULINCX, ARNOLD. B. 1624, Antwerp, Belgium. D. 1669, Leiden, Netherlands. Flemish metaphysician and moralist.

Born in Antwerp, Arnold Geulincx studied philosophy at Louvain, Belgium, where he was appointed professor of philosophy in 1646. Twelve years later, he was dismissed from Louvain on charges that were not made public and he left for Leiden, Netherlands. At the same time he renounced Roman Catholicism for Calvinism (see John Calvin*). In *The Ethics* (1665), Geulincx argues that mind, or soul, and body are mutually exclusive and do not act on each other. However, he agrees with Gottfried Leibniz* that there is some sort of preestablished harmony between mind and body.

GODWIN, WILLIAM. B. March 3, 1756, Wisbech, Cambridgeshire, England. D. April 7, 1836, London, England. English political philosopher and essayist.

Educated at Hoxtin, William Godwin entered the ministry in 1778 but lost his faith. Godwin became famous through a radical work entitled *The Enquiry Concerning Political Justice* (1793). In 1797 he married Mary Wollstonecroft, the author of *A Vindication of the Right of Women* (1798). She died in the same year, a few days after the birth of her daughter Mary, who later became the wife of Percy Bysshe Shelley (q.v.). At this time radicalism** had declined, and Godwin was fiercely attacked for his views. Godwin was a determinist (see determinism**) and an out and out anarchist. He saw the three types of society as corrupting their citizens. They corrupt because they create prejudice and prevent men from seeing reality as it is. To Godwin, "The ideal community must not be large and must not be highly organized. The citizen must never be a cog in a machine, unable to see the significance of his everyday activities. There must be no class distinctions which prevent us from seeing individuals as individuals" (*Encyclopedia of Philosophy*, edited by Paul Edwards. New York: Macmillan, 1972, vol. 3, 334, 360). Godwin was a radical and idealistic (see idealism**) political theorist. His major works include *Life of Chaucer* (1803), *An Essay on Sepulchres* (1809), *Of Population* (1820), *Thoughts on Man* (1831), and *Essay, Never before Published* (1873).

GORGIAS. B. ca. 485 B.C., Leontine, Sicily. D. ca. 380 B.C., Athens, Greece. Greek sophist and rhetorician.

Gorgias was born in Leontine, Sicily, and in 427 B.C. he travelled to Athens, Greece, on a diplomatic mission. Several years later he returned to Athens and made the city his home, although Gorgias travelled much in his lifetime throughout Greece, teaching rhetoric. His philosophy was negative in that he denied the existence of the visible world. He argued that, if anything did exist, it could not be known or communicated. As a rhetorician, Gorgias used commonplace occurrences in his arguments. Plato* named one of his dialogues concerning rhetoric after this Greek sophist and rhetorician. There are two extant works by Gorgias: *The Encomium on Helen* and *The Apology of Paramedes*.

HAECKEL, ERNST HEINRICH. B. February 16, 1834, Potsdam, Germany. D. August 9, 1919, Jena, Germany. German zoologist and monist philosopher.

Ernst Heinrich Haeckel studied medicine and science at Wurzburg,

Berlin, and Vienna, and in 1862 he received an appointment at the University of Jena to teach zoology. He was the first noted German scientist to accept Charles Darwin's* theory of organic evolution. His achievements in zoology brought him offers from famous institutions, but he chose to stay at Jena. A scientist, it is not surprising that in philosophy he favored empiricism** and rationalism.** He attempted a scientific account of the soul, and he advocated a monistic (see monism**) religious view which rejected revelation and theological faith. In his theory of knowledge, Haeckel rejected the thing in itself theory because he claimed it is unknown. According to Haeckel, the only genuine knowledge is that of nature. He held that both empiricism and rationalism are necessary to develop a satisfactory theory of knowledge. His works include *Anthropogenic* (1874), *Monism as Connecting Religion and Science* (1894), *Last Words on Evolution* (1906), and *The Wonders of Life* (1904).

HARTLEY, DAVID. B. August 8, 1705, Armley, Yorkshire, England. D. August 28, 1757, Bath, England. English association psychologist and moral philosopher.

David Hartley was educated at Jesus College, Cambridge. He became a physician and practiced medicine, but he never received a medical degree. As a philosopher he was not an innovator, but he excelled in the consolidation of ideas. An eclectic,** in the best sense, Hartley borrowed and synthesized several doctrines of his predecessors and offered a comprehensive account of human nature. He treats the mind and the body as parts of a coordinate system capable of influencing each other. One of Hartley's most interesting accomplishments lies in his account of the origin of ideas. He says that sensations remain in the mind for a short time, and through repetition of the sensations, simple ideas of sensation arise and then develop into complex ideas. His contribution to philosophy is his work *Observations on Man, His Frame, His Duty and His Expectations* (1749).

HEGEL, GEORG WILHELM. B. August 27, 1770, Stuttgart, Germant. D. November 14, 1831, Berlin, Germany. German philosopher and classical scholar.

Georg Wilhelm Hegel studied theology, philosophy, and classics at Tübingen, Germany, then went to Jena in 1801 as *Privat-dozent* in philosophy and became a professor there in 1805. Driven from the city by the invasion of the French army in 1806, he fled to Bamberg where he remained two years as the editor of a newspaper. The next eight years (1808–1817) he spent as director of the Gymnasium at Nürnberg. In 1816 he accepted a professorship at Heidelberg, and after two years he succeeded Johann Gottlieb Fichte* at the University of Berlin. Hegel's major works are concerned with the philosophy of religion, the history of philosophy, and the philosophy of history. Hegel espoused a theory which he called "the unhappy consciousness," a state in which the individual is divided within himself, if conscious of his own isolation, and attributes all that is good to the activity of God. Concerning the dialectic of morality, Hegel believed that institutions and rules are necessary to civilization because without these restrictions, the mind could not rise to the highest levels. Hegel's theories of aesthetics** are of interest to the world of art, music, and literature. In his works the *Phenomenology* and the *Encyclopedia,* he discussed the nature of art and beauty. One of his most important statements in aesthetics is that art is one of the manifestations of absolute mind. His works include *Phenomenologie des Geistes (The Phenomenology of Mind)* (1807), *Wissenchaft der Logik (Knowledge of Logic)* (1812–1816), and *Encyklopadie des philosophischen Wissenschaften im Grundrisse* (Encyclopedia of the Foundations of Philosophical Knowledge) (1817).

HEIDEGGER, MARTIN. B. September 26, 1889, Messkirch, Germany. D. May 26, 1976, Messkirch, Germany. German philosopher.

Martin Heidegger began his academic career in 1915 as a philosophy teacher at Freiburg in Bresgau where he completed his doctoral dissertation in 1916. In 1928 he succeeded his old teacher, Edmund Husserl,* and assumed the chair in philosophy at Marburg. During World War II, Heidegger was rector of Freiburg University. He later resigned, but the shame and disgrace of his collaboration with the Nazi regime followed him for the remainder of his life. Heidegger attempted a phenomenological (see phenomenology**) analysis of the temporal and historical character of human existence. Convinced that modern thinkers have forgotten or distorted the work of the great Greek philosophers, he argued that the only possible way to truth was through "destructive" (*Destruktion*) analysis of their thought. Søren Kierkegaard's* influence on Heidegger is reflected in his existential analysis of human existence in which the concepts of dread (angst**) and concern (sorge) play central roles (see existentialism**). In *Being and Time (Sein und Zeit,* 1927), he addresses the structures that explain the phenomenon of human existence in the temporal and historical world. His major works include *Duns Scotus* (1916), *Sein und Zeit* (1927), and *Vom Wesen des Grundes* (1929).

HERACLITUS. B. ca. 500 B.C., Ephesus, Asia Minor. Pre-Socratic philosopher.

It is interesting that the ancients nicknamed this philosopher "the obscure" since practically nothing is known about his life or the exact dating. He believed the world to be uncreated, and he spoke of the Logos from which all things take place. He never defined Logos, but it probably means the truth about things and the principle on which they function. Heraclitus believed in the unity of opposites. His greatest contribution to philosophy, however, is the theory of flux, which argues that in nature even apparently stable things are changing, although total balance is always maintained.

HOBBES, THOMAS. B. April 5, 1588, Wiltshire, England. D. December 4, 1679, Hardwick, Derbyshire, England. English philosopher and political theorist.

Thomas Hobbes was raised by a wealthy uncle and educated at Oxford. In 1608, after leaving Oxford, he became a tutor to the son of the Earl of Devonshire. In this position he met influential people and had access to a first-rate library. About this time, Hobbes determined to devote himself to the pursuit of learning, and he immersed himself in study of the classics. In 1628 he published a translation of Thucydides. His philosophical career began after his second visit to the continent. The Countess of Devonshire at this time had dispensed with Hobbes's services, and he took similar employment with Sir Gervaci Clinton. By 1637 he had arrived at his philosophical system, in which the method of geometry and the concepts of motion were applied to man in society. In Hobbes's natural philosophy (see naturalism**), he argues that varieties of motion are the causes of everything, including sensation. Here he assumed that things exist independently of our perceptions of them and that perceptions are really motions. His major works include *Elements of Law* (1640), *Leviathan* (1651), and *Human Nature* (1655).

HUME, DAVID. B. May 7, 1711, Edinburgh, Scotland. D. August 25, 1776, Edinburgh, Scotland. Scottish philosopher.

Although he attended the University of Edinburgh, David Hume did not graduate. As a young man, Hume studied law but abandoned it for studies in literature and philosophy. For several years, Hume settled in LaFleche, France, where he completed *A Treatise of Human Nature* (1739–1740). On returning to Scotland, Hume made a bid for the chair of philosophy at Edinburgh but failed to obtain the post. For some time he was a military attache, after which he took up residence in Edinburgh where he spent the remainder of his life. Hume led a very active public life, and in 1763 he served in France as secretary to the British ambassador. Hume's aim as a philosopher was to construct a Science of Man, that is, to study human nature by using the methods of physical science. His empirical position (see empiricism**) is expressed in his theory of knowledge. He argued that the mind is made up of impressions and that ideas are copies of impressions. His major works include *A Treatise of Human Nature, Essays Moral and Political* (1741–1742), *Principles of Morals* (1751), and *Dialogues on Natural Religion* (1779).

HUSSERL, EDMUND. B. April 8, 1859, Moravia, Czechoslovakia. D. April 21, 1938, Freiburg, Germany. German philosopher.

A mathematician before he was a philosopher, Edmund Husserl studied at Leipzig, Germany, and Berlin. He held teaching posts from 1887 to 1916 at Halle and Gottingen, but finally he settled down at Freiburg where he remained until his retirement in 1928. Although the term *Phanomenologie* (phenomenology**) had been current in philosophical discourse since the mid-eighteenth century (viz., Immanuel Kant* and Johann Heinrich Lambert), Husserl was the first to apply it to a philosophical system. In *Logische Untersuchungen* (Investigations of Logic) (1901), he defines phenomenology as descriptive analysis of subjective processes as opposed to psychology which Moritz Lazarus defines in his *Leben der Seele* (Life of the Soul) (1856–1857) as a search for causal explanations of mental phenomena. Husserl argues that phenomenology provides philosophy with the rigorous method, the method of science, which would lead to first principles and thereby establish the foundations for subsequent research. Like René Descartes,* his intent was to achieve a conception of consciousness that eliminates troublesome presuppositions and discovers the essence of things free of extraneous peripherals. His major works include *Philosophie der Arithmetik* (Philosophy of Arithmetic) (1891) and *Ideen zu einer reinen Phanomenologie und phanomenologischen Philosophie* (1913), trans. by W. R. Boyce Gibson, *General Introduction to Pure Phenomenology* (1931).

JAMES, WILLIAM. B. January 11, 1842, New York City, New York. D. August 26, 1910, Chocura, New Hampshire. American philosopher and psychologist.

William James was the oldest child of Henry James, a Swedenborgian theologian (see Swedenborgianism**), and the brother of Henry James (q.v.), the novelist. At first an art student, William James entered Harvard Medical School in 1863 and obtained his medical degree in 1869. Amid bouts of ill health and interrupted study in Germany, James eventually joined the Harvard staff as an instructor in anatomy and physiology (1873). He subsequently became a professor of philosophy at Harvard and remained at this post until 1897. In his *Principles*. James criticizes a priori metaphysics (see metaphysical**) as abstractions that philosophers arrive at apart from experience of the real world. The rendering of experience was an essential element in his philosophy, and he spoke of the world as "a world of pure experience." His major works are *The Varieties of Religious Experience* and *The Principles of Psychology* (2 vols., 1890). His teachings on pragmatism** and radical empiricism** are expressed in *Pragmatism* (1907) and *Essays in Radical Empiricism* (1912).

JASPERS, KARL. B. February 23, 1883, Oldenburg, Germany. D. February 26, 1969, Basel, Switzerland. German philosopher.

Jaspers began his career as a medical student; he did research in a psychiatric clinic and published *Allgemein Psychopathologie* (General Psychopathology) in 1913. From 1921 to 1937 he was professor of philosophy at Heidelberg but was dismissed because he had a Jewish wife. Deeply influenced by Friedrich Nietzsche* and Søren Kierkegaard,* Jaspers attempted an existentialist analysis (see existentialism**) of the human condition with particular emphasis on the problem raised by man's confrontations with the inevitability of death, guilt, and struggle. He addresses, in his works, the incompleteness and relativity of scientific research, the profoundest needs and demands of the individual, and the seemingly futile search for metaphysical truth. His major works include *Psychologie und Weltanschauung* (1919), *Die Geistige Situation der Zeit* (1931), *Vernunft und Existenz* (1935), and *Existenzphilosophie* (1938).

JUNG, CARL. B. July 26, 1875, Kesswil, Switzerland. D. June 6, 1961, Kusnacht, Switzerland. Swiss psychologist and psychiatrist.

Carl Jung attended the universities of Basel and Zurich (1895–1900) and then worked at the university psychiatric clinic in Zurich. Between 1907 and 1914, he collaborated with Sigmund Freud.* From 1933 to 1941, Jung served as professor of psychology at the Federal Polytechnical University in Zurich. In 1943, he was appointed professor of medical psychology at the University of Basel. Jung's major work was *The Psychology of the Unconscious* (1921). His major contribution was the development of concepts of the extroverted and introverted personality and research dealing with archetypes** and the collective unconscious.

KANT, IMMANUEL. B. April 22, 1724, Königsberg, Prussia. D. February 12, 1804, Königsberg, Prussia. German philosopher.

In 1740, Immanuel Kant entered the University of Königsberg where he studied the classics, physics, and philosophy. His life was ordinary by most standards, and it is said that in his lifetime he never travelled thirty miles beyond his native town. As a student, he was much influenced by a young philosophy professor, Martin Knutson, who introduced him to the rationalist philosophy (see rationalism**) of Gottfried Leibniz.* In 1770 he was appointed to the chair of philosophy at the same university. He revolutionized philosophy. Kant argues that the function of reason is to synthesize sense data, for which purpose it relies on the validity of such principles as "causality," principles which are not inductive generalizations from sense data but are rather a priori, formal, transcendental elements which the mind imposes on sense data. He recognizes two forms of the *sensibility:* space and time as formal demands of reason other than properties of things-in-themselves. The synthetic form of the *understanding* Kant designates as "categories," which are arranged in four groups of three each: quantity, quality, relation, and modality. Without these transcendental forms, there could be no understanding or knowledge of nature. Although reason is the lawgiver to nature, Kant argues that the will must be autonomous if the unconditional moral law, the "categorical imperative," is to have validity. His major works include *Critique of Pure Reason* (1781), *The Critique of Practical Reason* (1788), and *The Critique of Judgement* (1790).

KIERKEGAARD, SØREN. B. May 5, 1813, Copenhagen, Denmark. D. November 11, 1855, Copenhagen, Denmark. Danish philosopher and religious thinker.

Raised in a stern Christian environment, Søren Kierkegaard reacted early against orthodox religion. He was a sensitive, melancholy individual, who suffered intense frustrations. Until recently, Kierkegaard's influence was mostly felt in Scandinavian and German circles, but lately his unorthodox views have made an impact on the philosophical and literary worlds. Some of his views may be summarized as follows: sin is worse than suffering; man is an egoist and must suffer despair; God is beyond reason. Kierkegaard's works are not translated into English, but his *Sammtliche Werke* (collected works) are published in German. The works of Kierkegaard that have influenced literary figures the most are *Fear and Trembling* (1843) and *The Concept of Dread* (1844).

LANGER, SUSANNE. B. December 20, 1895, New York City, New York. D. July 17, 1985, New York City. American aesthetic philosopher.

Susanne Langer attended Radcliffe College and received both her bachelor's degree and her doctorate from that institution. In 1921 and 1922, she studied at the University of Vienna and then returned to Radcliffe as a tutor in philosophy. From 1927 to 1943 she was an instructor at the University of Delaware, and from 1945 to 1950 she was an instructor at Columbia University. In 1954 she went to Connecticut College for women and remained there as a professor of philosophy until 1963. Her first publication, *The Practise of Philosophy,* appeared in 1930. Her most successful philosophical work and the one that has assured her of a lasting reputation is *Mind: An Essay on Human Feeling* (3 vols: 1967, 1972, 1982). Her other works include *Problems of Art: Ten Philosophical Lectures* (1957) and many articles in philosophical journals.

LEIBNIZ, GOTTFRIED. B. July 1, 1646, Leipzig, Germany. D. November 14, 1716, Hanover, Germany. German philosopher.

Gottfried Leibniz entered the University of Leipzig at the age of fifteen to study philosophy, and then he went to Jena and Altdorf where he received his doctorate in law at the age of twenty-one. For some time, Leibniz served on diplomatic missions and enjoyed wide travels. In this capacity, he met Baruch Spinoza* and later became a critic of Spinoza's philosophy. Leibniz argued that the primary ingredient of things in the universe is not matter, but that objects consist rather of Monads which constitute the essential substance of things. Leibniz's most significant works include *New Essays on Human Understanding* (1765), *Essays in Theodicy* (1710), *Discourse on Metaphysics* (1686), *New System of Nature* (1695), and *Monadology* (1714).

LOCKE, JOHN. B. August 29, 1632, Wrington, Somerset, England. D. October 28, 1704, Oates, Essex, England. English philosopher.

John Locke was raised in a Puritan home and learned early the virtue of hard work. He was trained in the classics at Westminister School and then enrolled at Oxford University. Later he was appointed censor of Moral Philosophy. His interest in science led him to the study of medicine; in 1674, he obtained his medical degree and accepted a position as the personal physician of the Earl of Shaftesbury. In 1690 Locke published two books which were to make him famous as a philosopher and political theorist: *An Essay Concerning Human Understanding* and *Two Treatises On Civil Government.* With the first, he became "the first one to produce a full-length inquiry into the scope and limits of the human mind"

(Stumpf, 279). His views on religion and education are expressed in such essays as *The Reasonableness of Christianity* (1695) and *Some Thoughts on Education* (1693). Locke argued against the divine right of kings and insisted that ecclesiastical authority depended upon the consent of reason.

LUCRETIUS (TITUS LUCRETIUS CARUS). B. ca. 99 B.C., Rome, Italy. D. 55 B.C., Rome, Italy. Roman philosopher.

Although born of a good Roman family and well educated, Lucretius probably lived the life of a recluse. He is known only as the author of the famous *De Rerum Natura,* which is the most complete known exposition of Epicureanism.** Some scholars feel that Lucretius was an original thinker who was forced to rethink rather than merely restate Epicurus's teaching. He wrote in Latin and developed his own technical vocabulary. In the poem, which makes extensive use of the devices of simile and metaphor, Lucretius expresses the view that philosophy must be felt as well as thought. His most outstanding contribution to literature is his philosophy of history.

MARCUSE, HERBERT. B. July 19, 1898, Berlin, Germany. Naturalized U.S. citizen, 1940. D. July 29, 1979, Sternberg, East Germany. German/American social philosopher.

Herbert Marcuse obtained his doctorate at Freiburg and immediately became an associate of the Institut fur Sozial Forschung (Institute for Social Research) in Frankfurt. In 1934, he fled Nazi Germany to the United States where the institute was reestablished at Columbia University. In *Reason and Revolution* (1934), he stated that Karl Marx* was closer to the ideas of Georg Wilhelm Hegel* than the Soviet interpretation allowed, and he argued that all political and social systems were in need of drastic revision. His other major works include *Eros and Civilization* (1955); *One-Dimensional Man* (1964), which critics felt was addressed to the guilt-ridden American student population; *A Critique of of Pure Tolerance* (1965); and *Counterrevolution and Revolt* (1972).

MARITAIN, JACQUES. B. November 18, 1882, Paris, France. D. April 28, 1973, Toulouse, France. French philosopher.

Jacques Maritain studied for two years in Heidelberg, Germany (1905 to 1907) and then in Paris under the tutelage of Henri Bergson.* By 1906 he came under the influence of Leon Bloy and consequently was converted to the Catholic church. His first book, an attack on Bergson, appeared in 1913 under the title *La Philosophie Bergsonienne.* Soon Maritain, through lectures and numerous publications, became a defender of Catholic orthodoxy and the chief exponent of the neo-Thomistic movement in France. From 1945 to 1949, Maritain was French ambassador to the Vatican. In *L'Art et Scholastique* (Art and Scholasticism), a book on aesthetics,** he discussed the Thomistic doctrine of art. His other works include *True Humanism* (1938), *Man and the State* (1951), and *On the Use of Philosophy* (1961).

MARX, KARL. B. May 5, 1818, Trier, Germany. D. March 14, 1883, London, England. German philosopher and social critic.

Karl Marx was educated at the universities of Bonn and Berlin and received his doctorate in philosophy at Berlin in 1841. Very early in his career he became a left Hegelian (Georg Wilhelm Hegel*), then a Feuerbachian (Ludwig Feuerbach*). In 1842–1843 he was editor of the radical newspaper *Die Rheinische Zeitung*. By 1844 Marx had become a close friend of Friedrich Engels, and he now called himself a Communist. In 1845 and 1846, with Engels, he wrote *Die Heilige Familie* (The Holy Family) and *Die Deutsche Ideologie* (The German Ideology). In 1848 Marx and Engels published *The Manifesto of the Communist Party,* and at this time Marx began work on the *Neue Rheinische Zeitung* (New Rhine Newspaper). By 1859 he had written the foundation of his most famous work, *Das Kapital* (1867). In addition to his writings, Marx was engaged throughout his lifetime in practical political activity, especially in the labor movement. Marx, together with Engels, was the founder of the school of philosophy known as dialectical materialism,** which espouses an epistemological empiricism,** a strongly humanitarian theory of value, and a social theory based essentially on economic determinism.** Marx predicted the eventual demise of capitalism, to be replaced by socialism, leading ultimately to a classless, politically self-regulatory society.

MILL, JOHN STUART. B. May 20, 1806, London, England. D. May 8, 1873, Avignon, France. English philosopher and economist.

John Stuart Mill was trained by his father James Mill and Jeremy Bentham. As a young man, Mill worked as a civil servant in the East India Company, but overwork ended in a breakdown and depression that lasted for several months. In 1865 he was elected to Parliament where he fought for the exploited negroes in Jamaica and for the redistribution of land in Ireland. An empiricist (see empiricism**) in logic and epistemology, he arrived at his own version of utilitarianism** that was somewhat different than Bentham's. For Mill, the true utilitarian interprets the greatest happiness principle to mean not *my* greatest happiness but the greatest happiness of the greatest number. Mill's literary achievements consist of *System of Logic* (1843), *Principles of Political Economy* (1848), and *Utilitarianism* (1861).

NIEBUHR, REINHOLD. B. June 21, 1892, Wright City, Missouri. D. June 1, 1971, Stockbridge, Massachussetts. American theologian.

Reinhold Niebuhr received his Bachelor of Arts degree from Yale in 1914 and immediately began pastoral work in Detroit, Michigan, where he remained for thirteen years. In 1928 he became professor of applied Christianity at Union Theological Seminary in New York and remained there until his retirement in 1960. He eventually became interested in Marxism** and described himself as a Christian Marxist. In 1935, he expounded a radically perfectionist and transcendent position in his work *An Interpretation of Christian Ethics* (1935). After this publication, he was labeled "neoorthodox." He died in 1971, and to the very end his central interest was "the defense and justification of the Christian faith." His works include *Does Civilization Need Religion?* (1927) and *Moral Man and Immoral Society* (1932).

NIETZSCHE, FRIEDRICH. B. October 15, 1844, Rocken, Germany. D. August 25, 1900, Weimar, Germany. German philosopher.

Friedrich Nietzsche was one of the most renowned philosophical psychologists of the last century. He attended the University of Bonn where he studied theology. From 1864 to 1869 he attended the University of Leipzig where he gained a reputation as a brilliant student in classical philosophy. In a most surprising move, he was appointed professor of philosophy at the University of Basel at the early age of twenty-four. During the Franco-Prussian war, he served with the ambulance corps, but illness forced him to resign. In 1872 his first book, *The Birth of Tragedy,* appeared. In 1879 he resigned his chair at Basel and spent the remainder of his life writing. He was the first to recognize a difference between the philosopher and the scientist. He argued that the traditional values of western civilization are not applicable to the modern world, and he substituted his "will to power" as the essential principle in the development of the individual and society. Nietzsche attempted to develop a philosophy of life which would serve to enable one to withstand the misery of human existence. His other works include *Thus Spake Zarathustra* (1883), *Beyond Good and Evil* (1886), and *Genealogy of Morals* (1887).

ORIGEN. B. 185, Alexandria, Egypt. D. 254, Caesarea, Palestine. Christian theologian and exegete of the Bible.

Origen was born in Alexandria of Christian parents, and in 204 he was made head of a Christian school there. He taught until 231, when a conflict with the bishop forced him to leave for Caesarea where he taught until his death. His works include *De Principiis* (trans. 1936), in which he argues that Apostolic doctrine is incomplete; *On Prayer* (trans. 1954); and *Contra Celsum* (trans. 1953). Origen was a genuinely philosophical theologian who studied and drew from many philosophers including Plato,* the Stoics (see Stoicism**), and the Peripatetics.

PARMENIDES. B. Elea, Italy, and lived in sixth century B.C. Greek philosopher.

Plato* recorded that Parmenides visited Socrates* in Athens, Greece, in around 456 B.C. Otherwise, little is known about the man except that he was a contemporary of Heraclitus.* He was educated in the Pythagorean** tradition and developed his philosophy in a didactic poem entitled "On Nature." Here we see that he conceived the world as a unity and unchangeable. In one section of the poem, "On Opinion," Parmenides explains the sensory illusion of motion and change.

PASCAL, BLAISE. B. June 19, 1623, Clermont-Ferrand, France. D. August 19, 1662, Paris, France. French mathematician, physicist, inventor, philosopher, and theologian.

Blaise Pascal was a child prodigy who at the age of seventeen published an essay on mathematics that was acclaimed by René Descartes.* He invented the first digital calculator (1642–1644). Studies in geometry and hydrodynamics led him to invent the hydraulic press and to discover Pascal's law of pressure. In 1654 he entered the convent of Port-Royal where he wrote *Les Provenciales,* a defense of Jansenism against the Jesuits, and the *Pensées*. Pascal spent his last years in scientific research.

PLATO. B. 428 B.C., Athens, Greece. D. 348 B.C., Athens, Greece. Greek philosopher.

Born of an aristocratic Athenian family, Plato received the best elementary education possible. At the age of twenty, he joined the Socratic Circle and remained with them until the death of Socrates.* He traveled widely in Greece, Italy, Sicily, and Egypt, and in his travels he acquired a knowledge of Pythagoreanism (see Pythagorean**), the Heraclitean flux,** and other pre-Socratic philosophies. He founded his own school of philosophy in Athens in 387 B.C. For Plato the object of knowledge is Being, variously referred to as Ideas, Forms, Essences, Universals, which are discovered through reason and insight in nature, form the basis of reality, and are independently real as opposed to the phenomena of nature which are dependently real, and are approximations of Ideas. The soul, or mind, the seat of reason, is eternal, and virtue is achieved through knowledge of Being. Plato's aesthetics,** expressed in *Ion* and in Book X of *The Republic,* relegate the artist to an inferior ontological status since the objects of art are imitations of phenomena which are themselves imitations of Ideas. His works have been well preserved, and it is safe to say that no other philosopher (except perhaps Aristotle*) has influenced the history of philosophy more. An English translation, *The Dialogues of Plato* (trans. Benjamin Jowett, 4th ed., 4 vols., 1953) includes introductions and commentary.

PLOTINUS. B. 205, Lykopilis, Egypt. D. 270. The founder of Neoplatonism.**

Plotinus was born in Lykopilis, upper Egypt, and he may have been a Hellenized Egyptian. He studied philosophy under Amonius Saccas. Because of some political involvement, Plotinus was forced to flee to Antioch, in Asia Minor. He proceeded to Rome where he conducted a school of philosophy. After ten years he began writing, and at this time he gained influence with the new emperor Gallienus. At the end of his life, Plotinus probably left Rome and his pupils dispersed after the death of Gallienus, which suggests that Plotinus had been involved in some political intrigue. Plotinus's works, which have come down to us through his pupil Porphyry, are entitled *The Enneads* (trans. 1951–1959).

PYTHAGORAS. Ca. 560 B.C.–480 B.C. Greek philosopher and mathematician.

Little is known of Pythagoras's early life, but at one point he migrated to Croton in southern Italy and founded a philosophical and religious school which practiced vegetarianism and believed in reincarnation. Pythagoras and his followers were very concerned with numbers and mathematical practices. Much of the information on Pythagoras has come down to us from Aristotle's* *Metaphysics* and fragments of the book of Philolaus, a prominent Pythagorean** of the late 5th century B.C.

ROYCE, JOSIAH. B. November 20, 1855, Grass Valley, California. D. September 14, 1916, Cambridge, Massachusetts. American idealist philosopher.

Josiah Royce received his bachelor's degree from the University of

California in 1875 and his doctorate from Johns Hopkins University in 1878. He had also studied in Germany at Leipzig and Gottingen and had attended the lectures of Hermann Lotze. In 1882 he attended Harvard where he remained as one of the mainstays of the philosophy department. Royce attempted to resolve the problems raised by a religious view of reality through an eclectically structured metaphysical** system. His major works are *The Religious Aspect of Philosophy* (1885) and *The Problem of Christianity* (1913).

RUSSELL, BERTRAND. B. May 18, 1872, Trelleck, Wales. D. February 2, 1970, Penrhyndraeth, Merionetshire, Wales. British philosopher, mathematician, and social reformer.

Bertrand Russell's early education was at home with private tutors. He entered Cambridge University in October 1890 and studied mathematics and philosophy at Trinity College. He lectured there in philosophy from 1910 to 1916 when he was dismissed because of pacifist activities. From 1916 to the late 1930s, he supported himself through writing and public lectures. Russell's most significant contribution may be his work in logic and mathematical theory and his insistence on the identification of the methods of philosophical inquiry with those of science. He published *On Education, Especially in Early Childhood* in 1926 and *Education and the Social Order* in 1932. His other works include *Principles of Mathematics* (1903), *Introduction to Mathematical Philosophy* (1919), *Principia Mathematica* (with A. N. Whitehead), 3 vols. (1910–1913), *The Problems of Philosophy* (1912), and *An Inquiry into the Meaning of Truth* (1940).

SANTAYANA, GEORGE. B. December 16, 1863, Madrid, Spain. D. September 26, 1952, Rome, Italy. American philosopher.

The son of a Spanish father and an American mother, George Santayana was brought at an early age to the United States to receive a good Bostonian education that ended at Harvard. Santayana was never really Americanized, however, and after twenty-three years of teaching at Harvard, he settled first in England and then in Italy. An epistemological skeptic, he held that belief in the external world rests on an act of "animal faith." His works include *The Life of Reason* (1905), *Scepticism and Animal Faith* (1923), and *The Last Puritan* (1935), a best-selling novel.

SARTRE, JEAN-PAUL. B. June 21, 1905, Paris, France. D. April 15, 1980, Paris, France. French philosopher, novelist, dramatist, and critic.

Jean-Paul Sartre graduated from the École Normale Supérieure in 1929, and between 1931 and 1945 he was a teacher at the Lycée. His first novel was *La Nausée* (Paris, 1938, trans. R. Baldick, *Nausea,* Harmondsworth, 1965). Between 1936 and 1940 he published three monographs on the imagination and the emotions in the phenomenological (see phenomenology**) style of Edmund Husserl.* With the publication of his chief philosophical work, *L'être et Le Néant* (Paris, 1943, trans. E. Barnes, *Being and Nothingness,* New York, 1956), Sartre emerged as the leading existentialist thinker (see existentialism**). He continued to influence French philosophical and literary circles with such publications as *Critique de La Raison dialectique* (Paris, 1960, trans. A. M. Sheridan-Smith, *Critique of Dialectical Reason,* London, 1976). An important play that demonstrates his existential theories is entitled *Les Mouches* (Paris, 1943, trans. S. Gilbert, *The Flies,* London, 1946). As a literary critic, his most important work is *Qu'est-ce que la Litterature?* (Paris, 1947, trans. B. Frechtman, *What Is Literature?,* London, 1950).

SCHELLING, FRIEDRICH. B. January 27, 1775, Leonberg, Württemberg, Germany. D. August 20, 1854, Bad Ragaz, Switzerland. German idealist philosopher.

Friedrich Schelling was born at Leonberg in Württemberg, the son of a learned Lutheran pastor. While a student at Tübingen, he became friends with Georg Wilhelm Hegel* and Friedrich Hölderlin (q.v.), the great Romantic poet (see romanticism**). In 1798, at the unusually young age of twenty-three, he received a professorship at Jena, where he became a colleague and friend of Johann Gottlieb Fichte,* Germany's leading philosopher at the time. In 1802 and 1803, Schelling joined forces with Hegel and edited the *Kritisches Journal der Philosophie* (The Critical Journal of Philosophy). At this time, Johann Wolfgang von Goethe (q.v.) and Friedrich von Schiller (q.v.) were in nearby Weimar and at the heights of their careers. Schelling met both writers and became friends with Goethe. From 1803 to 1806, Schelling taught philosophy at the University of Würzburg. Schelling's major publications were *Ideen zu einer Philosophie der Natur* (Ideas for a Philosophy of Nature) (1797), *Von der Weltseele* (On the World Soul) (1798), and *Erster Entwurf eines Systems der Natur Philosophie* (First Design of a System of Natural Philosophy) (1798). During his lifetime, his main influence in England was in aesthetics,** and his lectures on the *Philosophy of Art* were translated into English in 1845.

SCHOPENHAUER, ARTHUR. B. February 22, 1788, Danzig (now Gdansk), Poland. D. September 21, 1860, Frankfurt am Main, Germany. German philosopher.

Arthur Schopenhauer attended schools in France, Switzerland, and Austria, and then he entered the University of Göttingen as a medical student. In 1811 he went to the University of Berlin where he studied philosophy and attended lectures of Johann Gottlieb Fichte.* He received his degree in 1813 and spent the next four years writing his major philosophical work, *The World as Will and Idea* (1818). The publication of this work helped him to obtain the post of lecturer at the University of Berlin. Because Georg Wilhelm Hegel* was lecturing at the university during the same hours as Schopenhauer, Schopenhauer advertised his opposition to Hegelian concepts. Nevertheless, Schopenhauer's lectures failed to attract students (Hegel's authority was too firmly grounded), and he did not attempt to establish himself further academically. From then on, he lived a solitary life, disappointed in his lack of recognition, but he continued to write. He published an essay *Über den Willen in der Natur* (Concerning the Will in Nature) (1836) and a volume on ethics *die Beiden Grundprobleme der Ether* (Both Basic Problems of the Ether) (1841). In 1851 he published *Parerga and Paralipomena,* which received considerable recognition in Germany and abroad. Discussions of his ideas appeared in journals, and by the time of his death he had a growing circle of admirers in England, Russia, and the United States.

SENECA, LUCIUS ANNUS (THE YOUNGER). B. ca. 4 B.C., Corduba, Italy. D. A.D. 65, Rome, Italy. Roman philosopher, statesman, and tragedian.

History states that Seneca was Rome's leading intellectual figure in the mid-first century A.D. He began a political career about A.D. 31, but for some unknown reason was banished to Corsica. On his return to Rome, after the murder of Emperor Claudius in 54, Seneca became a powerful political figure in Rome. When he retired from politics, he devoted himself to the writing of philosophical works and tragedies, which influenced the so-called revenge dramas of Renaissance** England.

SOCRATES. B. ca. 470 B.C., Athens, Greece. D. 399 B.C., Athens, Greece. Greek philosopher.

Very little is known about the life of this original and influential Greek philosopher. As a young man, he was familiar with the members of the Periclean circle. He served as a hoplite in the Peloponnesian War and exhibited courage in the campaigns of Potidaea, Delium, and Amphipolis. Socrates's personal life was subordinated to "the supreme Art of Philosophy." The teaching of Socrates has come down to us in the writings of Plato,* especially *Phaedo* and the *Apology*. The Socratic problem, that is, the question of facts about the historical Socrates as well as about his philosophical posture, is yet to be resolved. The Socratic method is a teaching technique which, through the process of asking pointed questions, the teacher elicits increasingly definite answers from the student as illustrated in Plato's dialogue, *Meno*. The method is based on Socrates's belief that man is born with knowledge which he cannot recall without the help of a teacher (the theory of reminiscence).

SPENCER, HERBERT. B. April 27, 1820, Derby, Derbyshire, England. D. December 8, 1903, Brighton, Sussex, England. English philosopher.

Herbert Spencer's early education was sporadic. At the age of seventeen, he began to study civil engineering, but nothing came of this. He exhibited an early interest in education, politics, and religion, and he attempted unsuccessfully to publish articles and reviews. In 1850, with a sketchy formal education behind him, he published his first book *Social Statistics,* which, nine years before the publication of *The Origin of Species,* advocated a theory of evolution similar to that of Charles Darwin's.* In 1854, despite his lack of systematic learning, he wrote and published *The Principles of Psychology.* His other works include *The First Principle* (1862) and *Principles of Ethics* (1879–1893).

SPENGLER, OSWALD. B. May 29, 1880, Blankenburg, Germany. D. May 8, 1936, Munich, Germany. German historian and philosopher.

Oswald Spengler studied philosophy, history, mathematics, and art at the universities of Munich and Berlin, where he received his doctoral degree in 1904. He started his academic career as a teacher of mathematics at the university of Munich. In 1918, there appeared the first volume of his remarkable philosophy of history, *Der Untergang des Abendlandes* (The Decline of the West, 1922–1928). The second volume appeared in 1922. In this work, Spengler predicted the disintegration of western European and American civilization. His other works include *Der Mensch und die Technik* (1931) (Man and Technology, 1932) and *Jahre der Entscheidung* (1933) (Hour of Decision, 1934).

SPINOZA, BARUCH. B. November 24, 1632, Amsterdam, Netherlands. D. February 21, 1677, The Hague, Netherlands. Dutch Jewish philosopher.

Baruch Spinoza was the greatest Jewish philosopher. He was a simple, humble man of great intellectual powers. He refused to accept the chair of philosophy at Heidelberg, in Germany, because he wanted to preserve his freedom to pursue his own ideas and search for truth. He felt that

exact knowledge of reality could be achieved by following the Cartesian**
method. Spinoza added to René Descartes's* method a highly systematic
arrangement of principles and axioms. Spinoza identified God with the
entire cosmos. In refining his knowledge of things, Spinoza moved from
imagination to reason and finally to intuition. Spinoza's major works are
Exposition More Geometric of Descartes' Principles (1633), *Tract Theol-
Politicus* (1670), *Ethics, Demonstrated in Geometrical Order* (1677),
Political Treatise (1677), and *De Intellectu Emendatione* (1677).

SWEDENBORG, EMANUEL. B. January 29, 1688, Stockholm, Sweden. D. March 29, 1772, London, England. Swedish scientist, mystic,
philosopher, and theologian.

Emanuel Swedenborg graduated from Uppsala, Sweden, in 1709 and
then spent the next five years traveling abroad where he gained new
insights in the natural sciences. He returned to Sweden in 1715 and
published the country's first scientific journal. In 1734 he produced his
Principia Rerum Naturalium (Principles of Natural Things). From 1740
Swedenborg devoted himself to Biblical and mystical writings. He
claimed to have direct knowledge of the spiritual world, and he defined
three levels of "being in God": Love, wisdom, and use. The Swedenborgian New (Jerusalem) Church was established in London in 1783. A
prolific writer, Swedenborg wrote in Latin, but the majority of his works
are available in translation, published largely by New Church societies.
These include *First Principles of Natural Things,* trans. A. Clissold
(1846); *The Infinite and Final Cause of Creation,* trans. J. J. Wilkenson
(1908); *A Philosopher's Notebook,* trans. A. Acton (1931); and *Psychological Transactions,* trans. A. Acton (1955).

TEILHARD DE CHARDIN, PIERRE. B. January 5, 1881, Sarcenat,
France. D. October 4, 1955, New York City, New York. French philosopher and paleontologist.

The son of a gentleman farmer, Pierre Tielhard showed an early interest
in geology. At the age of ten he began boarding at the Jesuit College of
Mongre, and at eighteen he entered the Jesuit novitiate at Aix-en-Prov-
ence. In 1912 he was ordained a priest and when World War I broke
out, he elected to serve as a stretcher bearer rather than a chaplain. His
courage on the battlefield earned him the Legion of Honor. In 1923 he
taught at the Catholic Institute of Paris. In the following years he made
several paleontological and geological missions to China where he was
involved in the discovery of Peking man. He returned to France in 1946,
but, frustrated in his desire to teach at the Collège de France, he moved

to the United States and spent the last years of his life at the Wenner-Gren Foundation in New York City. Teilhard was a first-rate paleoanthropologist, a scientist who never lost his sense of piety, or his faith, a sometimes confusing and paradoxical coalesence of the spiritual and the scientific. He accepts the Aristotelian** notion of the relationship between potency and act, and he argues for a spiritual evolution, guided by love, which will lead the universe toward an ''omega point,'' or transcendental consciousness. His major works include *The Phenomenon of Man* (trans. 1959), *The Appearance of Man* (trans. 1965), *The Divine Milieu* (trans. 1960), and *Hymn of the Universe* (trans. 1965).

VOLTAIRE (FRANCOIS-MARIE AROUET). B. November 21, 1694, Paris, France. D. May 30, 1778, Paris, France. French writer and self-styled philosopher.

Voltaire was born into a middle-class family and was educated by the Jesuits at the college of Louis-Le-Grand in Paris. For some time he studied law but finally abandoned it to become a writer. He wrote several classical tragedies but is known today by literary enthusiasts as the author of *Candide,* a satire on philosophical optimism. His only philosophical work, which was published in 1734, was *Lettres Philosophiques* (Philosophical Letters).

Glossary of Philosophical Terms, Concepts, and Movements

Absurdity: In philosophy, a statement or theory that is plainly not true, not sensible, or contradictory. Something that is foolish, ridiculous.

Aesthetics: The branch of philosophy that provides a theory of the beautiful and of the fine arts.

Allegory: The symbolic embodiment or generalization intended to reflect a given aspect of experience.

Altruism: Selfless concern for the welfare of others.

Angst: A German word meaning extreme anxiety.

Anima: A term used by Carl Jung to refer to the feminine side of man's personality. The corresponding masculine side of the woman's personality is call *animus*.

Anthropologist: A social scientist who deals with the origin and development of races, customs, and beliefs of mankind.

Apocolyptic: Pertaining to a prophetic revelation. From the Apocalypse or the Book of Revelation in the Bible.

Apollonian: A term borrowed by Friedrich Nietzsche* from Greek mythology to designate reason, culture, and moral rectitude (see Dionysian**).

Archetype: A primordial image, character, or pattern that recurs throughout literature.

Aristotelian: (Literary) method of analysis used by Aristotle* in the *Poetics*. This criticism is not centered in a historical or social context but finds its values within the work itself.

Atheism: Atheism is the denial of the existence of God, a position that excludes the possibility of a first principle. Atheism opposes religious belief and the worship of God. Several of the materialistic doctrines (see materalism**) in the period of the Enlightenment** express an atheistic posture. There is a famous refutation of Baruch Spinoza* to the charge that he was atheistic.

Atomism: The view that there are discrete irreducible elements of finite spatial or temporal span, for example, the atomic doctrine of Democritus* that the real world consists of atoms of diverse shapes.

Authenticity: A value term, prominent in existentialist philosophy; identified by Martin Heidegger* as the path to pure Being through individual self-identity.

Autocriticism: Self-criticism.

Buddhism: The philosophic and ethical teachings of Gautama Buddha. The basic assumptions in Buddhist philosophy are the following: a causal nexus in nature and man, the impermanence of things, and the illusory notion of substance and soul. Buddhists believe in the universality of suffering and in the relief of suffering through the cessation of craving, which is achieved through the Noble Eightfold Path: right views, right aspiration, right speech, right conduct, right livelihood, right effort, right mindfulness, and right contemplation.

Calvinism: The doctrine of John Calvin,* especially his affirmation of predestination and redemption by grace alone.

Cartesian: A term used originally in the seventeenth century to refer to the followers of René Descartes,* it means the resolution to doubt everything that cannot pass the test of the criteria of truth as being clearness and distinctness of ideas. Cartesians believe in three kinds of ideas: innate ideas, ideas produced in the mind, and ideas that come from without.

Contingency: An accidental happening or occurrence dependent on chance.

Creative Evolution: The theory that the cosmos is in a process of irreversible change toward increasing complexity and fulfillment.

Cultural milieu: A particular environment that is determined by a certain culture.

Darwinism: Named for Charles Darwin, the evolution of populations through natural selection, sexual selection, and inheritance. Natural selection involves variations that provide the organism with an advantage over the rest of the population in the struggle for life.

Deism: The belief that God created the world but has no relation with it, nor does he govern it. Deism sometimes refers to a group of seventeenth- and eighteenth-century thinkers in England and America who did not believe in revelation but held that reason is the touchstone to religious truth.

Determinism: The view that all things in nature behave according to inviolate and unchanging laws of nature, a theory inspired by the development of the physical sciences in the seventeenth and eighteenth centuries.

Dialectic: The art or practice of logical discussion involving the principles of logic.

Dialectical Materialism: See Marxism.

Dionysian: A term borrowed by Friedrich Nietzsche* from Greek mythology to designate the irrational and undisciplined (see Apollonian**).

Eclectic: Choosing the best from diverse sources.

Élan Vital: A term used by Bergson*; a vital force that serves as a source of efficient causation and evolution in nature (see vitalism**).

Empiricism: A proposition that the sole source of knowledge is experience or data of the senses only. In the form of denial, empiricism denies a priori knowledge, denies that there are universal truths, and denies innate or inborn knowledge.

Enlightenment: A movement of thought and belief concerned with the interrelated concepts of God, reason, nature, and man that gained wide acceptance among European intellectuals in the eighteenth and nineteenth centuries; its basic conviction was that through reason mankind could arrive at knowledge and happiness.

Epicureanism: A philosophical movement of ancient Greece founded by Epicurus,* which established a set of prescriptions recommending an ascetic way of life, a rejection or suppression of excess in any form, with the objective of achieving a state of tranquility. Epicurus argued for the incontestability of sense experience and for pleasure as the greatest good, pain the greatest evil. The Epicureans rejected belief in an afterlife as well as the belief in a controlling deity or deities. Man was not created, nor is he subjected to destiny. He is rather a propitious combination of atoms, subject only to the forces of nature, society, and his own will.

Evolution: The biological theory or process whereby organisms change with the passage of time so that descendants differ from their ancestors (see Darwinism**).

Existentialism: A philosophical movement that attempts to discover the meaning of human life in existence itself. The most important single thesis of existentialism is that the possibility of freedom and choice is the central fact of human nature. Among the foremost existentialists are Søren Kierkegaard,* Jean-Paul Sartre*(q.v.), Karl Jaspers,* and Martin Heidegger.*

Ex Nihilo: This is a Latin phrase which is translated "out of nothing." In theology, the expression is usually used to reinforce the idea that God created the universe out of nothing.

Expressionism: The term expressionism is used to describe movements in music and literature that took place in the early 1900s. In literature, expressionism was most visible in drama where the playwrights cut language to the bone and forced monosyllabic utterances to express feeling and emotions. Dramatic antecedents of expressionism included the later work of the Swedish playwright August Strindberg* and the works of the German Frank Wedekind, especially *Spring's Awakening*.

Fatalism: Determinism,** especially in its theological form, which asserts that all human affairs are predetermined by God.

Faustian: A view which argues that man is capable of transcending the human condition through the acquisition of universal knowledge which is available to him. It also refers to Faust's willingness to sacrifice his soul through a pact with the Devil to transcend the human condition.

Felicity: A Latin term meaning happiness, bliss, or good fortune.

Freudian: A term referring to the psychoanalytic school of Sigmund Freud,* which uses a combination of techniques including free association and dream interpretations.

Hedonism: A philosophical doctrine in which pleasure is the chief good of mankind. It follows the doctrine of the Cyreniac school of philosophy which was founded by Aristippos in the fifth century B.C. The chief good for the hedonist is the gratification of the senses, but for Epicurus,* the absence of pain is held to be the source of happiness.

Hegelianism: A philosophical school of thought based on the teaching of Georg Wilhelm Friedrich Hegel,* who argued that only the mind is real. Basic, as well, in the Hegelian system is the dialectical method illustrated in his own writings, which occur in dialectical triads consisting of thesis, antithesis, and synthesis.

Hellenism: A reference to the spirit of ancient Greece which exalts intellect and beauty.

Heraclitean flux: A theory of the pre-Socratic philosopher Heraclitus* that in nature even apparently stable things are constantly changing, although total balance is maintained.

Hinduism: A body of religious, philosophical, and social doctrines native to India.

Humanism: Any view in which the welfare and happiness of mankind in this life are primary concerns.

Idealism: The belief that material objects exist in our minds only as ideas and have no independent existence.

Jungian: This term refers to the work that Carl Jung* accomplished in the psychology of the unconscious. He proposed and developed the concepts of the extroverted and introverted personality and of the collective unconscious. The collective unconscious is that part of the mind that contains the memories and impulses of which the individual is not aware. Jung maintains that the collective unconscious is common to mankind as a whole and originates in the inherited structure of the brain. Finally, according to Jung, the collective unconscious contains universal primordial images and ideas.

Kantianism: The philosophy of Immanuel Kant*; also the critical philosophy, criticism, transcendentalism** or transcendental idealism, extending back to Kantianism.

Marxism: The philosophical, social, and economic theories developed by Karl

Marx* and Friedrich Engels. Philosophical Marxism is known as "dialectical materialism," which essentially states that the observable world is taken without reservations and does not receive its reality from any supernatural source (see materialism**).

Materialism: A doctrine which posits matter as primary and mind or spirit as secondary or nonexistent.

Metaphysical: Traditionally has reference to the study of things that transcend nature. In modern philosophy, especially since Immanuel Kant,* a priori conjecture or speculation on questions that do not lend themselves to scientific observation and experiment. In contemporary usage, the term is used with reference to the spiritual, the religious, and the occult.

Monism: A term that identifies metaphysical views that posit the oneness and/or unity of reality. First used by Christian Wolf (1679–1754) with reference to the mind/body controversy.

Mysticism: A type of religion that puts the emphasis on immediate awareness of the relation with God. Mysticism has been loosely used for esoteric types of knowledge which cannot be verified.

Naturalism: Naturalism maintains that the universe does not require a supernatural cause but "is self-existent, self-explanatory, self-operating, and self-directing" (Runes, 205). In aesthetics,** it is the doctrine that nature is the proper study of art. Artistic naturalism states that the sole function of the artist is to observe nature closely and to report faithfully the character and behavior of the artist's physical environment.

Nazism: A movement in Germany led by the Nationalsozialistische Deutsche Arbeiterpartei (National Socialist German Workers Party) known as the Nazi Party. Its leader from 1933 to 1945 was Adolph Hitler.

Neoplatonism: The philosophy of Plotinus* (who was probably a Hellenic Egyptian), which consists of elements of Platonism** mixed with pre-Socratic speculation, Oriental (Islamic) thought, and some aspects of Christianity. It continued to flourish in the medieval period and achieved considerable status in the Renaissance** and in seventeenth-century England (The Cambridge Platonist). It was not until the nineteenth century that Platonism was distinguished from Neoplatonism.

Nihilism: A philosophy of negation that involves the rejection of traditional morality and authority. Philosophically, it implies a skepticism in which the skeptic denies objective bases of truth. In nineteenth-century Russian literature, nihilism was popularized by the novelist Ivan Sergeyevich Turgenev. In modern French literature, it was an attitude Albert Camus (q.v.) attempted to overcome.

Occultism: That which relates to supernatural influence, agencies, or phenomena. Something that is beyond human comprehension.

Omnipotence: Possessing unlimited power; all powerful.

Paganism: Practices and beliefs that are incompatible with monotheism. It is often a designation of that which is neither Christian, Jewish, nor Islamic.

Pantheism: The doctrine that reality comprises a single being of which all things are projections. As a religious concept, pantheism is distinguished from deism by asserting the essential immanence of God in all creation.

Pessimism: The literature of pessimism (nineteenth century) considers the world the worst possible, believes man to be born to sorrow, and thinks him better if neither existed.

Phenomenology: A term used to refer to a descriptive study of phenomena prior to any attempt to explain the phenomena; a school of philosophy originating in Germany in the first decade of the twentieth century by a group of German thinkers, most notably Edmund Husserl.*

Platonism: The philosophical doctrines of Plato,* which posit a dualism that argues for the ascendency of mind over matter, assumes the existence of ideal forms or essences, and relates the problems of the universe and those of human beings to cosmic forces.

Positivism: The theory that science is the only valid knowledge and that philosophy should use methods that conform to scientific knowledge. Auguste Comte* adapted this theory, and the result was a great philosophical movement that was prevalent in the second half of the nineteenth century. The principle philosophical sources of positivism are the works of Francis Bacon* and the philosophers of the Enlightenment.**

Pragmatism: Pragmatism is a school of philosophy which was dominant in America during the first quarter of the twentieth century. It is based on the principle that the usefulness and practicality of ideas are the criteria of their merit. American philosophers, such as William James* and John Dewey,* stressed the priority of action over doctrine, and held that ideas get their meaning from their consequences.

Predestination: The act whereby God is believed to have foreordained all things.

Primitivism: (1) *Chronological primitivism:* a belief that the early periods of history were the best. (2) *Cultural primitivism:* the belief that civilization corrupts. The view, or doctrine, which argues that since primitive peoples live closer to nature, they are less subject to societal influences and are, therefore, nobler and more moral than those who live in civilized societies.

Promethean: This word was derived from Prometheus, who in Greek mythology was one of the Titans and the god of fire. Legend has it that Prometheus stole fire from the gods and gave it to man. As a consequence, he was punished. Zeus had him chained to a rock and sent an eagle to eat his immortal liver, which constantly replenished itself. He was eventually released by the Greek hero Hercules. In the literary work *Prometheus Bound,* by Aeschylus, the author depicts Prometheus as the bringer of fire to man, but also as their preserver who gave man all of the arts and sciences as well as the means of survival. (See the poetic drama *Prometheus Unbound* by Percy Bysshe Shelley [q.v.].)

Puritanism: An emphasis on the virtues of self-reliance, thrift, industry, and initiative. Puritanism has come to represent an undue repression of normal human enjoyments.

Pythagorean: The philosophy of Pythagoras* who argued for analogy between the unity of numbers and the unity of the universe. He believed in the immortality of the soul and in reincarnation. Escape from the cycle of reincarnation was to be achieved through a program of study, dietary rules, prohibitions, and permissions.

Radical empiricism: See empiricism.

Radicalism: Any position that advocates or supports the disruption or uprooting of that which is established; in philosophy, a movement initiated in the early nineteenth century by James Mill, John Stuart Mill,** and Jeremy Bentham among others, and more commonly known as Utilitarianism*.

Rationalism: This term implies that truth rests on the authority of reason rather than on sense perceptions. The early humanists (see humanism**) had insisted on the control of reason, and as early as 1624, Lord Herbert of Cherbury had drawn up certain rational principles which would be satisfactory to all existing religious factions. Thus, the rationalist movement through the ages has had a direct bearing on religious thought. An example would be the deists (see deism**) who followed reason and rejected revelation.

Realism: In medieval philosophy, the view that universals have a real, objective existence. In modern philosophy, the view that material objects exist independently of sense experience. Modern exponents include Samuel Alexander, William James,* G. E. Moore, and Bertrand Russell.*

Renaissance: A rebirth; revival. The humanistic (see humanism**) revival of art, literature, and learning in Europe especially the fourteenth through the sixteenth centuries.

Rosicrucianism: A secret worldwide brotherhood whose members claim to possess secret wisdom handed down from ancient times. The name derives from the order's symbol, the combination of a rose and a cross. The teaching of Rosicrucianism contains elements of occultism and a variety of religious beliefs and practices. Some regard Paracelsus, a Swiss alchemist who died in 1541, as the founder of rosicrucianism. Although reliable evidence traces the order's history no earlier than the seventeenth century, some claim that its origins go back to ancient Egypt.

Romanticism: A literary or philosophical posture that emphasizes the centrality of the individual in all experience and regards the intuitive and the imaginative as the surest paths to truth; in literature, an eighteenth- and nineteenth-century movement in Europe and England that reacted to the literary orthodoxy of the previous period.

Sacramentalism: A doctrine which accepts the efficacy of the sacraments.

Satanism: Devil worship. Worship of Satan. Satanism was traditionally considered as being an antithesis to Christianity and involving elements characteristic of black magic and witchcraft.

Scholasticism: Christian philosophy that was worked up by scholars in the schools of medieval Europe. The schools required curricular materials drawn from classical Greek and Roman sources as well as from Patristic Theology that were interpreted and discussed from a Christian viewpoint. The culmination of scholasticism took place under Thomas Aquinas* to the late scholastic period in the work of John Duns Scotus* and William of Ockham.

Skepticism: From the Greek term *skeptikis* meaning "inquirers." A position that questions the reliability of knowledge claims. The extreme skeptics have argued that the knowledge beyond immediate experience is not possible, and some (David Hume*) have doubted even this can be known.

Stoicism: The philosophical doctrine of the Stoics, Greek philosophers of the fourth century B.C. Stoicism extolls the virtues of endurance and self-sufficiency. Virtue consists in living in conformity to the laws of nature.

Superman: In the context of this reference book, the word superman is used as a free translation of the German *übermensch* as used by Friedrich Nietzsche.* This German philosopher used the term to mark an exceptional human being.

Surrealism: A modern movement in literature which attempts to show what takes place in the subconscious mind.

Swedenborgianism: A religious philosophy developed by Emanuel Swedenborg.* Swedenborg claimed direct spiritual knowledge. Swedenborgianism is often called the New Church (or New Jerusalem).

Symbolic logic: The adaptation of a set of symbols to represent any major segment of verbal argument of expression.

Symbolism: The use of one object to represent another; in literature, a literary movement that originated in France in the latter half of the nineteenth century and influenced both English and American literature into the twentieth century.

Theism: The view that all finite things are dependent in some way upon a supreme or ultimate being. In religion, one speaks of this being as God, who is regarded as beyond man's comprehension, is perfect and self-sustained, but is also involved in the world and its events.

Theodicy: The technical term for the problem of justifying the character of a good, creative, and responsible God in the face of the existence of evil in the universe.

Thomism: A term referring to the teaching (philosophy and theology) of Saint Thomas Aquinas.*

Totalitarianism: An organized society based on authoritarianism

Transcendentalism: An eclectic** American philosophical movement based on the teaching of modern European philosophers, especially Immanuel Kant* who argued that ideas such as self, cosmos, and God are transcendental because they do not correspond to any object in experience but are produced not by intuition but by pure reason alone. Because of the eclecticism and subjectivism, which characterize the so-called New England transcendentalists, it is difficult, if not impossible, to arrive at a single formula which characterizes the movement.

Utilitarianism: A doctrine that argues that the rightness or wrongness of an action is determined by its consequence.

Vitalism: A school of scientific and philosophical thought that dates back to Aristotle.* The term attempts to explain the nature of life that results from a vital force peculiar to living organisms. Vitalists hold that this force controls the form and development as well as the activities of the organism. Related somewhat to vitalism is the *élan vital*** of Henri Bergson's* philosophy which is described as the vital force, a source of efficient causation and evolution in nature.

Vorticism: A term used in reference to Descarte's* binomial theory of knowledge. More recently a term used by Ezra Pound as an extension of imagism.

Weltanschauung: A German word meaning "view of the world," or worldview.

Zen Buddhism: A form of Buddhism** that developed in India as a reaction to more traditional Buddhist positions; it found its most prominent expressions in China and Japan.

Selected Bibliography

Abbey, Cherie, ed. *Nineteenth-Century Literature Criticism*. Vol. 14. Detroit, Mich.: Gale Research, 1987.

Abrams, M. H. *The Mirror and the Lamp: Romantic Theory and the Critical Tradition*. New York: Oxford University Press, 1953.

Adams, Hazard. *The Interests of Criticism: An Introduction to Literary Theory*. New York: Harcourt, 1969.

Aiken, Henry D. *Reasons and Conduct. New Bearings in Moral Philosophy*. New York: Knopf, 1962.

Arendt, Hannah. *The Human Condition. A Study of the Central Dilemmas Facing Modern Man*. Chicago, Ill.: The University of Chicago Press, 1958.

Aristotle. *The Poetics*. Bilingual edition translated and edited by W. Hamilton Fyfe. Loeb Classical Library. 1960 Reprint. Cambridge, Mass.: Harvard University Press, 1973.

Armstrong, David M. *A Materialist Theory of the Mind*. London: Routledge, 1968.

Auerbach, Erich. *Mimesis: The Representation of Reality in Western Literature*. Translated by Willard R. Trask. Princeton, N.J.: Princeton University Press, 1953.

Ayer, Alfred J. *The Problem of Knowledge*. London, England: Penguin, 1956.

Ayers, M. R. *The Refutation of Determinism*. London: Methuen, 1968.

Bambrough, Renford. *Reason, Truth and God*. London: Methuen, 1969.

Barnes, Jonathon, ed. *Early Greek Philosophy*. New York: Penguin, 1987.

Barthes, Roland. *Criticism and Truth*. Minneapolis: University of Minnesota Press, 1987.

Baxandall, Lee, ed. *Radical Perspectives in the Arts*. Baltimore, Md.: Penguin, 1972.

Beardsley, Monroe C. *Literature and Aesthetics*. Indianapolis, Ind.: Bobbs-Merrill, 1968.

Bennett, Tony. *Formalism and Marxism*. New York: Routledge Chapman & Hall, 1979.

Bhattacharyya, Kalidas. *Alternative Standpoints in Philosophy*. Calcutta, India: Cupta, 1953.

Bickman, Martin. *The Unsounded Center: Jungian Studies in American Romanticism*. Chapel Hill: University of North Carolina Press, 1980.

Birenbaum, Harvey. *Tragedy and Innocence*. New York: University Press of America, 1983.

Bloom, Harold. *The Anxiety of Influence: A Theory of Poetry*. New York: Oxford University Press, 1973.

Bochenski, I. *The Logic of Religion*. New York: New York University Press, 1965.

Bolling. *Philosophy and Literature*. New York: Haven Publications, 1986.

Bremmer, Jan. *The Early Greek Concept of the Soul*. Princeton, N.J.: Princeton University Press, 1987.

Bronowski, Jacob. *The Identity of Man*. New York: Heinemann, 1966.

Browne, Lewis. *Wisdom of the Jewish People*. Hichmount, N.Y.: Aronson, 1988.

Buckley, Vincent. *Poetry and the Sacred*. London: Chatto and Windus, 1968.

Bush, Douglas. *Mythology and the Renaissance Tradition in English Poetry*. New York: Norton, 1963.

Campbell, Joseph. *The Hero with a Thousand Faces*. 2nd ed. Princeton, N.J.: Princeton University Press, 1968.

Cascardi, Anthony J., ed. *Literature and the Question of Philosophy*. Baltimore, Md.: Johns Hopkins University Press, 1987.

Cassirer, Ernst. *An Essay on Man. An Introduction to a Philosophy of Human Culture*. New Haven, Conn.: Yale University Press, 1945.

Caudwell, Christopher. *Illusion and Reality: A Study in the Sources of Poetry*. New York: International, 1963.

Chisholm, Roderick M. *Perceiving a Philosophical Study*. Ithaca, N.Y.: Cornell University Press, 1957.

Craig, Edward. *The Mind of God and the Works of Man*. New York: Oxford University Press, 1987.

Craige, Betty J., ed. *Relativism in the Arts*. Athens, Ga.: University of Georgia Press, 1983.

Daiches, David. *Critical Approaches to Literature*. Englewood Cliffs, N.J.: Prentice-Hall, 1956.

Danto, Arthur C. *Mysticism and Morality: Oriental Thought and Moral Philosophy*. New York: Columbia University Press, 1988.

Devaraja, N. K. *The Philosophy of Culture*. Allahabao: Kitab Mahal Private, 1963.

Dewey, John. *Art as Experience*. New York: Minton, Balch, 1934.

Dray, William H., ed. *Philosophy of History*. London: Oxford University Press, 1957.

Eagleton, Terry. *Marxism and Literary Criticism*. Berkeley: University of California Press, 1976.

Ehrenzweig, Anton. *The Hidden Order of Art: A Study in the Psychology of Artistic Imagination*. Berkeley: University of California Press, 1967.

Eliot, T. S. *The Sacred Wood: Essays on Poetry and Criticism*. 2nd ed. London: Methuen, 1972.

Encyclopedia of Philosophy, edited by Paul Edwards. 4 vols. New York: Macmillan, 1972.

Ernst, Kenneth. *A Continued Examination of the Human Condition*. New York: Carlton Press, 1988.

Farrer, Austin. *The Freedom of the Will*. London: Black, 1958.

Feder, Lillian. *Ancient Myth in Modern Poetry*. Princeton, N.J.: Princeton University Press, 1971.

Fiedler, Leslie. *Love and Death in the American Novel*. 2nd ed. New York: Stein and Day, 1966.

Findlay, John N. *Language, Mind, and Value. Philosophical Essays*. London: Allen & Unwin, 1963.

Gallie, Walter B. *Philosophy and the Historical Understanding*. London: Chatto & Windus, 1964.

Gardner, Helen. *Religion and Literature*. London: Faber, 1971.

Gilson, Etienne. *The Unity of Philosophical Experience*. 1937. Reprint. New York: Scribner, 1955.

Goldmann, Lucien. *Cultural Creation in Modern Society*. Translated by Bart Brahl. St. Louis, Mo.: Telos, 1976.

Griffiths, A. Phillips, ed. *Philosophy and Literature*. Cambridge, England: Cambridge University Press, 1984.

Hans, James. *Imitation and the Image of Man*. Philadelphia, Pa.: Benjamins, John, North American, 1987.

Hartshorne, Charles. *Creativity in American Philosophy*. New York: Paragon House, 1985.

Heller, Erich. *The Disinherited Mind: Essays in Modern German Literature and Thought*. 4th ed. New York: Harcourt Brace Jovanovich, 1975.

Hook, Sidney. *Dimensions of Mind. A Symposium*. New York: New York University Press, 1960.

Horden, Peregrine, ed. *Freud and the Humanities*. New York: St. Martin's Press, 1985.

Huxley, Aldous. *Literature and Science*. New York: Harper, 1963.

Kenny, Anthony. *Rationalism, Empiricism & Idealism*. New York: Oxford University Press, 1986.

Kermode, Frank. *The Classic: Literary Images of Permanence and Change*. Cambridge, Mass.: Harvard University Press, 1983.

Kim, Yong C. *Oriental Thought: An Introduction to the Philosophical and Religious Thought of Asia*. Totowa, N.J.: Littlefield, 1981.

Langer, Susanne K. *Problems of Art: Ten Philosophical Lectures*. New York: Scribner, 1957.

Lesser, Simon O. *Fiction and the Unconscious*. Boston: Beacon, 1957.

Lewis, John. *Science, Faith, and Scepticism*. London: Lawrence & Wishart, 1959.

Lonergan, Bernard. *Insight: A Study of Human Understanding*. London: Longman & Greene, 1958.

Magee, Brian. *Modern British Philosophy*. New York: Oxford University Press, 1986.

Martin, James A. *The New Dialogue between Philosophy and Theology*. New York: Seaburg, 1966.

Montefiore, Alan, ed. *Philosophy in France Today*. New York: Cambridge University Press, 1983.

Moore, G. E. *Some Main Problems of Philosophy*. New York: Macmillan, 1953.

Murdock, Kenneth B. *Literature and Theology in Colonial New England*. Cambridge, Mass.: Harvard University Press, 1949.

Niebuhr, Rheinhold. *The Nature and Destiny of Man: A Christian Interpretation*. New York: Scribner, 1941.

Philips, Dewi S. *Faith and Philosophical Inquiry*. London: Routledge, 1970.

Raju, P. T. *Spirit, Being, and Self: Studies in Indian and Western Philosophy*. Columbus, Mo.: South Asia Books, 1986.

Righter, William. *Myth and Literature*. London: Routledge & Kegan Paul, 1975.

Roland, Alan, ed. *Psychoanalysis, Creativity and Literature: A French-American Inquiry*. New York: Columbus University Press, 1978.

Runes, Dagobert David, ed. *Dictionary of Philosophy*. New York: Philosophical Library, 1983.

Sartre, Jean-Paul. *What Is Literature?* Translated by Bernard Frechtmann. New York: Philosophical Library, 1949.

Sontag, Susan. *Against Interpretation*. New York: Farrar, 1966.

Spender, Stephen. *The Destructive Element: A Study of Modern Writers and Beliefs*. Boston: Houghton, 1938.

Spitzer, Leo. *Classical and Christian Ideas of World Harmony*. Baltimore, Md.: Johns Hopkins University Press, 1963.

Strawson, P. F., ed. *Studies in the Philosophy of Thought and Action*. London: Oxford University Press, 1968.

Stumpf, Samuel Enoch. *Philosophy: History & Problems*. 4th ed. New York: McGraw-Hill, 1989.

Tymienlecka, A. T. *The Philosophical Reflection of Man in Literature*. Norwell, Mass.: Kluwer Academic, 1982.

Upadhyaya, K. N. *Early Buddhism and the Bhagavadgita*. Delhi, India: Molital Banarsidass, 1971.

Warnock, G. J. *Contemporary Moral Philosophy*. London: Oxford University Press, 1967.

Watt, Ian. *The Rise of the Novel*. Berkeley: University of California Press, 1962.

Wellek, Rene, and Austin Warren. *Theory of Literature*. 3rd ed. New York: Harcourt, 1962.

Williams, Raymond. *Culture and Society, 1780–1950*. New York: Columbia University Press, 1958.

Winters, Yvor. *In Defense of Reason*. Denver, Colo.: Swallow, 1947.

Index

Page numbers in **bold** indicate main entry.

About the Authors

EDMUND J. THOMAS is Professor of English at Niagara County Community College, New York. He is also the author of *College Prep Reader*.

EUGENE G. MILLER is Associate Professor of English at Niagara County Community College, New York.

123212